Politics and
the Emotions

Politics and the Emotions

The affective turn in contemporary political studies

Edited by

PAUL HOGGETT
AND
SIMON THOMPSON

continuum

Continuum International Publishing Group

80 Maiden Lane
Suite 704
New York NY 10038

The Tower Building
11 York Road
London SE1 7NX

www.continuumbooks.com

Library of Congress Cataloging-in-Publication Data
A catalog record for this book is available from the Library of Congress.

ISBN: HB: 978-1-4411-7381-2
PB: 978-1-4411-1926-1

Typeset by Newgen Imaging Systems Pvt Ltd, Chennai, India
Printed and bound in the United States of America

Contents

Acknowledgements

The origins of this book lie in a series of research seminars entitled 'Politics and Emotions', which was very generously supported by the Economic and Social Research Council (award/grant reference RES-451-25-4281).

List of contributors

Marian Barnes is Professor of Social Policy in the School of Applied Social Science, University of Brighton, United Kingdom. A major theme of her work for the last 20+ years has been user involvement and user movements, public participation, citizenship and new forms of democratic practice. Her books include: *Power, Participation and Political Renewal* (2007) (with Janet Newman and Helen Sullivan); and *Subversive Citizens: Power, Agency and Resistance in Public Services* (2009) (with David Prior), both Policy Press.

Michael Cunningham is Senior Lecturer in Politics at the University of Wolverhampton, United Kingdom. His principal research interests are Northern Irish politics on which he has published widely including *British Government Policy in Northern Ireland 1969–2000* (Manchester University Press, 2001) and, more recently, the politics of apology on which he has published several articles.

Tim Dartington is a researcher and social analyst in health and social care and associate at The Tavistock Institute in London and the Tavistock & Portman NHS Trust. He is a member of Organisation for Promoting Understanding of Society (OPUS) and of the International Society for the Psycho-Analytic Study of Organizations (ISPSO). He is the author of *Managing Vulnerability, the Underlying Dynamics of Systems of Care* (Karnac Books, 2010).

Deborah B. Gould was involved in ACT UP for many years as well as the Chicago activist group, Queer to the Left, and is a founding member of the art/activism/research collaborative group, Feel Tank Chicago. She is an Associate Professor of Sociology at the University of California, Santa Cruz. Her scholarly interests are in contentious politics and political emotion. Her book *Moving Politics: Emotion and ACT UP's Fight against AIDS* was published by the University of Chicago Press in 2009.

Paul Hoggett is Professor of Social Policy at the University of the West of England and a psychoanalytic psychotherapist. He is the author of several books in social policy but also has a long-standing interest in understanding public life from a nonrationalist perspective. His books in this area include *Partisans in an Uncertain World* (Free Association Books, 1992), *Emotional*

Life and the Politics of Welfare (Macmillan, 2000) and *Politics, Identity and Emotion* (Paradigm, 2009).

Mary Holmes is a Senior Lecturer in Sociology at Flinders University, Adelaide, Australia. Her research interests are in emotions, politics, gender and sexuality and in the sociology of intimacy. She has published many articles on these topics and is the author of *What is Gender?* (Sage Publications, 2007) and *The Representation of Feminists as Political Actors* (VDM Verlag, 2008).

Steven Kaindaneh completed the PhD study programme at the Centre for Peace and Reconciliation Studies, Coventry University, United Kingdom. His research interest is in war memory and its significance in healing and coexistence in post-conflict societies. Before coming to Coventry in 2006 to study for the MA in Peace and Reconciliation Studies, he worked in Sierra Leone, Guinea and Sudan – countries that have experienced bitter and protracted armed conflicts.

Scott Lucas is Professor of American Studies at the University of Birmingham, where he has worked since 1989. A specialist in US and British foreign policy, he has written and edited nine books, more than 40 major articles, and a radio documentary, and he has co-directed the 2007 film Laban! A journalist since 1978, Lucas is also the founder and editor of the leading international website EA WorldView (www.eaworldview), which specializes in coverage of US foreign policy and global affairs, especially in the Middle East, North Africa and Iran.

Michael Northcott is Professor of Ethics in the School of Divinity at the University of Edinburgh. He is author of *The Environment and Christian Ethics* (Cambridge University Press, 1996), *An Angel Directs the Storm: Apocalyptic Religion and American Empire* (I B Tauris, 2004) *and A Moral Climate: The Ethics of Global Warming* (Darton Longman and Todd, 2007). He is also an Episcopal Priest and a trustee of Traidcraft.

Andrew Rigby is Emeritus Professor of Peace Studies at Coventry University, United Kingdom, where he was the founding director of the Centre for Peace and Reconciliation Studies. He has a long-term interest in the emotional dynamics of nonviolent action for change. His most recent book is *Palestinian Resistance and Nonviolence* (East Jerusalem, PASSIA, 2010).

Simon Thompson is Reader in Political Theory at the University of the West of England, Bristol. He is author of *The Political Theory of Recognition* (Polity, 2006) and co-editor of *The Politics of Misrecognition* (Ashgate, 2012), *Emotions, Politics and Society* (Palgrave Macmillan, 2006) and *Richard Rorty:*

Critical Dialogues (Polity, 2001). He has published articles in a wide range of journals including *Constellations, Contemporary Political Theory, European Journal of Political Theory,* and *Philosophy and Social Criticism.*

Bas van Stokkom is a philosopher and sociologist. He is currently Assistant Professor at the Criminological Institute, Radboud University, and lecturer at the Faculty of Social Sciences, Free University, Amsterdam. His research concentrates on the fields of freedom of speech, deliberative democracy, restorative justice and punishment ethics. He is secretary of the Dutch-Flemish journal *Tijdschrift voor Herstelrecht* (Journal of Restorative Justice).

Cas Wouters is a sociologist who studies twentieth-century social and psychic processes, focusing on regimes of manners and emotions in relationships between classes, sexes and generations, and interpreted as a process of informalization. Two recent books are *Sex and Manners: Female Emancipation in the West 1890–2000* (Sage, 2004) and *Informalization: Manners and Emotions Since 1890* (Sage, 2007). Cas works at the universities of Utrecht and Amsterdam.

1

Introduction

Paul Hoggett and Simon Thompson

Social science and human feelings

It seems odd that, while acceptance of the role of the emotions in public and political life was once commonplace, it is only now being rediscovered after decades of neglect. The Greeks debated the role of the emotions in public rhetoric, Machiavelli analysed the contribution of love and fear to the exercise of power, and Hume examined the contribution of the moral sentiments to human reason. But for much of the last century political studies eschewed consideration of the emotions. It was assumed that political subjects were essentially rational actors busily maximizing their strategic interests even while sometimes constrained by their limited information-processing abilities. This strange and lopsided account of the political subject split cognition from emotion, and reason from passion. To some extent, what happened in political studies simply echoed what was going on elsewhere in the social sciences, where, throughout much of the period after the Second World War, the grip of positivism and behaviouralism was powerful. Only slowly was this tide to be turned: first, through what has sometimes been referred to as the 'discursive turn' in the social sciences – that is, through the interest in language, meaning and discourse which gathered force in the 1980s; second, and more recently, through what is sometimes referred to as the 'affective turn' in the social sciences.

This renewal of academic interest in human feelings has been greatly facilitated by a number of traditions and disciplines. One strand within continental philosophy, focusing primarily on the affective dimension of our feeling lives, can be traced from Nietzsche through Bergson and Scheler to the postmodernists such as Deleuze and Guattari (1999). Almost as enduring has been the contribution of psychoanalysis, from Freud through Klein and Lacan to the present day (Anderson, 1992; Dor, 1999). More recently, developments in mainstream psychology involving the work of Ekman (1994), Plutchik (2002) and Tomkins (2008) have facilitated greater understanding of the different categories of human feeling, including distinctions between basic and secondary emotions. Contemporary psychological theories in turn have influenced and been influenced by advances in neuroscience which have provided scientific evidence of the distinctive location, functioning and organization of the 'feeling brain' (Damasio, 2000; Dennett, 1992). Finally, the human sciences themselves, particularly sociology (e.g. Hochschild, 1983), have provided us with ways of understanding the cultural and institutional organization of feelings, so that we now are beginning to realize that, although feelings are individually experienced, they are often embodied in the cultures of occupations and corporations.

Of course, it might be argued that by means of these theoretical developments the social sciences have done no more than begin the long process of catching up with the world that unfolds around them. It seems bizarre that the determined refusal to admit the feeling world into the social sciences and political studies occurred in a global society characterized by eruptions of nihilistic hatred (the Holocaust and, later, ethnic cleansing in Bosnia and Rwanda), rule by terror and paranoia in successive communist regimes, the background threat of Mutually Assured Destruction and its flashpoints during the Cuban Missile Crisis, and, later, the Tehran hostage crisis. To brighten the landscape, the refusal to admit feelings also occurred at the same time as the waves of hope-fuelled progressive social movements swept across the West in the 1960s, Eastern Europe in the late 1980s, and the 'Arab Spring' today. Indeed, to bring matters up to date, we have seen repeated evidence of the powerful and formative role of human feelings in public life in the last decade from the waves of contagious panic which fuelled the crash in the financial markets in 2008, to the triumph of Barack Obama's 'politics of hope' over the Republicans' 'politics of resentment' in the same year.

Conceptual distinctions

In one sense, the so-called 'affective turn' in the social sciences to which we have just referred is misleadingly named. This is because we can distinguish between *affect* and *emotion* as two forms, overlapping and not mutually exclusive, that human feelings can assume. Affect concerns the more embodied, unformed and less conscious dimension of human feeling, whereas emotion concerns the feelings which are more conscious since they are more anchored in language and meaning. An affect such as anxiety is experienced in a bodily way, while an emotion such as jealousy is directed towards objects (a lover, a rival) which give it meaning, focus and intentionality. The distinctive thing about anxiety is the way in which its object constantly shifts from one thing to another, almost as if the object is secondary to the feeling. Thus, whereas emotion is embedded in discourse, affect appears to be more detached from it. We typically know if someone is anxious by how they look, walk, carry themselves, by the gestures they deploy, by the tension that may be visible in their bodies; all this we register even before they speak.

In making this distinction between affect and emotion, we want to suggest that purely cognitivist accounts of human feelings, such as that developed by Robert Solomon (2007), give insufficient account of that dimension of our feeling lives which is more impulsive, indeterminate and unformed. We believe that this is important for analyses of the role of human passions in political life. Because affect is less anchored in discourse, it is more labile and fluid, and thus more susceptible to spreading rapidly through groups, even beyond face-to-face groups. Originally such movement was construed by Freud and others in terms of 'contagion' (Freud, 1921); nowadays we are more likely to understand it in terms of the operation of 'affective networks' (Hoggett, 2009, pp. 10–11). The affective dimension of feelings therefore helps us understand their unruliness and unpredictability. Nowhere is this more so than in public life where anxiety, rage, panic, paranoia and other feelings, once they gather momentum, become difficult forces to control. Political actors, such as populist politicians who seek to manipulate such feelings, are just as likely to be destroyed by the forces they try to control.

For methodological individualists, the idea that a feeling such as anxiety or guilt may be a property of a group is likely to prove puzzling. Seeing the individual as the basic unit in society, they are led to assume that feelings, like meanings and intentions, are somehow the 'property' of the individual. This under-socialized concept of the human subject, one shared by some traditions within mainstream psychology, is unable to see how feelings bind the group, contributing substantially to its coherence. Affect and emotion shape the structure and texture of society at its various levels, from the family group, through to organizations and beyond to the wider social movements in civil society. Various concepts have been put forward recently as ways of trying to grasp such socially structured feelings. For example, Debbie Gould, a contributor to the present volume, has suggested the concept of 'emotional habitus' (Gould, 2009) as a way of grasping the tacit, taken for granted, affective patterns that characterize social movement subcultures. In a similar vein, James Jasper, in his study of political mobilization, distinguishes between fleeting emotional reactions and what he terms 'abiding affects'. These are enduring and organized feelings such as fear or anger which provide the motivational basis for political action (Jasper, 1998). Another valuable concept is that of 'structures of feeling', an idea developed by the Marxist literary critic Raymond Williams (Williams, 1977). For Williams, a structure of feeling may characterize a whole society or group of societies during a particular period of history. So, for example, the pervasive nature of moral and risk anxiety in advanced capitalist societies such as the United States, United Kingdom and Japan could be seen as a 'structure of feeling' which manifests itself in everything from the design of homes and buildings, patterns of use of outdoor urban spaces, film, art and music and even in everyday public interaction. To illustrate the latter, some of our own recent research revealed how many men living in working-class areas of the city no longer say 'hello' to strangers in their neighbourhood for fear of being thought of as 'weird' or even a 'paedo' (Beedell et al. 2010).

Feelings in politics: some themes

This volume is based upon a seminar series which ran over a period of 18 months between December 2006 and June 2008. The series, called 'Politics and the Emotions', was supported financially by the United Kingdom's Economic and Social Research Council. We sought to use this series as a way of taking a closer look at some of the thematic areas which were emerging as foci for study and debate in political studies, and in the social sciences more widely. Some of these themes, such as the 'politics of fear' surrounding 9/11 and subsequent Western interventions in Iraq and Afghanistan, were current and very topical. Others, such as the rise of therapeutic culture and its impact on public policy, related more to trends covering several decades. While work in this whole field of politics and the emotions is still quite scattered, it is now becoming easier to discern some of the contours and clusters, only some of which we have managed to include in this volume.

First, and this takes us right back to Aristotle and the Greeks, there is the relation between the emotions and political discourse, narrative and rhetoric. At times, some of the more rationalist currents within political studies have tacitly assumed that if discourse is to be truly reasonable it should be free of passion. Indeed, we have argued that at times accounts of political deliberation have posited an ideal of communicative rationality shorn of the emotions (Hoggett and Thompson, 2002). Of course such an ideal assumes that our reasoning capacities are enhanced when freed from emotion. We argue, quite to the contrary, that so long as these emotions are not overwhelming, they provide both the motivational basis for our intellectual lives and enhance our reasoning capacities. Thus, for example, George Marcus (2002) has found that moderate levels of anxiety facilitate the search for, and processing of, political information among voters: anxious voters are likely to be more discerning voters, so long as this anxiety is contained within comfortable limits. The same is true of the anger voters feel when they perceive an injustice has been done. This emotion motivates them to search out information, and to take a more critical stance towards arguments which they may have previously accepted at face value. And, in terms of their communication to others, strong feelings can make their own arguments more powerful.

For the Greeks, the use of emotion in political argumentation was the subject of much debate. Avoiding the more rationalist strain in Plato, Aristotle saw rhetoric as essential to practical debate and the ability to win over the soul of the other. More generally, we suggest that all communication has what might be called 'affective registers' (Newman, 2011), and such communication includes the narratives elicited through interviews conducted by political journalists. The affective register may support the narrative content as, for example, when a policymaker speaks hopefully about a new development. But the affect may not support the narrative, and it is these incongruities between affect and discourse which take us into the complexities of rhetoric – the threat lurking in the warm words of the authoritarian ruler, the condescension present in the reasoned tone of the political patrician, and so on.

Second, and this is illustrated to some extent by the contributions of Cunningham, Kaindaneh and Rigby in this volume, feelings are integral to the dynamics of conflict and post-conflict situations. This is vividly illustrated in situations of conflict where hatred of the other group is inextricably bound to love of one's own group. Paradoxically, therefore, love, the basis for 'fellow feeling', can provide the platform for highly regressive and authoritarian forms of group bonding (Ahmed, 2004). The patterning of love and hate in conflict situations also provides a glimpse of the way in which feelings contribute to the dynamic ordering of public life. As Žižek (1993) has noted, since we enjoy our hatreds, they are not easily given up. In fantasy, aggressors imagine themselves to be the victim, wrapping themselves up in the victim's moral virtue. In conflict situations, aggressors cannot be 'educated' out of their misdeeds; for change to occur, the emotional roots of group identities have to be understood. Change for both real victims and real perpetrators involves loss, guilt and regret, and some now argue that institutional mechanisms providing for reparative justice – for example, memorializations, truth commissions – need to be constructed if such feelings are to be worked through (Minow, 1998).

Third, the role of feelings in social movements has been a subject of considerable interest. The renewed interest in the role of passion in politics was largely prompted by the work of political sociologists in the United States such as Jeff Goodwin and James Jasper who have analysed the role of feelings such as love, shame, anger and humour in the mobilization of political and social movements (Goodwin et al. 2001). These writers have tended to draw on sociological and anthropological accounts which emphasized the way in which feelings were socially constructed through movement discourses and the 'framing' activities of activists and elites. Gould, for example, has looked at the efforts of gay and lesbian movement activists in the United States during the AIDs crisis in the 1980s to reshape the shame and loss that pervaded their community into pride and anger, thereby enabling this community to move from being positioned as an object of fear, anxiety and contempt to the position of an active political subject (Gould, 2001, 2002).

A fourth area where an understanding of the emotions can contribute to politics is in the area of political campaigning and communication. Ever since the early work of Philip Converse (1964), the idea that voters are rational information processors or dispassionate reasoners has been subject to challenge. The typical voter makes decisions on small amounts of information which have been selectively filtered. They make little use of abstract categories such as 'egalitarianism'. There may be little consistency in the opinions that they have, and they can be powerfully influenced by how they imagine 'people like us' think and feel about the same issues (Luskin, 2002). In a powerful critique of Democratic Party campaigning, Drew Westen (2007) has argued that Republicans had been consistently more adept in understanding the 'non-rational' dimensions of voter behaviour including, for example, the power of narratives (good stories) as well as facts and information. Drawing on recent advances in neuroscience which have revealed the role of the emotions in thinking, reasoning and decision-making, Westen has concluded that political campaigning is about winning both hearts and minds, and that the Democrats have lost out to their opponents in the past by focusing only on the latter.

Fifth, the emotions are also intimately involved in the processes of governance and policymaking. In late modernity, the state becomes the focus of social anxieties which manifest themselves in recurrent moral and risk panics. What attitude does the state take to such anxieties? Does it face them proactively or reactively? Does it even recognize the emotional ground upon which it is working? If governments cannot contain such anxieties, then they will project, enact or embody these feelings. *Projection* occurs where a government colludes with powerful anxieties by focusing them upon a particular target group which becomes construed as a social problem. *Enactment* occurs when a government, faced with a panic of some form, succumbs to the intense pressure to be seen to be doing something. This is very much the territory of Murray Edelman's 'symbolic policy making' (Edelman, 1964).

Alternatively, the state and its institutions may come to *embody* social anxieties through its rules, systems, structures and procedures. The state may seek to deal with recurring risks through ever-increasing attempts at control, thereby proliferating rules, rigidifying procedures and structures. Such reactions can be seen as 'social defences against anxiety' (Menzies, 1959). The idea that policies and institutions may embody unreflexively organized defences or coping responses provides a valuable contribution to our understanding of the propensity of the state towards bureaucracy. Here the resort to hierarchical control by, for example, forcing staff to adhere rigidly to detailed procedure manuals, can be an illusory quest to eliminate risk in complex situations – such as child protection, street crime and immigration – which provoke massive social anxieties.

A sixth area which has been developed recently concerns the contribution that an understanding of the emotions can make to the humanitarian impulse in politics. Interesting arguments have developed concerning the nature of compassion, its normative dimensions, its relation to other feelings and impulses such as sympathy and pity, and its connections to altruism and other forms of social solidarity (Berlant, 2004; Linklater, 2007; Monroe, 1996; Nussbaum, 1996, 2001; Whitebook, 2002). The attempt to restore the status of compassion as a political virtue has had to deal with important objections (Arendt, 1973), but in a globalized society the need to expand the reach of democratic principles and practices has motivated the search for ways of enriching and deepening democratic values, and for some writers compassion captures this idea of a sentiment or impulse which is both democratic and cosmopolitan.

Finally, there has been a recent emergence of interest in emotion in international relations (Mercer, 2005; Ross, 2006). The contributions by Northcott and Lucas in this volume represent one very specific aspect of this – the role of fear and paranoia in the post-9/11 world. This closely parallels growing interest in the role of fear, humiliation and 'group love' in what might be called 'the politics of violence', particularly with reference to the Middle East (Ayyash, 2010; Fattah and Fierke, 2009; Melander, 2009; Sasley, 2010).

A typology of political feelings

Another way of explaining the importance of an understanding of the human passions to public life is by developing typologies of human emotions and then observing the connection between each of these different typologies and politics. Several attempts have been made in mainstream psychology to typologize emotions in this way, from Paul Ekman's attempts to isolate the 'basic emotions' (Ekman, 1994) through to Robert Plutchik's 'wheel of emotions' (Plutchik, 2004). The following categorization of feelings draws upon some of these previous typologies.

Positive moral emotions: There are a range of feeling states which are specifically bound up with our moral and ethical lives; these can be divided between positive and negative moral emotions. Positive moral feelings, such as compassion, concern, sympathy and forgiveness, draw us towards the object of our emotion. We have already mentioned the extensive ongoing debate about the nature of compassion by political theorists. These debates also have considerable practical relevance. For example, in the United Kingdom a group of leading NGOs engaged in action around humanitarian and environmental issues, produced the report *Common Cause* as a way of highlighting the deepening relevance of 'pro social' values in market-driven societies. As they put it:

> The values that must be strengthened – values that are commonly held and which can be brought to the fore – include: empathy towards those who are facing the effects of humanitarian and environmental crises, concern for future generations, and recognition that human prosperity resides in relationships – both with one another and with the natural world. (Crompton, 2010)

Negative moral emotions: By contrast, negative feelings repel us from their object. The most powerful negative moral emotions aimed at the other are disgust and contempt. These are often implicated in the powerful moral reactions which characterize moral panics (Cohen, 1972; Glassner, 1999) where a particular outgroup – 'paedos', 'trailer trash', 'chavs', 'feral' children – are subject to organized moral hostility. While such feelings can be directed towards the self, more common self-directed negative feelings include guilt, remorse and regret. These feelings are clearly implicated in the 'politics of forgiveness', but whether they are the necessary condition for the emergence of such a politics is an issue explored by Michael Cunningham in this volume.

Positive feelings (of attraction): The organization of good feelings in public life, although a pervasive phenomenon, has still not been systematically examined. Good feelings mediate both horizontal and vertical social relations, and there is also a third cluster of good feelings which seem to refer more to an internal state having no particular object. Feelings such as love, trust and gratitude play a key role in mediating our relations with each other. This remains relatively under-explored, the one exception being the study of trust and the vital role it plays in maintaining social networks, contracts and inter-organizational relations (Fox, 1974; Granovetter, 1992), and as a basic currency in the formation of social capital (Sullivan and Transue, 1999). Love, admiration and awe also mediate our positive relations to something higher, whether this be a loved political or religious leader, or a set of beliefs or symbols. Studies of charisma clearly reveal the idealization of political leaders, even those of the most autocratic nature (Overy, 2004). But 'leader love' is not necessarily the creation of charismatic relations; it may be based upon non-idealized love and gratitude towards political figures who have earned such respect through their courage, fortitude or generosity. The third group of positive feelings are in some ways the most intangible; perhaps closely approximating to affects, they include hope, optimism, joy, happiness and enthusiasm. Within millenarian traditions, including political belief systems with strong millenarian foundations, optimism is based upon a teleology which suggests that history is somehow on the movement's side. As is well known, the Italian Marxist Antonio Gramsci sought to counter this impulse within the early communist movement by insisting that the only realistic foundation for optimism would come from 'a pessimism of the intellect' (Gramsci, 1971) – that is, the capacity to face the world as it is rather than as we would like it to be. Nevertheless, there is evidence that 'positive illusions' can play an important role in sustaining health and well-being (Snyder, 1989). Perhaps for most of us, Gramsci's paradox – think critically and face reality unblinkingly while retaining an unswerving hope in the capacity of oneself and one's fellows to change life for the better – is just too difficult to sustain. Indeed, psychoanalysts such as D.W. Winnicott made precisely this point when insisting that imagination, as opposed to delusion, plays an essentially constructive role in individual and cultural development (Winnicott, 1971). Like other affects, optimism has a propensity towards contagiousness, something revealed vividly in the recent credit-fuelled bubble that preceded the 2008 financial crash. Here we could say that at some point 'positive illusions' became transformed into 'negative delusions' as the contagion amplified the initial optimism into something which became uncontainable. The concept of positive illusions takes us to the issue of happiness, something which has become a focus for both researchers and policymakers in recent years. Martin Seligman has become particularly associated with the development of what has become called 'positive psychology', the focus of which is the study of happiness or well-being (Seligman, 2011). Given the accumulating evidence (Lane, 2000; Layard, 2005; Rutter and Smith, 1995) that at a certain point the correlation between increased material prosperity and increased well-being begins to lessen, policymakers in the prosperous West have become increasingly preoccupied with the search for alternative measures of 'wealth' to GDP. The work of Amartya Sen has been very influential here, not only in informing the Human Development Index for the United Nations but, more recently, in influencing both the UK and French governments. Sen (1999) and Nussbaum (2001) have argued for the continued relevance of Aristotelean notions of human flourishing as against more narrowly utilitarian notions of happiness.

Negative feelings (of repulsion): The strongest negative feelings towards the other include hatred, envy, spite, malice and loathing. In public life, this cocktail of toxic feelings is most closely associated with the phenomenon of *ressentiment*, a particular kind of resentment first glimpsed by Nietzsche, then analysed further by Max Scheler (1992), and now widely understood to be the affective foundation for reactionary and authoritarian forms of populism (Brown, 1995; Demertzis, 2006; Hage, 2003). Ressentiment is seen as the feeling of the powerless who are forced to suppress the resentment and anger they feel about their position so that their bitterness turns in upon itself. In ressentiment, the original object of grievance is given up but the affect is held on to; the sense of grievance is nursed, finding expression in a litany of complaints, criticisms and denigrations which becomes the material for populist politicians and movements. Racism, nationalism and welfare chauvinism (hostility to those perceived as non-nationals who are benefiting from public services such as education and health care) are routes through which ressentiment may be channelled. There is also a group of more intangible negative feelings whose 'object' is not so much the other but life or time itself. Here we can include pessimism, cynicism and despair. Peter Sloterdijk (1984, 1988) was one of the first to examine cynicism as an organized cultural phenomenon, and several studies have now been conducted of cynicism in institutions such as the police force (Regoli, et al. 1989) and education (Southwell and Welch, 2006). For some, the modernization of politics and the creation of new political/media elites has led to a growing disenchantment with democratic processes and institutions giving rise to a generalized cynicism and disengagement.

Feelings associated with loss: The feelings associated with loss – grief, sorrow, disappointment, disillusionment, sadness, melancholy – are among some of the most powerful to be experienced by individuals and groups. As Peter Marris has argued, all change involves loss (Marris, 1974), and therefore loss and the feelings attendant upon it are the inevitable accompaniment of social and economic change, including experiences of urbanization and development, industrial restructuring and migration. The more recent tradition of postcolonial studies sees loss as the companion to domination, and melancholia as integral to racialized, gendered and other 'othered' subject positions (Eng and Kassanjian, 2003). If loss can be worked through by accessing the symbolic resources (politics, literature, music, film) necessary for the loss to be mourned, then new collective identities (cultural, national, etc.) can be constructed. From a different direction, the creative uses of grief and grieving have also been examined, particularly by Gail Holst Warhaft (2000) in her fascinating study *Cue for Passion: Grief and its Political Uses*. One of the possibilities that emerges from this work concerns the possibility of 'frozen grief' which – unlike the 'inability to mourn' of melancholia – assumes the form of a 'refusal to mourn' as, in the celebrated case of the Mothers of Disappeared in Argentina, the victims of the junta use their grief to sustain their struggle for justice.

Feelings associated with hurt: Groups which are the object of negative emotions such as hatred, disgust and contempt will be affected by such sustained attacks. Any social group requires a degree of healthy narcissism to sustain its positive sense of itself. Injuries to such narcissism, the consequence of unequal relations of power, result in shame and humiliation. For example, in an almost routinized way, social-class differences are reproduced through processes of disrespecting and shaming (Reay, 2005; Sennett and Cobb, 1993). Similar processes can occur along lines of cultural difference, particularly where these have become racialized. In his influential book *The Geopolitics of Emotion* (2010), Dominique Moisi argues, in an implicit critique of Samuel Huntington's thesis concerning the clash of civilizations, that tension between the West and Middle Eastern countries is best understood in terms of the relationship between a culture of fear in the United States and a culture of Arab and Muslim humiliation, the legacy of at least two centuries of colonial and imperial interference. The role of rage as a defence against feelings of shame and humiliation has been examined by Thomas Scheff among others (Scheff and Retzinger, 1991). Scheff suggests that shame and rage have played an important role in sustaining some forms of conflict such as that in Northern Ireland. To take a final case, based on face-to-face interviews with militant Islamists in the post-9/11 period, Jessica Stern, in her book *Terror in the Name of God*, traces the links between humiliation and religious rage (Stern, 2004).

Feelings associated with injustice: Anger, resentment, grievance and outrage lie at the heart of the emotions of protest. However, the mediating role of framing processes crucially influence the perception, or failure to perceive, injustice. Thompson (2006) has argued, against Axel Honneth, that anger is not the automatic response to misrecognition, nor is it intuitively guided towards the source of injustice. It all depends crucially upon the way in which the experience is framed.

Feelings related to 'flight': Anxiety, fear, terror and horror can have a powerful influence on public life. For example, fear and sometimes even terror typically accompany the eruption of moral and risk panics (Sunstein, 2005). Paranoia constitutes a particular and interesting form of fear where the object of the fear response is largely imaginary. The 'paranoid style' of politics in the

United States has been a focus of analysis since the McCarthy period of the 1950s (Hofstadter, 1979; Rogin, 1987), and, as we have just noted, it surfaces again in Moisi's (2010) analysis of the culture of fear in the United States. The contributions of Northcott and Lucas in the present volume continue this line of analysis, adding to the literature on the climate of paranoia in the United States after 9/11 (Clarke and Hoggett, 2004).

Chapter by chapter

Part I of this book focuses on the complex and multi-faceted relationships between emotions, antagonism and deliberation. In Chapter 2, Marion Barnes focuses on the place of emotions in the various sorts of deliberative forums which are now quite commonly used in policymaking processes. In particular, she seeks to determine which sort of forum is best able to handle the emotional experience of welfare service users in order to shape policies for these users in the fairest and most effective way. To this end, Barnes investigates two particular cases. The first, a citizens' jury held in Belfast in 1998, sought to find out how people felt about proposed changes to health and social-care services. The second case is that of a legislation subcommittee which was charged with implementing reforms to Ontario's community mental health services. Barnes contrasts the understanding of these forums as spaces in which reasoned argument is intended to lead to good policymaking with the importance of values and emotions in motivating action within social movements. Her conclusion is that, since the expression of legitimate and important emotional experiences needs to have its place in deliberation about social policies, 'deliberative forums should be judged on their capacity to encompass such expression'.

Bas van Stokkom's argument in Chapter 3 complements Barnes's well. Like Barnes, he argues for a broader conception of deliberation than that characteristically assumed by the designers of deliberative spaces. He does so in the belief that the argumentation process can be enriched by drawing upon affective and narrative types of communication within public discussion. To make this point, van Stokkom examines a number of Dutch interactive policy experiments in the fields of urban and landscape renewal. Focusing on the emotional dynamics of such experiments, he notes that it is not rational argumentation which changes the views of the participants, but rather their encounter with particular stories, metaphors or design-presentations. The emotional energy that comes with these encounters may change not just the views but also the very identities of the participants. Barnes would not disagree with van Stokkom's conclusion that 'we are in need of deliberative bodies in which persons do not have to leave their emotions behind'.

In Part II, the authors address the intimate and powerful role that fear plays in our political lives. For Michael Northcott, the shape of the contemporary politics of fear is most clearly seen in the doctrine of the 'war on terror' which emerged after 2001. He argues that the US government used this idea in order to sustain an 'atmosphere of fear' in which it was possible to ensure the quiescence of the American public as a reinvigorated set of foreign policy objectives was developed. However, Northcott argues, 'far from reducing the risk of terrorist attacks, and fear of such attacks, the war on terror actually advanced both the fear and the reality of terror and violence'. Taking a step back from contemporary events, Northcott suggests that the origins of the modern politics of fear may be traced back to Thomas Hobbes' *Leviathan*. For Hobbes, fear is the quintessential political emotion, since it is only fear that is capable of forcing us into political association with one another. Northcott ends his chapter by asking 'where we might find resources for the recovery of a more hopeful and peaceable vision of politics'. For him, Augustine may provide the answer. In sharp contrast to Hobbes' dark vision of Leviathan, Augustine's 'commonwealth is a multitude of people who are bound together by their "common objects of love"'.

In his contribution to this book, Scott Lucas agrees with Northcott that 'a far-from-benign "culture of fear"' is to be found in contemporary American political discourse. Such a culture, Lucas argues, plays an important role in the making of US foreign policy, both now and in the past. The Soviet Union of the 1950s, and the Islamist terrorists of today, are both 'constructed nightmares' which are used 'to justify the projection of American power around the world'. Just as anti-communism justified American policy during the Cold War, so the war on terror now justifies the US government's attempts to secure a worldwide 'preponderance of power'. Lucas's worrying final thought is that it is not clear how this contemporary politics of fear may be exhausted, since, 'unlike the Cold War, there is no symbolic marker – no fall of the Wall, no end to an enemy system such as Communism – that can offer long-term absolution of the fear that has been cultivated in past generations and, in particular, in the first years of this century'.

Part III of this book examines what we have called the affective dimension of political mobilization. In her chapter, Deborah Gould conducts an intriguing examination of the nature of political despair. This sense that nothing can be done, that nothing will change, may of course lead to the demoralization and demobilization of would-be political activists. More surprisingly, Gould argues, this emotion may also have productive potential. Despair and its companion feelings – such as hopelessness, desperation and a sense of being overwhelmed – may actually inspire political action. In order to make these arguments, Gould draws on the case of the direct action AIDS movement in the United States, ACT UP. After a moving account of the workings of despair in this movement, she concludes on a more hopeful note. Without seeking to deny or repress feelings of despair, Gould suggests, it may be possible for political activists to acknowledge, collectivize, politicize and even mobilize on the basis of despair. Her account of the First Annual Parade of the Politically Depressed held in Chicago on May Day 2003 suggests that there might even be playful ways of facing up to and dealing with despair.

In Chapter 7, Mary Holmes agrees with Gould that the connections between the emotions and political mobilization are complex. For evidence of this, she looks at the tangle of emotions involved in feminist political processes, drawing in particular on second-wave feminist writings from the 1970s and first half of the 1980s in Aotearoa/New Zealand. In examining this body of writing, Holmes draws our attention to 'the importance of emotional reflexivity in navigating a complex contemporary world and especially in using political means to try and change that world'. By taking such reflexivity into account, we can see that people are not just moved by emotions, almost against their knowledge and will, but rather that they understand who they are, and they present themselves to the world, in terms of certain emotional dispositions. In shaping their organizations, the feminists on whom Holmes focuses sought to reject 'the cold rationality traditionally associated with political decision making in favour of more (emotionally) expressive participatory models'. However, their attempts continually to establish consensus meant that these feminists struggled to acknowledge and thus to deal with dissent. Too often, their answer was to exclude or silence the dissenters. Holmes ends on a more positive note: 'Experience helped some feminists find emotional styles and practices that worked for them rather than against them, and many were able to turn their undoubted emotional commitment to women's interests to impressive political effect.'

The penultimate part of this book focuses on the emotions at work in the politics of reparation. In Chapter 8, Michael Cunningham investigates the role of the apology in politics. More specifically, he considers the relationship between the apology and emotions, presents an analysis of the emergence of the public apology in the contemporary period, considers the philosophical issues such an apology raises, and finally asks whether it has any use in politics today. With reference specifically to emotions, Cunningham's suggestion is that 'guilt, shame and remorse may be features of the apologizing party and hurt and anger may be features of the party seeking or being granted an apology'. However, since in many instances state actors are apologizing for events long in the past – such as Tony Blair's 1997 apology for the Irish

Famine – he suggests that emotions are less likely to play a role in these cases. Cunningham's conclusion is that apologies 'demonstrate that citizens and their leaders can reflect critically on past actions for which they, or at least some of the citizenry, feel shame or regret'. Hence such public declarations 'can attend, at least in part, to the hurt and humiliation of other groups'.

In their chapter, Steven Kaindaneh and Andrew Rigby investigate the role of emotions in efforts to build peace in 'post-conflict' situations. Focusing on the case of Sierra Leone, they suggest that emotions play a vital role in efforts 'to promote co-existence and harmony between those that have been divided through destructive and violent conflict'. Skilfully sketching an 'emotional history' of Sierra Leone before, during and after the civil war of the 1990s, Kaindaneh and Rigby show how important a part 'anger, fear and anxiety' played in this case. On the basis of this analysis, they argue that if peace-building after violent conflict is to be successful, it must find ways to cultivate 'more positive emotions such as compassion, forgiveness, trust and hope'. The conclusion that Kaindaneh and Rigby reach is that 'those who seek to engage in constructive conflict transformation work should factor into their analysis and practice not only the emotional dynamics of any conflict, but also the centrality of emotions in any peace-building project'.

In different ways, both of the authors in Part V of this book address what we have called 'politics and the triumph of the therapeutic'. In Chapter 10, Tim Dartington argues that within neo-liberal welfare regimes, the importance of relationships has become eroded in the development of personalized services that are responsive to an opportunity agenda of social policy. He argues that the apparent emphasis on relationship in a culture which is both therapeutic and performative obscures the ways that relationship is in fact discounted and discredited through a distorted vision of the rights and responsibilities of the consumers and providers of public goods and services. For example, in the NHS today, patients are regarded as consumers of services efficiently delivered by doctors, rather than as one half of the doctor–patient relationship. In parallel, Dartington suggests that we also live in a therapeutic culture that holds out the promise of 'quick fixes' – such as short courses of therapy focusing on individuals in isolation, to the neglect of the relationships in which they are inevitably located. After insightfully analysing these developments, Dartington concludes that they are intimately connected: against the anxieties created by 'the freedoms of a market economy', 'a therapeutic culture that indulges the fantasy of personal growth and salvation without the necessity for a committed relationship provides a very necessary defensive environment'.

In the final chapter of this book, Cas Wouters takes a long-term view of what he refers to as 'processes of informalization of manners and "emancipation of emotions"'. During the late nineteenth and throughout the twentieth century, emotions that had been denied and repressed (re)gained access to consciousness and wider acceptance in more informal social codes. As an example of such emotional emancipation, while soldiers in the Second World War could not admit to feeling fear, it was almost expected that those who fought in the Gulf War would do so. Drawing on his own highly regarded work on the history of manners, Wouters suggests that such an emancipation calls for a stronger and yet more flexible self-regulation. Towards the end of his chapter, he considers a counter-trend: in societies in which all individuals are regarded as each other's equals, it becomes necessary to repress feelings of superiority or inferiority. Wouter's final question is this: will what he calls the *controlled decontrolling of emotional controls* come to include these feelings too?

References

Ahmed, S. (2004), *The Cultural Politics of Emotion*. Edinburgh: Edinburgh University Press.

Anderson, R. (1992), *Clinical Lectures on Klein & Bion*. London: Tavistock/Routledge.

Arendt, H. (1973), *Crises of the Republic*. Harmondsworth: Penguin.

Ayyash, M.H. (2010), 'Hamas and the Israeli state: A "violent dialogue"', *European Journal of International Relations*, 16(1), 103–23.

Beedell, P., Wilkinson, H., Hoggett, P. and Garner, S. (2010), *Report on Focus Group Research into the Impact of Recession and the Barriers to Community Cohesion in Six Bristol Wards*. Bristol: Bristol Partnership Board.

Berlant, L. ed. (2004), *Compassion: The Culture and Politics of an Emotion*. New York: Routledge.

Brown, W. (1995), *States of Injury: Power and Freedom in Late Modernity*. Princeton: Princeton University Press.

Clarke, S. and Hoggett, P. (2004), 'The empire of fear: the American political psyche and the culture of paranoia', *Psychodynamic Practice*, 10(1), 89–105.

Cohen, S. (1972), *Folk Devils and Moral Panics*. London: MacGibbon and Kee.

Converse, P. (1964), 'The nature of belief systems in mass publics', in D. Apter, ed., *Ideology and Discontent*. New York: Free Press, pp. 206–61.

Crompton, T. (2010), *Common Cause: The Case for Working with Our Cultural Values*. London: World Wildlife Fund.

Damasio, A. (2000), *The Feeling of What Happens: Body and Emotion in the Making of Consciousness*. London: Heinemann.

Deleuze, G. and Guattari, F. (1999), *A Thousand Plateaus*. London: Athlone Press.

Demertzis, N. (2006), 'Emotions and populism', in S. Clarke, P. Hoggett and S. Thompson, eds, *Emotion, Politics and Society*. Basingstoke: Palgrave Macmillan.

Dennett, D. (1992), *Consciousness Explained*. London: Allen Lane, The Penguin Press.

Dor, J. (1999), *The Clinical Lacan*. New York: Other Press.

Edelman, M. (1964), *The Symbolic Uses of Politics*. Champaign, IL: University of Illinois Press.

Ekman, P. (1994), *The Nature of Emotion: Fundamental Questions*. Oxford: Oxford University Press.

Eng, D. and Kazanjian, D. eds (2003), *Loss: The Politics of Mourning*. Berkeley, CA: University of California Press.

Fattah, K. and Fierke, K.M. (2009), 'A clash of emotions: The politics of humiliation and political violence in the Middle East', *International Journal of International Relations*, 15(1), 67–93.

Fox, A. (1974), *Beyond Contract: Work, Power and Trust Relations*. London: Faber and Faber.

Freud, S. (1921), *Group Psychology and the Analysis of the Ego*, S.E. 18, pp. 67–143.

Glassner, B. (1999), *The Culture of Fear: Why Americans Are Afraid of the Wrong Things*. New York: Basic Books.

Goodwin, J., Jasper, J. and Poletta, F. eds (2001), *Passionate Politics*. Chicago: Chicago University Press.

Gould, D. (2001), 'Rock the boat, don't rock the boat, baby: ambivalence and the emergence of militant AIDS activism', in J. Goodwin, J. Jasper and F. Poletta, eds, *Passionate Politics*. Chicago: University of Chicago Press, pp. 135–57.

—(2002), 'Life during wartime: emotions and the development of ACT UP', *Mobilization*, 7(2), 177–200.

—(2009), *Moving Politics: Affect, Emotions, and Shifting Political Horizons in the Fight Against AIDS*. Chicago: University of Chicago Press.

Gramsci, A. (1971), 'The modern prince', in *Selections from the Prison Notebooks of Antonio Gramsci,* ed. and trans. Q. Hoare and G.N. Smith, London: Lawrence and Wishart.

Granovetter, M. (1992), 'Problems of explanation in economic sociology', in N. Nohria and R. Eccles, eds, *Networks and Organisations: Structure, Form and Action*. Boston, MA: Harvard Business School Press, pp. 25–36.

Hage, G. (2003), *Against Paranoid Nationalism: Searching for Hope in a Shrinking Society*. London: Merlin Press.

Hochschild, A. (1983), *The Managed Heart: The Commercialization of Human Feeling*. Berkeley, CA: University of California Press.

Hofstadter, R. (1979), *The Paranoid Style in American Politics and Other Essays*. Chicago: University of Chicago.

Hoggett, P. and Thompson, S. (2002), 'Toward a democracy of the emotions', *Constellations*, 9(1), 106–26.

Hoggett, P. (2009), *Politics, Identity, and Emotion*. Boulder, CO: Paradigm.

Holst-Warhaft, G. (2000), *Cue for Passion: Grief and its Political Uses*. Cambridge, MA: Harvard University Press.

Jasper, J. (1998), 'The emotions of protest: affective and reactive emotions in and around social movements', *Sociological Forum*, 13(3), 397–424.

Lane, R. (2000), *The Loss of Happiness in Market Democracies*. New Haven, CT: Yale University Press.

Layard, R. (2005), *Happiness: Lessons from a New Science*. London: Penguin.

Linklater, A. (2007), 'Distant suffering and cosmopolitan obligations', *International Politics*, 44(18), 19–36.

Luskin, J. (2002), 'From denial to extenuation and finally beyond: political sophistication and citizen performance', in J. Kuklinski, ed., *Thinking about Political Psychology*. Cambridge: Cambridge University Press, pp. 281–305.

Marcus, G. (2002), *The Sentimental Citizen: Emotion in Democratic Politics*. University Park, PA: Pennsylvania State University Press.

Marris, P. (1974), *Loss and Change*. London: Routledge and Kegan Paul.

Melander, E. (2009), 'The geography of fear: regional ethnic diversity, the security dilemma and ethnic war', *European Journal of International Relations*, 15(1), 95–124.

Menzies, L.I. (1960), 'A case study in the functioning of social systems as a defense against anxiety', *Human Relations*, 13(2), 95–121.

Mercer, J. (2005), 'Rationality and psychology in international politics', *International Organization*, 59, 77–106.

Minow, M. (1998), *Between Vengeance and Forgiveness: Facing History after Genocide and Mass Violence*. Boston, MA: Beacon.

Moisi, D. (2010), *The Geopolitics of Emotion: How Cultures of Fear, Humiliation and Hope are Reshaping the World*. New York, NY: Anchor.

Monroe, K. (1996), *The Heart of Altruism*. Princeton, NJ: Princeton University Press.

Newman, J. (2011), 'Activism, emotion, affect and performance: problems of theory and method', Paper given to the Fourth Interpretive Policy Analysis Conference, UK: University of Cardiff.

Nussbaum, M. (1996), 'Compassion: the basic social emotion', *Social Philosophy and Policy*, 13(1), 27–58.

—(2001), *Upheavals of Thought*. Cambridge: Cambridge University Press.

Overy, R. (2004), *The Dictators: Hitler's Germany, Stalin's Russia*. London: Allen Lane.

Plutchik, R. (2002), *Emotions and Life: Perspectives from Psychology, Biology and Evolution*. Washington, D.C.: American Psychological Association.

Reay, D. (2005), 'Beyond consciousness? The psychic landscape of social class', *Sociological Review*, 39(5), 911–28.

Regoli, R.M., Crank, J.P. and Culbertson, R.G. (1989), 'Police cynicism, job satisfaction, and work relations of police chiefs: an assessment of the influence of department size', *Sociological Focus*, 22(3), 161–71.

Rogin, M. (1987), *Ronald Reagan the Movie, and Other Episodes in Political Demonology*. Berkeley, CA: University of California Press.

Ross, A. (2006), 'Coming in from the cold: constructivism and the emotions', *European Journal of International Relations*, 12(2), 197–222.

Rutter, M. and Smith, D. eds (1995), *Psychosocial Disorders in Young People: Time Trends and their Causes*. New York, NY: Russell Sage Foundation.

Sasley, B. (2010), 'Affective attachments and foreign policy: Israel and the 1993 Oslo Accords', *European Journal of International Relations*, 16(4), 687–709.

Scheff, T. and Retzinger, S. (1991), *Emotions and Violence: Shame and Rage in Destructive Conflicts*. Lexington, MA: Lexington Books.

Scheler, M. (1992), *On Feeling, Knowing, and Valuing,* ed., H. Bershady. Chicago: Chicago University Press.

Seligman, M. (2011), *Flourish: A Visionary New Understanding of Happiness and Well-being.* New York, NY: Free Press.

Sen, A. (1999), *Development and Freedom.* Oxford: Oxford University Press.

Sennett, R. and Cobb, J. (1993), *The Hidden Injuries of Class.* London: Faber and Faber.

Sloterdijk, P. (1984), 'Cynicism – the twilight of false consciousness', *New German Critique,* 33, 190–206.

— (1988), *Critique of Cynical Reason*, Minneapolis, MN: University of Minnesota Press.

Snyder, C.R. (1989), 'Reality negotiation: from excuses to hope and beyond', *Journal of Social and Clinical Psychology,* 8(2), 130–57.

Solomon, R. (2007), *True to Our Feelings: What Our Emotions are Really Telling Us.* New York, NY: Oxford University Press.

Southwell, M. and Welch, J. (1995), 'Reflections on professional cynicism in education and the management of educational organizations', *Education Action Research,* 3(3), 337–45.

Stern, J. (2004), *Terror in the Name of God: Why Religious Militants Kill.* New York, NY: Harper.

Sullivan, J. and Transue, J. (1999), 'The psychological underpinnings of democracy: a selective review of research on political tolerance, interpersonal trust and social capital', *Annual Review of Psychology,* 50, 625–50.

Sunstein, C. (2005), *Laws of Fear: Beyond the Precautionary Principle.* Cambridge: Cambridge University Press.

Thompson, S. (2006), 'Anger and the struggle for justice', in S. Clarke, P. Hoggett and S. Thompson, eds, *Emotion, Politics and Society.* Basingstoke: Palgrave Macmillan.

Tomkins, S. (2008), *Affect, Imagery, Consciousness: The Complete Edition.* New York, NY: Springer.

Westen, D. (2007), *The Political Brain: The Role of Emotion in Deciding the Fate of the Nation.* Washington, D.C.: Public Affairs.

Whitebook, M. (2002), 'Compassion as a political virtue', *Political Studies,* 50(3), 529–44.

Williams, R. (1977), *Marxism and Literature.* Cambridge: Cambridge University Press.

Winnicott, D.W. (1971), *Playing and Reality.* London: Routledge.

Žižek, S. (1993), *Tarrying with the Negative.* Durham, NC: Duke University Press.

PART ONE

Emotion, antagonism and deliberation

2

Passionate participation
Emotional experiences and expressions in deliberative forums

Marion Barnes

Introduction

The expansion of participatory governance has created multiple forums within which citizens, service users and public officials discuss issues of welfare and well-being. These forums have been characterized as partnerships, invited spaces, contested spaces, deliberative spaces, spaces for change (e.g. Cornwall and Coelho, 2007). In this chapter, I consider these as emotional spaces: spaces in which identities are negotiated, constructed and possibly transformed, righteous anger, pain and frustration are expressed, and hopes and aspirations are pursued. My approach here is less concerned with the emotional dynamics of interaction within participatory forums (Thompson and Hoggett, 2001; Van Stokkom, 2005), than with the relationship between the emotional content of the issues being debated and the capacity of dialogue within these forums to realize welfare, well-being and justice. As the distinction between invited and free spaces becomes increasingly fluid because of the adoption of 'empowerment' and participation as official policy, it is important to understand what happens to those who try to operate in both arenas: as activists within social movement organizations and participants within officially sponsored deliberative forums. It is also important to consider what kind of spaces might be necessary to encompass the emotional dimension of the experiences of those subject to social policies who seek to draw from personal experience to inform social policymaking.

By way of introduction, the issues I will be exploring can be illustrated with two incidents from studies of such forums. The first comes from a study I conducted of a citizens' jury in Belfast (Barnes, 1999). This was convened to explore citizens' views about proposed changes to the structure of health and social care services. In order to evaluate this process I observed deliberations, collected data about immediate responses to the process from jurors, and undertook telephone interviews with jurors, witnesses and those who commissioned the jury a few weeks after this had taken place. During an interview a health service manager who had acted as a witness made an observation that ran counter to much of the received wisdom at the time about the value of deliberative forums such as citizens' juries. This woman had previous experience of public consultations on health and health service issues and compared the citizens' jury experience unfavourably with public meetings. She commented on the absence of opportunities for interaction with members of the jury and described the process as one in which the jurors posed questions, because that was what they were there to do, and she answered them. There was no follow-up discussion and she had no sense of why the questions were asked, or whether they reflected broadly held views among the jurors. She contrasted this with public meetings which are often characterized by angry people coming with views to express, but where she felt she understood more about what those views were and why they were held, and thus more able to provide a helpful response and engage in an exchange about this than she did in the citizens' jury.

The other example concerns the dynamics of psychiatric survivor participation in a legislation subcommittee with responsibilities for implementing proposals for community mental health services in Canada (Church, 1996). Many of the officials involved in this process found the angry and emotional input from service users very hard to handle. One young woman started to cry as she told her story and challenged officials to act quickly because if they didn't it would be too late for her – she would be dead. Officials thought the approach adopted by service users was too confrontational and tried to rule personal stories – that they described as 'horror stories' – as outside the remit of the committee. Questioning of officials was described as 'grilling' and overall the behaviour of service users was constructed as 'bad manners'. Church concluded that the service users were not so much rude as playing from a different standard for politeness and reason. She wrote:

> they used the public hearings to express the pain in their lives. They wanted a professional/bureaucratic response to the emotional as well as the cognitive aspects of their speaking out. The fact that they rarely received it was more than a breach of decorum. (Church, 1996, p. 41)

Thus, in the first case, we see the absence of emotion among the jurors being cited as grounds for questioning the authenticity of their interest in the issues they are deliberating. There is a sense that they are 'going through the motions', that they do 'not really care' about the issues in any significant sense. In the other example the presence and expression of emotion is considered to rule much of what is being said as 'outside the remit' of the committee and as evidence of bad manners on the part of the participants. This suggests emotionality is linked to ways of assessing the authenticity of both the motivations and style of participants, but that these judgements may be contested.

In this chapter I will address the theory and practice of two different modes of participation: action within social movements and participation in deliberative forums constituted by public officials to involve 'the public' in policymaking and service delivery. Focusing on the significance of emotionality within both contexts, I will illustrate the tensions that are evident when social movement activists take part in deliberative policymaking. I will then offer a perspective from relational ethics that I suggest offers a way of broadening our conception of deliberative practice that might resolve such tensions – at least at an analytical level, but which may also perhaps offer a clue about practical ways of achieving a better understanding between officials and citizens in such contexts and of enabling deliberation to deliver welfare, well-being and justice.

Emotions, identity and social movements

Different social movement theorists offer different explanations for why people take part. The perspective I am adopting draws primarily from a sociocultural perspective, emphasizing the significance of value systems, the way in which actors make sense of their own situations and their responses to dissatisfactions with institutional or broader social norms, rather than from a position deriving from rational choice theory (see e.g. Crossley, 2002, ch. 4). However, theorists who have argued that it is necessary to bring emotions back into the understanding of motivations for participation in social movements and the strategies adopted within them can take both cultural and structural positions on this issue (Goodwin et al. 2001; Kemper, 2001).

Those who are better integrated into social networks are more likely to be recruited to social movements (Della Porta and Diani, 1999). The significance of social networks in affecting individual decisions to get involved, as well as the significance of networks in sustaining social movements, has been extensively researched (Diani and McAdam, 2003). The extent, intensity and overlap between various types of networks are important and there is not a simple linear relationship among networks, community and movement participation. For Melucci and other cultural theorists who reject rational choice theory, networks represent the context in which interactions among individuals produce both the cognitive and affective schemas that can connect individuals to collective action (1996, p. 65). This suggests the importance of understanding the nature of the social relationships of those who become engaged in action not only in structural terms, but also at a micro level. Kemper (2001) argues that structural relationships of power and status can explain the emergence of emotions such as fear, anger, resentment and hope that help explain why social movements arise, amass and sustain necessary levels of support. But he does not address the specific contexts within which individuals experiencing such emotions actually decide to get involved. It is within social networks and relationships that we might find the production of *motivations for* participation – a concept which can be distinguished from the 'incentives' that rational choice theorists invoke in explaining the evaluation of costs and benefits of participation – and which has an affective as well as a cognitive dimension.

There are two aspects of this that are of particular significance for my argument here. The first concerns the significance of values as motivating factors in participation and in constructing identities, and the second relates to what have been variously referred to as 'stigmatized' or 'spoiled' identities. I will start with the issue of values.

Gecas (2000) suggests that the significance of values as a basis for identity has been neglected in comparison with social structural contexts for identity formation. He argues 'an equally strong case can be made for the significance of value identities, in linking individuals to cultural systems and to social groups or collectivities with similar value identities, as is typically the case in social movements' (Gecas, 2000, p. 94). However, he also recognizes the interplay between group and value based identities as the valuing of group or role identities can be incorporated into value systems, many role identities have value components (such as the caring associated with nurses), and group membership usually implies values such as solidarity and loyalty. The distinction between role- and group-based identity and value-based identity is that value-based identities are less situation specific and usually transcend membership of any specific group or occupation of any specific role.

Values have both cognitive and affective dimensions and the emotionally charged nature of values can provide a strong motivation to action. Emotions can sustain commitments and lead those who experience them to accept courses of action that would not be taken by those who do not share such emotions (Barbalet, 2006). Goodwin et al. (2001, p. 6) suggest: 'Cognitive agreement alone does not result in action' and they consider the significance of emotions such as anger or outrage at injustice in generating the frames through which common objectives can be defined as a basis for action. Examples of this from research I conducted with colleagues (Barnes et al. 2006b, 2007) include activists in an initiative to develop fuel poverty strategies who were driven by, for example, the injustice of old people dying of cold, and participants in a Local Agenda 21 Sustainability Forum who were passionately committed to green issues. Distinctions have been drawn between 'instrumental' and 'terminal' values corresponding with a 'means'–'end' distinction (Rokeach, 1979). Terminal values, such as 'freedom' or 'social justice' also signify desired goals and underpin political, philosophical or religious systems of values – the ideologies that provide a frame and a common vocabulary within which social movement participants develop their objectives and plan their strategies. The development of collective identities within social movements is given meaning by the shared worldview which offers a moral basis on which action is built and which becomes a significant reference point for individuals' sense of who they are.

The second part of this analysis relates to social movements that are more obviously based around shared identities and that have particular relevance to the field of social welfare. Collective action among those whose identities relate in part to poor health, abusive experiences and/or dependency on welfare services can be built around various negative or damaging experiences:

- The pain and fear associated with illness, disability and, in some cases, ageing.

- Shame, fear and self-loathing resulting from physical or sexual abuse.

- Frustration and anger associated with receiving services that are disrespectful, unresponsive or which undermine people's sense of who they are.

- Lack of recognition of people as autonomous agents capable of making their own decisions.

- Experience of discrimination, stigmatization and injustice in their daily lives.

There is evidence of the significance of collective action both motivated by and transforming such experiences among different groups: for example, people who live with mental health problems (Barnes and Bowl, 2001; Barnes and Shardlow, 1996); survivors of child sexual abuse (Whittier, 2001); adolescents in the transition to adulthood (Kaplan and Liu, 2000); women experiencing post-partum depression (Taylor, 2000); and disability (Campbell and Oliver, 1996). Action in social movements is motivated not only by emotionally charged negative experiences, but also by anger at experienced injustices. A key purpose and outcome of collective action is the generation of a positive identity out of what some have called 'spoiled identities', of positive emotions such as anger and pride out of shame and fear. Participation in such activities can be directly related to well-being. The following words of activists in a mental health user group indicate the significance of this:

> In some ways it turned out to be a positive step for me. It changed my life around from something that was killing me, virtually, to something that I finally got some kind of reward in. It's given me a life and without it I wouldn't have dreamed of doing half the things I do now. It's given me confidence, assurance . . . I get up now and speak at a conference quite happily. A few years ago I would have no more done that than fly! (Barnes and Shardlow, 1996)

Drawing on research exploring organization among mothers experiencing post-partum depression Taylor (2000) identifies the way in which the development of solidarity with others elicits what she refers to as 'vitalising' emotions – emotions such as pride and joy with the group's new positive collective self-definition. Similarly Whittier (2001) highlights the politicized emotional interpretation of the experience of coming out among child sexual abuse sufferers that can transform fear and shame into empowerment and resistance. This is explicit in the adoption of the term 'Mad Pride' among some within the mental health user movement. A key strategy in this respect (which was first fully articulated within the women's movement) is the sharing of personal experiences and allowing, indeed encouraging, participants to express the fear, anxiety, guilt or other emotions that characterize their response to living with mental illness.

Within the disability movement the dominant emotion motivating early organization was anger at discrimination and injustice, that is, a more obviously politically focused emotion than those evident in other groups highlighted here (Barnes, 1991). However, more recently disabled activists have started to question the adequacy of an approach that downplays the significance of impairment, and this opens up the possibility for more personal emotions to find their place within disability activism (Shakespeare, 2006).

In some cases, for example, collective action among lay carers, gaining recognition for a new social identity is a central purpose of organization (Barnes, 1997, ch. 5). That has both a political dimension, claiming rights for service support in their own right, and a personal dimension, offering spaces in which those who may have been isolated can experience both practical and emotional support. The following quote from a woman who had cared for a son with both learning difficulties and mental health problems demonstrates the way in which finding others with similar experiences can offer a sense of being part of a 'community':

> We have weekly meetings and you actually feel, it's like being in a foreign country and nobody understands the lingo you speak. Then all of a sudden you come back home and everybody understands. (Barnes, 2006, p. 127)

In summary, my argument here is that action within social movements requires an understanding of the emotionality that both motivates and is generated by action. The emotional dynamics will be different in different contexts and emotionality is linked both to values and to the nature of the identity experiences that motivate participation. But in both contexts emotions are central to the purpose and the processes of organizing. We should not then be surprised if social movement activists bring emotionally charged perspectives into deliberative arenas when they move into those spaces.

Deliberation

I now turn to consider the way in which deliberation has been theorized in the context of the 'participatory turn' in governance (e.g. Dryzek, 2000; Fishkin, 1991). In setting out key aspects of 'deliberative democracy', it is important to understand that the 'deliberative ideal' has now been extensively demonstrated to be unachievable in practice (see e.g. Davies et al. 2006) and that the concept of 'deliberation' may be used loosely in referring to a range of participatory practices, many of which are not designed explicitly to follow the tenets of deliberative practice. But the ideal has had a considerable impact in shaping a new imaginary of what participative policymaking might look like.

Deliberation aims to bring decision-making out of the hidden back rooms in which bargaining takes place among interest groups, and enable 'ordinary citizens' to engage in dialogue with both the issues and the decision-makers. The practice of deliberative democracy is intended to open knowledge previously restricted to specific scientific or other communities to lay scrutiny, as well as to open up political arenas to more direct processes of citizen involvement. Underlying such initiatives is the belief that technical or expert knowledge alone is inadequate for the resolution of policy problems, since the issues such problems raise are also political and ethical. Thus it has an educative purpose, creating a more informed citizenry who are better able to engage with the complex issues which form the substance of policymaking. It also has a cohesive purpose as it is believed to generate better decisions that hold greater legitimacy because they are more open and informed, and because the intention is that participants will arrive at a consensus about the best course of action or the most appropriate position to adopt in order to achieve the greatest public good (Bobbio, 2003). Where it is not possible to arrive at a shared position, there should be an account of the reasoning that led to the different conclusions reached by different participants. Deliberation aims to make transparent the reasoning behind positions that are adopted and to enable reflection on the differences that emerge through the process of debate. This notion of *transforming* views, rather than simply aggregating preferences (as happens in voting) is central to the concept of deliberative democracy. In this respect Young (2000) argues for the importance of democratic practices that increase the chances that people will move from positions based on self-interest to those that are more likely to deliver social justice as a result of having to listen directly to others whose positions and circumstances are different from their own.

In order to achieve all the above, Habermas (1984) prescribed what he referred to as 'an ideal speech situation' as a necessary condition for deliberation. This requires that anyone who is competent to speak and act is allowed to take part in the process of deliberation; that all those taking part in the process of deliberation are allowed to introduce any assertion they wish to make and to question any assertion made by others; that all are allowed to express their attitudes and wishes; and that no speaker should be prevented from exercising those rights – either as a result of internal or external pressure.

The privileging of reasoned argument by theorists of deliberative democracy has led to the design of deliberative spaces that are intended to create the conditions outlined above. This has been interpreted in some cases to mean that those with a particular interest in the topic being deliberated should be excluded and has led to what might be considered a self-censoring process to avoid raising issues that might generate heated disagreement (Barnes, 1999).

However, Young (2000) suggests that assuming that deliberation has to be based solely on *reason* – which is usually defined as neutral and dispassionate, and conducted solely through rational argument – will exclude many people. She argues instead for the importance of recognizing and valuing other styles of speech in deliberative processes and identifies greeting, rhetoric and storytelling as modes of speech that are excluded by deliberative theorists. For example, the concept of 'greeting' or public acknowledgement is absent in those cases where individuals or groups who have tried to make claims in public forums have found themselves ignored, stereotyped or otherwise insulted; while telling individual stories of experiences (narrating) can often be dismissed as 'mere anecdotes' rather than valid evidence. Experience of initiatives to secure the involvement of, for example, older people and mental health service users clearly demonstrates the way in which storytelling can be dismissed and delegitimized as a basis on which to draw conclusions about policy and service issues (Barnes, 2004; Church, 1996). Rhetoric, a committed and passionate attempt to persuade others, is usually regarded as aiming to manipulate rather than to reflect a genuine expression of the emotional meaning and content of the position being represented.

Young argues that situating deliberation, rhetoric, narrative and greeting in relation to one another provides a more sophisticated understanding of the elements that may be necessary to enable dialogue between citizens and public officials to take place in a way that is capable of generating alternative discourses and transforming policymaking. Empirical work such as that by Davies et al. (2006) also identifies the way in which emotional engagement with a topic (on the part of both 'witnesses' and citizens) can enhance cognitive engagement and thus enhance deliberation. Their study of the Citizens' Council of National Institute for Health and Clinical Excellence (NICE) indicated that exchanges were more deliberative in style 'when the content under discussion concerned concrete cases and when they were responding to strong invested statements from witnesses and could identify and mobilise their own strongly held opinions in response' (p. 129).

Social movement activists in deliberative forums

The 'new spaces' that have been created to enhance public participation in policymaking are unfamiliar territory to most of those who take part. As I have suggested, some deliberative practices, such as citizens' juries, aim to exclude anyone who might be regarded as having a 'special interest' in the topic under debate and thus those known to be active in social movement organizations, voluntary sector organizations or professional associations that are relevant to the topic would be disallowed. But these highly formalized deliberative practices are not typical and such exclusions do not apply to many of the participatory initiatives that have been developed by local government, the National Health Service (NHS) and other public bodies and that are influenced by the deliberative ideal. Indeed, recruitment may often involve identifying relevant groups and organizations and inviting representatives from these. Thus many of those who do take part in such initiatives have experiences in other contexts where the objectives – which include those of influencing and shaping public policies or service delivery – are similar (Barnes et al. 2007). These experiences derive from involvement in diverse groups and organizations that might be considered to constitute social movements, in more traditional forms of politics and trades union activity, and in voluntary sector organizations which encompass campaigning activities. People bring to deliberative forums experiences of how they operate in other contexts and this influences the way in which they respond to the opportunities offered by these new spaces and indeed the way in which such spaces are themselves constituted (Barnes, 2005; Davies et al. 2006).

This clearly generates tensions that relate substantially to the way in which emotion is handled in such contexts. This was evident in the example of the Canadian mental health policy process discussed in the introduction. Another example from the mental health sphere was a facilitator of a mental health service user council in a psychiatric hospital 'translating' the angry words of users in order to avoid negative responses from psychiatrists and being rebuked by users as a result (Barnes and Wistow, 1994). A similar focus for conflict was evident in an initiative that intended to engage young people in a deprived neighbourhood in planning a youth conference (Barnes, 2007a). The young people who were members of an autonomous youth forum were angry at what they saw as the injustice meted out to the area in which they lived and saw the youth conference as a way of seeking redress. Youth workers charged with facilitating this process sought to train young people to express their opinions in a way that would not 'scare' councillors and local officials. They saw this as an opportunity to educate young people to become responsible participating citizens. The tension between two rather different objectives was focused around the perceived legitimacy of this particular group of young people expressing their feelings in a conflictual manner.

In her study of the child sexual abuse survivor movement Whittier (2001) highlights the very different ways in which emotion is handled in different contexts. In demonstrations and other contexts controlled by the movement emotions of resistance are strongly expressed in a public coming out that is experienced as powerfully transformative. In contrast, survivors appearing in talk shows demonstrated pain and fear, often in a childlike manner – for example, by holding teddy bears. This reflected the construction of talk shows as a route to therapeutic catharsis (see also Lunt and Stenner, 2005). And when activists seek a response from the legal system for the damage that has been done to them: 'displaying grief, hurt, lack of trust, fear, or shame is virtually mandated in order to be a legitimate subject deserving of compensation' (Whittier, 2001, p. 245). The emotion management Whittier describes reflects the different dimensions and purposes of social movements. Movement activists are determining what the 'right emotions' are (Stenner, 2005), not only to feel but also to express in different situations. But other evidence discussed in this chapter suggests that public officials find *any* emotion – whether it be anger, pain or despair – difficult to handle in the context of deliberation directed at issues of policy or service delivery. The onus on managing emotions thus rests with the service users or citizens taking part; officials can invoke institutional rules and norms to define what is acceptable in contexts they control.

So is it possible to conceive of a deliberative practice that can also accommodate the emotionality of those who choose to engage in social movement organizations because of their commitments to the values pursued in such groups, or because through collective action they are able to develop a positive sense of their own identity? Must deliberation be reserved for circumstances in which the 'public' that is engaged is a dispassionate public? If so, what are the consequences for any notion that deliberative processes are capable of contributing to social justice and well-being? The evidence from Davies et al.'s (2006) study suggests that it would be a mistake in empirical terms to reserve deliberation for dispassionate participants, but beyond this empirical evidence of the value of emotionality in facilitating deliberation is the question of the *morality* of excluding those most directly affected by the decisions to be reached through deliberation. Indeed, one of the principles articulated for deliberation is that all those actually or potentially affected by the decisions that flow from such practices should have the opportunity to be involved in the deliberative process. In a social policy context this means those whose lives are most affected by the nature and quality of welfare services and policies, and by the impact of poor health, impairment, poverty, abuse and other experiences which impact negatively on emotional health.

I started this chapter by identifying the contested link between emotional expression, authenticity and legitimacy in the context of deliberation. I now want to suggest that we need to understand authenticity as linked both to the value-based identities of actors and to the way in which action within social movements can transform negative into positive identifications. Both processes are emotionally charged. If deliberation is to enable debate on issues that are significant, in terms of the impact of the decisions that flow from such debate on the way in which we live together, in terms of the moral disagreements that characterize politics (Gutmann and Thompson, 1996), and in terms of the life chances and emotional health of those directly affected by decision outcomes, then it must be capable of engaging not only with strongly held views based in different value positions, but with the hurt and anger of those who have experienced unfairness and injustice. Deliberation must be capable of engaging with the emotional content of experiences that are brought into the deliberative sphere. Deliberation cannot be restricted to the purely rational or cognitive because to do so is to exclude many of those directly affected by the policy decisions that may flow from deliberation. This does not mean that 'rational argument' should be replaced with a slanging match, but it does mean that the tendency to avoid engaging in issues because they are too emotionally charged, or to rule the emotional content of experience as outside the remit of public deliberation, cannot be acceptable. Participants need to learn how to engage with the consequences of this.

If, as Gutmann and Thompson argue, deliberation requires moral argument with the aim of reaching provisional moral agreement, then I would argue that it has to encompass what I refer to as 'emotional morality' – by which I mean recognition and respect for the emotional content of experiences and values and the authentic expression of these as a necessary part of dialogue on issues that are directly relevant to such experiences and values. One reason for this is that the claims that are made in this register are not simply personal claims for individual recognition. Social movement activists do not speak solely for themselves, but express a position that is shared by many others. They call attention to the situation of all those who, for example, are stigmatized by a diagnosis of mental illness, or who suffer as a result of poor treatment by public services. They seek outcomes that are morally acceptable and capable of contributing to justice and well-being within a context of inequality and moral disagreement.

Gutmann and Thompson (1996, p. 40) ask, 'If democracy must be moral at its foundations and in its outcomes, then should it not also be moral within its everyday processes?' How then might we understand the moral processes of deliberative democratic practices that can encompass what I have called emotional morality? Gutmann and Thompson do not consider emotionality directly, but they do emphasize the necessity of recognizing that moral arguments take place in specific contexts and that the arguments that are pursued begin from where we are and have to appeal to those with whom we now live. This suggests that we need to develop a concept of deliberative democracy that also embraces a relational ethics. Such an ethic – an ethic of care – has been developed by feminist political philosophers. Applying this framework to an analysis of deliberative practices offers a rather different perspective on what might be the criteria for assessing 'good' deliberation, that is, deliberation that is capable of encompassing the emotional as well as the rational, rather than criteria that have been formulated on the basis of Habermas' 'ideal speech situation' (Webler, 1995).

Deliberating with care

The concept of care has usually been seen to be restricted to the personal and to the realm of service delivery. However, recent feminist work has developed a political analysis of the significance of care and it is this analysis that I draw on here. Tronto and Fisher offer the following definition of care:

> On the most general level we suggest that caring can be viewed as a species activity that includes everything we do to maintain, continue and repair our 'world' so that we can live in it as well as possible. That world includes our bodies, ourselves and our environment, all of which we seek to interweave in a complex, life-sustaining web. (cited in Tronto, 1993, p. 103)

This definition has been criticized for being too all encompassing, but the point behind it is to emphasize that 'care' is not solely something that should be present within interpersonal relationships. Both Tronto and Sevenhuijsen (1998) argue that care is as much a political as personal value, and Sevenhuijsen and others have considered the value base of social policies and offered ways of analysing such policies within an ethic of care framework (e.g. Sevenhuijsen et al. 2003; Williams, 2001). Key to this analysis is the recognition that not all citizens are equal, but that the achievement of equality is a political goal. This point is eloquently pursued by Eva Feder Kittay (1999) who argues that equality will remain elusive as long as we hold to universalistic egalitarian traditions and fail to develop approaches to equality that also recognize dependency. Elsewhere I have argued that care performs social and political functions in the context of disadvantaged and oppressed communities and that the work of, for example, community activists and peer advocates can be understood as evidence of care in practice (Barnes, 2007b).

Care is both a value and a practice and a caring orientation is acquired through engaging in caring practices and reflecting and debating the values and virtues necessary for care. Thus the notion of 'deliberating with care' can be understood to relate both to the attention given to policy outcomes that are capable of reflecting the contribution of care to justice and well-being, and also to the way in which deliberation takes place. At its most basic Sevenhuijsen (1998) suggests that in the public sphere, care as a democratic practice requires the potential for decision-making roles and positions to be open to diverse participants. But I suggest we can go further than this.

Tronto (1993) outlined four moral principles of care:

- Attentiveness: to recognize and be attentive to others.
- Responsibility: to take responsibility for action.
- Competence: caring work should be competently performed.
- Responsiveness: the position of the care-receiver should be considered from their perspective.

Sevenhuijsen added a fifth principle: 'trust'. She argues that trust is always interwoven with power and responsibility and that a willingness to use power in a positive and creative manner is a necessary aspect of care.

These principles can be applied to the process of deliberation in order to suggest what deliberative practices that are capable of encompassing the emotionality of those subject to social policies might look like. Deliberative practices which enable dialogue about different experiences which derive from the disadvantage and marginalization resulting from, for example, disability, old age or mental distress, can encourage attentiveness to such experiences and give recognition to them (see e.g. Barnes, 2004; Barnes et al. 2006a). But such attentiveness requires that public officials are prepared to listen and to hear things that are said in ways that make sense to the speaker – which may well be very different from ways of speaking familiar to public officials. Emotional expressions emphasize the significance of the issues that are the substance of debate and the particularity of the situations that demand a response. Such emotions provide important information that policymakers need to recognize in determining what action is necessary in order to produce positive outcomes. They then have a responsibility to take action on the basis of this.

The focus on positive outcomes reflects the importance of the principle of competence. An intention to enable people to take part in policymaking, and even taking responsibility to provide opportunities for this to happen, but then failing to conduct deliberation in a way that enables people to feel their contributions are recognized and valued, means that the purpose of participation is not fulfilled. Webler (1995) has argued that 'cognitive competence' is necessary to creating the ideal speech situation required for deliberation. But if deliberation is to be capable of encompassing emotionality then this implies that 'affective competence' is also necessary.

The principle of responsiveness refers to the need to understand how those receiving care respond to it, that is, it emphasizes care receiving as a key part of the practice of care. But it also recognizes that we do not start from positions of equality – that those who are very young, old and frail, or ill are more vulnerable than many of those who make decisions about their care. Thus it emphasizes the importance of understanding *their* experiences rather than assuming we can 'put ourselves in their place' and so speak on their behalf.

Finally, effective participation requires reciprocal trust (Barnes and Prior, 1998). Disregarding or ruling out of order contributions to debate on the basis that they are not expressed in the right way will undermine such trust and may deepen existing negative self-perceptions.

I suggest that adopting this perspective offers a way of conceptualizing the emotional morality that I have argued is necessary to deliberation in the context of public policymaking – particularly with respect to deliberation that is capable of delivering welfare, well-being and justice. Such a morality addresses the likelihood that participants will have an emotional investment in the issues being debated because of the significance of the outcomes for their lives, and understands that emotional expression will often be necessary to communicate the substance of the issues to be addressed. The cognitive emphasis on increasing the information available as a basis on which to enhance understanding prior to reaching decisions will be enhanced by practices that enable understanding of the consequences of decision-making. The potential for transforming the way in which all participants – both citizens and officials – think about policy issues is enlarged, as is the likely level of reciprocal trust between them.

Conclusion

In this chapter I have concentrated on the emotional substance and expression of experiences that service users and citizens bring to the process of deliberation about social policies. I have argued that this represents a legitimate and important contribution to the process of making and assessing social policies and that deliberative forums should be judged on their capacity to encompass such expression. The implication of this is that emotional management should not solely be the responsibility of social movement activists who engage in deliberative forums. Emotion cannot be ruled out of order and public officials cannot claim that good manners dictate that strong feelings be left at the door.

I have not addressed the issue of the emotions that may be felt by public officials in such contexts: either those that relate to their anxiety about how they might handle the emotionality of others, or those deriving from feelings that may reflect something of the experiences expressed to them. Public officials themselves may live with mental health problems, have experienced sexual abuse, or be balancing the demands of paid work with unpaid care. They may themselves be activists in social movements. Such an analysis is worth undertaking. Wadsworth and Epstein (1998) have demonstrated the way in which emotional defences can be built up by workers apparently sympathetic to the idea that mental health service users should take part in service planning. In this context it was the emotions of the staff that got in the way of constructive dialogue. But this reinforces the importance of the perspective I have taken here. In officially sponsored deliberation forums officials wield most power. If such spaces are to be routes towards increased well-being and social justice, then the key challenge is how to enable those who are often subject to others' decision-making to be heard in ways that make sense to them.

References

Barbalet, J. (2006), 'Emotions in politics: from the ballot to suicide terrorism', in S. Clarke, P. Hoggett and S. Thompson, eds, *Emotions, Politics and Society*. Basingstoke: Palgrave, pp. 31–55.

Barnes, C. (1991), *Disabled People in Britain and Discrimination*. London: Hurst Calgary.

Barnes, M. (1997), *Care, Communities and Citizens*. Harlow: Addison Wesley Longman.

—(1999), *Building a Deliberative Democracy: An Evaluation of Two Citizens' Juries*. London: Institute for Public Policy Research.

—(2004), 'Affect, anecdote and diverse debates: user challenges to scientific rationality', in A. Gray and S. Harrison, eds, *Governing Medicine: Theory and, Practice*. Maidenhead: McGraw-Hill/Open University Press, pp. 122–32.

—(2005), 'Same old process? Older people, participation and deliberation', *Ageing and Society*, 25(2), 245–59.

—(2006), *Caring and Social Justice*. Basingstoke: Palgrave.

—(2007a), 'Whose spaces? Contestations and negotiations in health and regeneration fora in the UK', in A. Cornwall and V.S. Coelho, eds, *Spaces for Change: The Politics of Citizen Participation in New Democratic Arenas*. London: Zed Books, pp. 240–59.

—(2007b), 'Participation, citizenship and a feminist ethic of care', in S. Balloch and M. Hill, eds, *Communities, Citizenship and Care: Research and Practice in a Changing Policy Context*. Bristol: Policy Press, pp. 59–74.

Barnes, M. and Bowl, R. (2001), *Taking Over the Asylum: Empowerment and Mental Health*. Basingstoke: Palgrave.

Barnes, M. and Prior, D. (1998), 'Trust and the competence of the welfare consumer', in A. Coulson ed., *Trust and Contracts: Relationships in Local Government, Health and Public Services*. Bristol: Policy Press, pp. 129–42.

Barnes, M. and Shardlow, P. (1996), 'Identity crisis? Mental health user groups and the "problem" of identity', in C. Barnes and G. Mercer, eds, *Exploring the Divide: Illness and Disability*. Leeds: The Disability Press, pp. 114–34.

Barnes, M. and Wistow, G. (1994), 'Learning to hear voices: listening to users of mental health services', *Journal of Mental Health*, 3, 525–40.

Barnes, M., Davis, A. and Rogers, H. (2006a), 'Women's voices, women's choices: experiences and creativity in consulting women users of mental health services', *Journal of Mental Health*, 15(3), 329–41.

Barnes, M., Newman, J. and Sullivan, H. (2006b), 'Discursive arenas: deliberation and the constitution of identity in public participation at a local level', *Social Movement Studies*, 5(3), 193–207.

Barnes, M., Newman, J. and Sullivan, H. (2007), *Power, Participation and Political Renewal: Case Studies in Public Participation*. Bristol: Policy Press.

Bobbio, L. (2003), 'Building social capital through democratic deliberation: the rise of deliberative arenas', *Social Epistemology*, 17(4), 343–57.

Campbell, J. and Oliver, M. (1996), *Disability Politics*. London: Routledge.

Church, K. (1996), 'Beyond "bad manners": the power relations of "consumer participation" in Ontario's community mental health system', *Canadian Journal of Community Mental Health*, 15(2), 27–44.

Cornwall, A. and Coelho, V.S. eds (2007), *Spaces for Change: The Politics of Citizen Participation in New Democratic Arenas*. London: Zed Books.

Crossley, N. (2002), *Making Sense of Social Movements*. Buckingham: Open University Press.

Davies, C., Wetherell, M. and Barnett, E. (2006), *Citizens at the Centre: Deliberative Participation in Health Care Decisions*. Bristol: Policy Press.

Della Porta, D. and Diani, M. (1999), *Social Movements: An Introduction*. Oxford: Blackwell.

Diani, M. and McAdam, D. eds (2003), *Social Movements and Networks: Relational Approaches to Collective Action*. Oxford: Oxford University Press.

Dryzek, J. (2000), *Deliberative Democracy and Beyond*. Oxford: Oxford University Press.

Fishkin, J.S. (1991), *Democracy and Deliberation*. New Haven: Yale University Press.

Gecas, V. (2000), 'Value identities, self-motives and social movements', in S. Stryker, T.J. Owens and R.W. Whites, eds, *Self, Identity and Social Movements*. Minneapolis: University of Minnesota Press, pp. 93–109.

Goodwin, J., Jasper, J.M. and Polletta, F. eds (2001), *Passionate Politics: Emotions and Social Movements*. Chicago: University of Chicago Press.

Gutmann, A. and Thompson, D. (1996), *Democracy and Disagreement*. Cambridge, MA: Belknap Press.

Habermas, J. (1984), *The Theory of Communicative Action*, Vol. 1. Boston: Beacon Press.

Kaplan, H.B. and Liu, X. (2000), 'Social movements as collective coping with spoiled personal identities: intimations from a panel study of change on life course between adolescence and adulthood', in S. Stryker, T.J. Owens and R.W. Whites, eds, *Self, Identity and Social Movements*. Minneapolis: University of Minnesota Press, pp. 215–38.

Kemper, T. (2001), 'A structural approach to social movement emotions', in J. Goodwin, J.M. Jasper and F. Polletta, eds, *Passionate Politics: Emotions and Social Movements*. Chicago: University of Chicago Press, pp. 58–73.

Kittay, E.F. (1999), *Love's Labor: Essays on Women, Equality and Dependency*. New York and London: Routledge.

Lunt, P. and Stenner, P. (2005), 'The Jerry Springer Show as an emotional public sphere', *Media, Culture and Society*, 27(1), 59–81.

Melucci, A. (1996), *Challenging Codes: Collective Action in the Information Age*. Cambridge: Cambridge University Press.

Rokeach, M. (1979), *Understanding Human Values: Individual and Societal*. New York: Free Press.

Sevenhuijsen, S. (1998), *Citizenship and the Ethics of Care: Feminist Considerations on Justice, Morality and Politics*. London and New York: Routledge.

Sevenhuijsen, S., Bozalek, V., Gouws, A. and Minnaar-McDonald, M. (2003), 'South African social welfare policy: an analysis using the ethic of care', *Critical Social Policy*, 23(3), 299–321.

Shakespeare, T. (2006), *Disability Rights and Wrongs*. London: Routledge.

Stenner, P. (2005), 'Emotions and rights: or: the importance of having the right emotions', *History and Philosophy of Psychology*, 7(1), 11–21.

Taylor, V. (2000), 'Emotions and identity in women's self-help movements', in S. Stryker, T.J. Owens and R.W. Whites, eds, *Self, Identity and Social Movements*. Minneapolis: University of Minnesota Press, pp. 271–99.

Thompson, S. and Hoggett, P. (2001), 'The emotional dynamics of deliberative democracy', *Policy and Politics*, 29(3), 351–64.

Tronto, J.C. (1993), *Moral Boundaries: A Political Argument for an Ethic of Care*. New York and London: Routledge.

Van Stokkom, B. (2005), 'Deliberative group dynamics: power, status and affect in interactive policy making', *Policy and Politics*, 33(3), 387–409.

Wadsworth, Y. and Epstein, M. (1998), 'Building in dialogue between consumers and staff in acute mental health services', *Systemic Practice and Action Research*, 11(4), 353–79.

Webler, T. (1995), '"Right" discourse in citizen participation: an evaluative yardstick', in O. Renn, T. Webler and P. Wiedemann, eds, *Fairness and Competence in Citizen Participation: Evaluating Models for Environmental Discourse*. Dordrecht: Kluwer Academic Publishers, pp. 35–86.

Whittier, N. (2001), 'Emotional strategies: the collective reconstruction and display of oppositional emotions in the movement against child sexual abuse', in J. Goodwin, J.M. Jasper and F. Polletta, eds, *Passionate Politics: Emotions and Social Movements*. Chicago: University of Chicago Press, pp. 233–50.

Williams, F. (2001), 'In and beyond New Labour: towards a new political ethics of care', *Critical Social Policy*, 21(4), 467–93.

Young, I.M. (2000), *Inclusion and Democracy*. Oxford: Oxford University Press.

3

Deliberative rituals
Emotional energy and enthusiasm in debating landscape renewal

Bas van Stokkom

This chapter argues that the argumentation process within interactive policymaking processes can be enriched by drawing upon affective and narrative types of communication. To illustrate this 'broadened deliberation', I focus on the emotional dynamics typical of some Dutch experiments in the fields of urban and landscape renewal. It is suggested that it is not rational argumentation which changes the views of the participants, but being confronted with particular stories, metaphors or design-presentations. These projects can be viewed as transition rituals, in which collective emotional energy may bring about a new identity formation. Creative experts may have some grip upon the conditions under which group enthusiasm can arise. The possibilities and risks of these projects are discussed, especially the pitfalls of group identification.

Introduction

Many theorists of deliberative democracy stress that a dialogue should be free of strategic views, rhetoric and emotions. Rhetorical statements and passionate debating are generally viewed as obstructive, hampering the formation of rational agreements. These theorists idealize communication settings free of power and domination, and divert the attention away from 'real settings', which often have rowdy and turbulent forms of political com-munication (van Stokkom, 2005). The emotional dynamics in these 'messy' interactive projects form – no matter how – a part of public communication. In some cases, initial feelings of anger, indignation or fear can be overcome and the process may take a turn that stimulates positive cooperation. In other cases, the initial approval gives way for different emotions, for example, aver-sion and disappointment. It seems fruitful to understand these 'non rational' group dynamics in order to improve the organizational setting and develop realistic expectations (Thompson and Hoggett, 2001).

In this chapter I will focus on emotional dynamics in a group of Dutch interactive experiments in the fields of urban and landscape renewal. In these interactive projects the role of designers is of great importance: they can take the lead in transforming conflicting local commitments into a 'project identity'. These projects often function as 'transition rituals' in which 'being part of the process' and 'experiencing collective enthusiasm' seem decisive for consensus formation. I will argue that participation in these symbolically charged events may release an 'emotional energy' that reinforces designs or plans that are deemed attractive or important. It is not rational argumentation which changes the views of the participants, but being confronted with sto-ries, metaphors or design-presentations.

Design professionals and other creative experts can bring in options to high-light the intuitions and preferences of the participants (Forester, 1999). They can shift the attention from antagonistic and polarizing arguments to relevant historical, ecological or architectural issues with which the participating parties are unacquainted. This may include narrative knowledge of the local environ-ment and landscape designs that evoke an unexpected, attractive coherence (Hajer, 2003). Creative experts and other heterodox experts like historians and writers may provide unconventional views that function as eye openers.

In this chapter I will examine these processes of artistic and narrative learning. The participants may identify with the special and unique character-istics of a plan or proposal, like a renovated neighbourhood or a redeveloped wetland. The attraction of particular and scenic places is an important factor: identification with these places is defined by physical and spatial character-istics and historical antecedents. During such projects the creative input of architect teams, like visual material and reports of the field, are attuned to the knowledge and experiences of the participants. Presenting photographs and historic information about the location may start up a process of identification (Hajer, 2003, 2005). Possibly the individuals, opponents and unknown persons who meet each other during these projects may see the plans and designs as a valuable collective undertaking. In this way deliberation may culminate in temporary forms of consensus seeking: the willingness to shape and support the project together. This means that the dynamic of identification moves to the centre of the process of deliberation. The participants may grow towards one another, approve the plans discussed, and become enthusiastic.

Of course this process does have its dark sides. It may bring along risks and drawbacks: the group-identification process may be too greedy and raise oppressive feelings, critical notes and discrepant views are not really heard, opponents may find themselves in the margins of the event or give up.

In this chapter the possibilities and risks of these dynamics are dealt with. By doing so, I will explore the boundaries of deliberative democracy. Is it meaningful to bring about consensus by means of 'non-rational' strategies? Is it acceptable in terms of deliberative democracy? Does 'deliberation' occur at all during such group processes? I will first portray some planning projects in the context of urban and landscape renewal in which architects and other creative experts take the lead. How do they mobilize the public? Which methods are used to detach participants from their initial views and augment their receptiveness to new designs? In the next section I will theorize the emotional dimensions of narratives and the process of identity formation. In what respects is this process manageable? What is the role of the group rituals and the released emotional energy? I will sketch the contours of a theory of collective transition rituals, which might indicate which conditions are relevant for group enthusiasm. Finally I want to raise some critical comments, related to group identification and 'ritualistic consensus formation'. My overall conclusion will be that identity formation and narrative competence deserve far more attention within deliberative democracy. There is no reason to reduce learning to a rational exchange of arguments.

Developing 'project identities'

One of the Dutch interactive projects in which I am interested took place on the island Hoeksche Waard. In the 1990s there were many controversies concerning the future of the region. Urbanization from Rotterdam and the growth of industrial activities put considerable pressure on the island (Dijkink en Hajer, 2001; Hajer, 2005). During the cultural manifestation Air Southward in Rotterdam (1999), future plans for Hoeksche Waard were presented. However, this event was not supported by the island inhabitants because the plans were experienced as queer and alien. Many inhabitants denigrated the Rotterdam initiative as plans prepared 'for' the citizens, not 'by' the citizens. In their view the region was presented as weak-willed malleable material.

Subsequently, some moral entrepreneurs started a Hoeksche Waard Initiative in which they unfolded their own plan and story, detached from the 'arrogant' cultural scene in Rotterdam. During these Air Plus activities, the inhabitants were consulted and the involved landscape architects were eager to show the variety of ways in which the inhabitants make use of their natural environment. The architects approached the public in subtle ways. They did not suggest that something 'great' was going to happen; neither did they present plans that might overwhelm the public. Rather they presented a multitude of pictures, detailed fieldwork, photographs, designs and maps, all multi-interpretable and intended to evoke curiosity.

At the same time the landscape architects wanted to break through existing visions: upsetting and unbinding existing representations by offering many opposing pictures that for instance refer to landscape functions in earlier times. They created a 'proximity' that evoked emotional reactions and tried to make the language of the local physical and cultural *Lebenswelt* productive. In this way the participants in the meetings – the potential local users of the area – were forced to reorient themselves; some designs that were organized around specific metaphors did attract the public, although for different reasons.

The Air Plus creative process culminated in a storyline that explicitly took into consideration the diversity of wishes of the region. But this storyline was also able to develop the shared meanings of the region, formulated against the usurping ambitions of the nearby metropolis Rotterdam. The Dutch political scientist Maarten Hajer points out that in Hoeksche Waard a new discourse coalition was created, in which different groups endorsed the same story for different reasons. First an 'identity of resistance' was shaped, a social and cultural opposition to the interference of Rotterdam, which subsequently gave way to a 'project identity', that anticipated the formulation of a future plan starting from clear and self-conscious feelings (see also Castells, 1997, p. 9).

In another Dutch interactive policy project, the Position of Amsterdam, landscape architects were involved in the formulation of a conservation plan (Gomart et al. 2003). The Position of Amsterdam is a fallen fortification system that lost its original function but still is observable in the landscape, although most parts are hidden. The architects intended to preserve and strengthen the Position as a recognizable cultural and green zone of connections in the Amsterdam region. By means of consulting citizens, the province of Noord-Holland tried to gain commitment and support of the public.

In the first stage of this project the architects and designers wanted to break through existing views, trying to dislocate and detach: to dislodge the Position from familiar representations by means of presenting conflicting images (referring to other historical periods or, on the contrary, portraying details released from historical functions). The alternative designs presented were intended to make a lively contact with the environment by installing 'closeness' and evoking recognizable perceptions. These designs also intended to dissociate the public, and drag them out of passivity. Some suggestions by the participants were included in the plans.

During the Day of Participation in 2001 the organizing team tried to select ideas that could make 'the difference' and could withstand critique and resistance. Doing so the team was working up to a coherent and accessible design. The presentation of a well-known novelist proved to have a converging effect. He described the fallen fortification system in a nostalgic way, introducing a unity of suggestions and allusions. He coined the term 'Stiltestelling', which might be translated as 'stillness position' or 'stillness trenches'. A quote may illustrate the generaltone (cited in Gomart et al. 2003, p. 142):

Hier hoort land bij stad.
Hier hoort vooruitgang bij stilstand.
Zo kalm, zo mooi, zo stil, in het zicht van een helse metropool: een wonder is het.

Here land belongs to city
Here progress belongs to stagnation
So calm, so beautiful, so still, in sight of a hellish metropolis: it is a wonder

After his intervention this concept became the leading metaphor of the project and the Position of Amsterdam received a nostalgic emotional turn. How can the successful reception of this metaphor be explained? What is the 'magic' of storytelling? Which emotions are in play here? In the sections below I will first theorize the emotional dimensions of narratives and subsequently I will deal closely with the process of identity formation, the group rituals and the growth of collective enthusiasm.

The organization of identification

Designing tropes

These Dutch interactive projects show that it is not the exchange of arguments, facts or options that does the work of changing the opinions of the public, but the attractiveness of storylines. Specific stories can reduce complex questions to some simple formulas or metaphors. The power of a story does not consist in logical consistency, but in being multi-interpretable. Participants get the opportunity to understand the question of landscape planning in their own ways, to give their own meanings to the ambiguous profile of the story (Hajer,

1995). Metaphors such as 'home' or 'yard' are burdened with emotions and are often experienced in a subconscious way. Metaphors, but also visual presentations, activate memories, fantasies and impressions; they renew experiences. Exactly because they act out a story, they sensitize and act upon our emotions. Successful designs seem to have a paradoxical combination of variety and simplicity: voicing different experiences of the public on the one hand and introducing guiding metaphors on the other.

Stories embody a narrative rationality that appeals to concrete experiences and the imagination; stories can be moving, suggestive and seductive. By stirring the emotions we are in a better position to recognize, identify and create self-consciousness. Stories bring about something because of their specification: it's 'us' who are involved. Events are often voiced in intimate concepts. Therein lies the potential for change: adding new experiences and referring to particular feelings of inhabitants, their expectations and fantasies that are embedded in local stories about their city or region (Abma, 2001, 1997; Fisher, 1984).

The openness and indefiniteness of narrative forms guarantee personal attachments and reconstructions of everyday realities. The reader or listener makes a plausible interpretation of a complex question that often is strongly polarized or raises divided opinions. But stories may represent reality in a more coherent and meaningful way. Providing coherence and order in a complex and often politicized environment can be called 'narrative organisation' (Wagenaar, 1997).

Metaphors and tropes allow us to attribute meaning to events or incidents (motives, causes, qualities, etc.); they change information into lived experience. The audience is able to situate the event, to compare meaningfully, to get hints for action. Of course, because metaphors are polysemic, one separate event can generate many different narrative interpretations. For instance, people can interpret a metaphor in a positive way and fantasize around it. In respect to interactive meetings related to environment planning, figures of speech that attribute 'oneness' and 'unique qualities' seem to be of special importance. Psychoanalyst Yiannis Gabriel (1998) emphasizes the emotional dimensions of stories. Some stories, in particular epic stories that refer to courage and perseverance, succeed in raising pride and admiration in listeners. Using the notions of Gabriel, one could place environmental or urban plans and designs in the genres of epic and romantic stories. Comical and tragic stories do not seem to be really suitable. The epic story has a typical progressive storyline in which fortune smiles upon the principal role player. The combining emotions are elevating and cheering. Epic aspects play a role when a city or landscape renewal project concurs with other rival projects. In that case often merit, performance and success are stressed, combined with pride, or, on the contrary, jealousy when rival towns or regions do perform better. During citizen forums that aim to construct an attractive future town vision, the non-performance of rival municipalities is often stressed. Sigmund Freud (1921) would have called this the 'narcissism of minor differences'. In this way epic stories might contribute to a shared feeling, for instance by using 'we'-terms or grandiose names for building projects.

In romantic stories the central themes generally are love, care and devotion. These themes are connected with metaphors and tropes of attributing feelings (for instance: 'the plans are affecting'), merit ('this region deserves a nice future') and quality ('authentic architecture'). According to Gabriel the emotions these stories generate are caring, warmth, pride and especially nostalgic feelings, the affectionate orientation to and longing for characteristics of the past, or sharing in the quality of an untouched past (see van Stokkom, 1997).

The attribution of merit, achievement and quality to a local project could be interpreted as an attempt at 'self-elevation'. According to sociologist Pierre Bourdieu (Bourdieu 1984; see also Ashforth, 2001) especially well-educated people identify more with symbols that reveal distinction. Conforming to their 'habitus', they tend to judge designs and building projects rather upon their prestige. Distinction creates a sharp contrast between members and non-members, which strengthens the salience of one's own identity. Presenting attractive symbols is thus partly a status phenomenon: citizens tend to pride themselves on the uniqueness of their residential environment.

Introducing identity claims

Is it possible to structure the conditions under which collective enthusiasm for specific designs may arise? I think landscape architects, writers and artists have some grip upon these conditions and that the design process may be attuned to these conditions.

In respect with this question the classic stages that the psychologist Kurt Lewin developed are of special importance. He introduced the concepts of 'defreezing', 'moving' and 'refreezing' in a collective learning process (Ashforth, 1998, 2001; Lewin, 1976; Pratt and Barnett, 1997). These three stages can be reinterpreted as follows.

Defreezing/detaching identities

The process of 'unlearning' or 'detaching' suggests taking distance from familiar knowledge and initiating ruptures with the past. Unlearning responds to doubt, uncertainty and dissatisfaction, so that the participants are thrown off balance. Unlearning techniques force them to reorientate themselves and check what really counts. Raising conflicting emotions seems to stimulate this process: emotional tension and excitement, on the one hand, and dissatisfaction, on the other, seem to be the key to becoming detached from familiar and routine views (Pratt and Barnett, 1997).

Moving/re-identification

As pointed out, the real creative process of design is tailored to the development of attractive new concepts, metaphors and stories. It deals with restructuring: displaying new connections in the middle of artistic stimuli. During this process there could arise a growing recognition of certain values. It concerns tentative and provisional claims on an identity, and anticipation of new applications of the local environment, testing the viability of options, without taking too much risk. Apparently small events can be reinterpreted as new storylines. A large variety of artistic stimuli allows us to test these figures of speech, to adapt them and reintegrate them into new coherent connections.

Refreezing/confirming new identities

Kurt Lewin's term 'refreezing' is somewhat unfortunate because identities always change and keep on being ambiguous. Nevertheless, claims of new identity formation need to be confirmed, disseminated and made known if they want to be attached. Identity claims have to be made urgent and salient in public.

Probably the first stage does not bring along many problems. Creative experts can easily employ methods and techniques that estrange and disengage participants. The second stage is more difficult: much depends on the group interaction rituals that I will discuss below. Making new identity claims permanent is without doubt the most difficult stage. Of course, organizers who have taken great pains in developing new identities do not really have grip upon what is happening beyond the interactive meetings.

Transition rituals: rousing emotional energy

Designing identity claims is one thing, to get them embedded in the group is another. Some storylines seem to be reinforced during group rituals. What is the role of the group process and the collective emotions in this?

Typical of rituals is that group processes as such – and especially the physical aspects – are of more importance than the content of what is being said. If we participate in rituals we are in a way forced to see others as partners; in a public setting we behave as if we already identify with the new plans or future projects. In rituals and ceremonies 'acting together' culminates in 'becoming'. As psychologist Blake Ashforth says: heart and head follow the hands (Ashforth, 2001).

In particular, transition rituals seem to be inviting and seductive because they evoke new identity claims. In these rituals there seems to be more scope to explore in collectively attractive ways. Excitement ('this is what we are going to do') seems to go hand in hand with anticipating the joy of collective future 'achievements'.

Sociologist Randall Collins (1990, 2004) points out that group rituals are contagious: the participants are assimilated into the speed of the collective play. He calls the long-term affective effect of group events 'emotional energy'. High emotional energy suggests enthusiasm and loyalty, being prepared to take the initiative. Low emotional energy indicates that participants do not feel attracted to group activities. They would prefer to avoid them. Individuals in the group generally show emotional passivity.

Because of their infectious quality, positive emotions may be felt more intense during meetings, for instance when a collective achievement or breakthrough is celebrated. Often enthusiasm is generated by a group leader or other vital and prominent participants. These persons function as an accumulator of emotional expression. According to Collins short-term positive emotions as enthusiasm, passion and in particular the expression of emotionally charged symbols, build up a supply of emotional energy. These emotions are often experienced as shared power, status and esteem. Intense group events and experiences and the related tropes and storylines may reinforce each other, and generate an emotional multiplier effect, a synergy that could bring forward a progressive movement of excitement. In that way the perception of so-called 'magical moments' has self-fulfilling characteristics: the ultimate plan that is endorsed by the participants is coloured by preceding group rituals. Sometimes these 'magical moments' will be called 'recognition', sometimes 'chemistry'. Collins also stresses that emotional energy tends to extinguish and dissolve when it is not renewed and revived through ritual, energizing events.

Enthusiasm is evidently contagious: seeing or hearing other people's enthusiasm makes us feel it too, often in an irresistible manner. What functions does enthusiasm have? The term 'enthusiasm' is derived from the Greek 'en theos', meaning 'having a God inside'. Enthusiast persons feel omnipotent, just like a god (Poggi, 2007). They are in a state of exultation, fervour and elation, a state that is close to other emotions in the area of joy. It is felt during or even before the pursuit of a goal. Collective plan-making is often exciting because the participants anticipate the joy of its achievement. Enthusiasm gives also a sense of power and self-efficacy: the achievement of the plans is 'in our hands'. The participants believe with a high degree of certainty that they will achieve their goals. In this sense, enthusiasm includes the hope of success, although hope is less self-confident because hopeful people are mostly aware of external conditions and have a more accurate perception of reality (Miceli and Castelfranchi, 2010; Webb, 2007). Thus enthusiasm is an activating, energy-providing emotion which is felt during action. In that sense it has also dark and dangerous aspects: enthusiasm may be triggered in irrational ways, without reality checks, and it may lead to fanaticism.

In a group dynamic of enthusiasm there is typically an element of novelty. We feel enthusiastic when supporting something creative, when we are doing something deemed important or beautiful, in terms of adding value and establishing something. Enthusiasm is typically related to innovative images and aesthetic goals (Poggi, 2007). Thus I think it would be beside the point to suppose that people's enthusiastic responses are only governed by already learned and mastered habits (MacKuen et al. 2010; Marcus, 2002). Of course capitalizing on enthusiasm, as is the case in political advertisments, may cause people to rely more heavily on prior political beliefs (that are felt attractive), but still these people expect leaders to accomplish something. Enthusiasm fades away when there is no foreshadowing of something important.

Prolonged feelings of excitement?

How can positive commitments be preserved when the interactive meetings have terminated? How to go on when the excitement of collective experiences is ebbing away? This seems easier to realize in organizations in which members meet each other regularly than in *ad hoc* organizations. It is not clear whether the originally endorsed visions will survive during the implementation of the plans. Maybe former conflicts of interest will flare up again. Thus, the question is how to keep the attractive stories coupled to the plan alive. How is it possible to prevent only a subgroup siding with the new plan, while the interest of the majority of the stakeholders dwindles? How is it to keep the plan on course, in the midst of other concurring policy options?

If stories contain powerful 'we-images', then the core symbols of those images might become part of the project identity of a certain region or neighbourhood. The real art is to translate ritual process experiences into symbols that can be transmitted easily (Boyle, 1995; Downing, 1997). As set out before, stories contain a whole range of meanings and allow different interpretations. This abundance of meanings may be opened up by telling stories again and again, so they can be passed through multiple perspectives. Each renewed performance may introduce other story-layers and nuances (Abma, 1997).

Probably charismatic personalities can play a role here. In many interactive projects (informal) leaders come to the fore, functioning as opinion-makers and boosters. The participants generally like sympathetic and inspiring leaders who have a challenging style and with whom they can easily identify. Although the project might be dominated by such persons – the gurus, architects with name and fame – they might reinforce and regain the feelings of 'collective excitement' (Weierter, 2001). After finishing the interactive meetings, these entrepreneurs keep on playing a relevant role, especially to consolidate the often vulnerable project identity.

It should be noted, however, that many interactive projects easily find a 'gentle death' (van Stokkom, 2005). The majority of interactive projects in the Netherlands seem to end up in an uphill struggle, resulting in difficult compromises from which the original aspects of the proposals have been chipped away. Often the motives to develop new plans are barely recognizable. Sometimes administrators are obstructive or hold up the process, so the expectation of tangible results dwindles away. Many participants gradually believe that administrators fail to appreciate the value of their input. They have the impression that the end products of the project are not taken seriously. In other cases the lack of commitment and openness of local officials evokes sceptical attitudes. When it becomes clear that the chosen plan would only play a minor role, several participants point to the futility of the process. They start arguing for a more confrontational form of dialogue in which politicians are criticized for falling short of citizens' desires for reform.

Creative identity formation: some characteristics

Nevertheless, the creative group process during the planning meetings may be rewarding and promising. Enthusiasm thrives when the group is collectively experiencing an expectation of coming success. This process of 'artistic' identity formation does have its own logic and sequences. Let's describe three peculiar characteristics. First, identification is by no means a polished process and often is the outcome of struggle and conflict. To realize that you are forced to take distance from formerly valued views (the 'unlearning') or that idealized designs are not achievable, causes considerable dissatisfaction. Not all participants are willing to displace their interests.

Secondly, participants are encouraged to reconsider their aims and views, and explore attractive points of recognition. The creative experts are working towards a 'narrative organization': providing coherent designs or stories in the midst of conflicting opinions and interests. Stories that anticipate the needs of various publics have a greater chance of getting accepted. They seem to have a paradoxical combination of variety and simplicity: on the one hand incorporating the diverse experiences of the public and on the other hand introducing guiding metaphors.

Thus, narrative knowledge seems to be more promising than rational argumentation. Suggestive and seductive language is indispensable to create shared intuitions and desires as 'being at home'. The participants think they share something precious; although all remain strangers, they have the feeling that they developed a shared identity.

Thirdly, profiling is partly a status phenomenon. This may explain why modern citizens are so concerned with the promotion and upgrading of their environment. A profiled story about the local future envisions a world that represents one's own views and beliefs, and makes one's geographical setting more meaningful and more authentic. Stories appeal to the desire of participants to substantiate their own striking images. Therefore creative experts tend to strengthen and amplify special local and historical meanings.

The dark side of group identification

In discussing interactive policy formation as group rituals, we have been moved far away from the principles of deliberative democracy. Habermas and other protagonists of deliberative democracy would probably reject these ritualistic ways of consensus formation. Enthusiasm and other collective affects are conceived as misleading and carry us away from argumentation.

Of course, pursuing consensus and unanimity has been criticized on good grounds. Consensus formation disregards the opinions of minorities or dissidents. In this context Cass Sunstein (2003) introduced the term 'enclave deliberation': deliberation among like-minded persons. The affective relationships in these groups do reduce the amount of divergent arguments and augment collective influence upon individual choices. In other words: the warmer the feelings, the fewer the protests. Psychologists call this phenomenon groupthink. Groupthink precludes putting alternative options on the agenda or discussing these options properly; decisions may be of lower quality (Steenbergen et al. 2004). Sunstein also points to a 'law of group polarisation': during the discussions the whole group is moving towards a more extreme position. An inflamed group dynamic may culminate in a radicalized collective viewpoint. Each organization, political party, social movement or NGO which mobilizes participants may pass through such a route of group polarization.

However, it is questionable whether this radicalization is typical for interactive meetings in the context of urban and landscape renewal. As stressed earlier, contradictory interests keep on playing a role behind the collective approval of the plan. Moreover, identification is more changeable than the theory of groupthink suggests: cues of identification are not traditionally given, but are readjusted, developed or obtained individually. In a postmodern society personal identities are continuously changing and they are often reframed and reworked in cooperation with others (Brewer, 2004; Castells, 1997; Hajer, 2000).

Still, an ascending consensus may hinder a critical dialogue and may prevent particular perspectives from being put on the agenda. Iris Young (2000) stresses that pursuing consensus may put some participants at a disadvantage, because they would be forced to give up their specific views; their viewpoints are excluded from the discussion. But again one may reply, if participants embrace a collective design or story, each of them is stressing specific meanings that are connected to their own interests and views. When participants agree to go on with the group process and approve agreements, they may do so for very different reasons (see Dryzek, 2000; Pellizzoni, 2001).

However, unconditional identification with the group process conflicts with democratic principles (i.e. autonomous decision-making; equal respect). Group dynamics may rule out sound judgements; the participants may be carried away by the general enthusiasm. For these reasons we need some clear conditions to keep group processes within the contours of democratic communication. First, emotions should be stylized in terms of mutual respect. For instance, the group dynamics should not overwhelm in terms of following others slavishly, nor incite coercion. The organizers could regularly make a time-out to check everybody's experiences. Secondly, affective stories should refer to public interests. Communication that cannot relate the particular to the general does not have much political meaning. Thirdly, narrative communication should draw back in favour of argumentation when the political question 'what are we going to decide' comes in (Dryzek, 2000). In the phase of decision-making, critical argumentation should be of overriding importance. However, in the phase of plan formation the participants could focus freely on creative methods and techniques. This is important because meetings with (over)rationalized discussions often fail to generate innovative plans or culminate in flattened out plans with the lowest common denominator (van Stokkom, 2005).

Conclusion

I conclude that in the stage of plan formation we could broaden the argumentation process, and make use of various types of communication, including affective and narrative ones. There is no reason to reduce participation to speaking, and learning to knowing (Forester, 1999). Nor is there any reason to see participants as carriers of abstract opinions and experiences, because that would obscure their particular interests and needs, and the specific narrative contexts from which they think, feel and act (see also Young, 2000). Learning cannot be restricted to rational argumentation. Learning processes are best addressed in terms of sensibility and attraction, through which the participants commit themselves to the aims of the project. In particular, texts and metaphors are bearers of important insights and may have a catalysing role. Narrative learning appeals to taste and articulates from sensitizing registers, through which the participants are affected and moved.

Passion and rhetoric raise commitment and give deliberation its liveliness and power. During the group process particular opinions and visions are dramatized and experienced in a collective way; these experiences often bring to the fore deeper meanings that may occupy individual memories. Thus, the group ritual may sharpen motives and choices, and reinforce specific attractive future visions. It may therefore also support decision-making processes.

I think that for those reasons narrative knowledge and competence deserve far more attention within deliberative democracy than they have hitherto received. Deliberation could be widened, absorbing more passionate and intuitive meanings, so that the learning process can be enriched. Delimiting deliberative democracy to a bleak 'rational exchange of arguments' seems to be a dead end. A cold debate is not in itself more valuable than an emotional group ritual.

Emotional democracy: some afterthoughts

In our postmodern times more and more aesthetic methods are being used to script and stage (unforeseen) shared identities. Appealing to attractive images is part of developments within popular culture, in which there is a cultivated prominence of feeling. Citizens are addressed via highly aestheticized imagery, which aims to generate emotional resonance in the public mind (Richards, 2004).

Identity formation seems to occur within an 'emotional democracy', the many everyday spaces of 'fear-free communication' (Giddens, 1994; van Stokkom, 1997). In a democratized world people can speak out freely; they do not have to hide behind status positions. Emotional life is emancipated: emotions that had been denied and repressed have gained access to individual consciousness and wider acceptance in informal social codes. This tendency is accompanied by a stronger and yet more flexible self-regulation in which emotions are expressed but kept under control (Wouters, 2007). But emotional democracy does also bring along with it a worrying development: dissatisfaction is easily expressed and citizens seem less willing to compromise; the scope of open and manifest conflicts and controversies seems to grow wider.

Both tendencies – controlled and impetuous expression – are part of contemporary mass politics. On the one hand there is a strong tendency to process emotional life and to address anxiety, anger and frustration. In the language of psychotherapy: there is an effort at containment and the working through difficulties, rather than expression through acting out (Richards, 2004). But at the same time we are witnessing a rising popular 'discourse' of raw opinion, mudslinging and the denouncing of political correctness.

This last tendency raises the problem of demagogy, which is often – mistakenly – equated with emotion in politics. As media-researcher Barry Richards says, it is important to emphasize the distinction between the exploitation and manipulation of feeling characteristic of the demagogue, and the articulation and management of feeling that is the role of politicians who reach for containment. So we have to distinguish between manipulative and containing forms of emotionalized rhetoric.

I think that Richards' analysis is on the right track. The majority of citizens does not like political tactics that sneer and pull down the 'enemy'. We resent grandiose idealizations of leaders and their idealized images: it incites disbelief or boredom. Many creative trends within popular culture – cabaret, music and docudramas – point to other directions: there is an increasingly demand for more authentic, ironic and playful political representations. The argument is not to rush into 'personality politics', as Richards says, but for the enrichment of political communication. Many political leaders and opinion-makers seem to respond to these needs and develop a style which is attuned to today's emotional democracy: presenting emotionally compelling narratives and appealing to citizens' best impulses and desires. They shape identities in positive ways and try to bridge the interests of diverse publics.

What role is left for 'rational' deliberative democracy in this emotionalized culture? At first sight, deliberative democracy, encompassing bodies in which citizens can deepen their thoughts, seems to have only a marginal place within the mass media. Still I think that bodies such as citizens' juries and deliberative polls will continue to be influential, especially as correction devices in which many distorted mass media opinions may be readjusted.

These forms of 'counter-populism' may be important, but citizens cannot be simply educated out of political passions. Moreover, and that's the concern of this contribution, we are in need of deliberative bodies in which persons do not have to leave their emotions behind (Hoggett and Thompson, 2002). In these interactive domains citizens can reveal their needs and engage in creative identity formation.

References

Abma, T. (1997), 'Machtige verhalen', *Beleid en Maatschappij*, 24(1), 21–31.

—(2001), 'Narratieve infrastructuur en fixaties in beleidsdialogen', *Beleid en Maatschappij*, 28(2), 66–79.

Ashforth, B. (1998), 'Becoming: how does the process of identification unfold?' in D.A. Whetten and P.C. Godfrey, eds, *Identity in Organizations: Building Theory through Conversation*. Thousand Oaks: Sage, pp. 213–22.

—(2001), *Role Transitions in Organizational Life. An Identity-Based Perspective*. Mahwah New Jersey: IAE.

Bourdieu, P. (1984), *Distinction. A Social Critique on the Judgement of Taste*. London: Routledge.

Boyle, M. (1995), 'Collective centring and collective sense-making in the stories and storytelling of one organization', *Organization Studies*, 16(1), 107–37.

Brewer, Marilynn (2004), *Self and Social Identity. Perspectives on Social Psychology*. Malden, MA: Blackwell.

Castells, M. (1997), *The Power of Identity*. Oxford: Blackwell.

Cohen, J. (1989), 'Deliberation and democratic legitimacy', in J. Bohman and W. Regh, eds, *Deliberative Democracy: Essays on Reason and Politics*. Cambridge: MIT Press.

Collins, R. (1990), 'Stratification, emotional energy and the transient emotions', in Th. Kemper, ed., *Research Agendas in the Sociology of Emotions*. Albany: State University of New York, pp. 27–57.

—(2004), *Interaction Ritual Chains*. Princeton, NJ: Princeton University Press.

Dijkink, G. et al. (2001), *De Zuidvleugel van de Randstad: Instituties en discoursen*. Amsterdam: AME.

Downing, S. (1997), 'Learning the plot: emotional momentum in search of dramatic logic', *Management Learning*, 28(1), 27–44.

Dryzek, J. (2000), *Deliberative Democracy and Beyond. Liberals, Critics, Contestations*. Oxford: Oxford University Press.

Fisher, W. (1984), 'Narration as a communication paradigm: the case of the public moral argument', *Communication Monographs*, 51, 1–22.

Forester, J. (1999), *The Deliberative Practitioner. Encouraging Participatory Planning Processes*. Cambridge Mass: MIT Press.

Freud, S. (1921) 'Group psychology and the analysis of the ego', in *Standard Edition of the Complete Psychological Works of Sigmund Freud*, Vol. 18. London: Hogarth Press. pp. 67–143.

Gabriel, Y. (1998), *Storytelling in Organizations. Facts, Fictions and Fantasies*. Oxford: Oxford University Press.

Giddens, A. (1994), *Beyond Left and Right: The Future of Radical Politics*. Cambridge: Polity.

Gomart, E., Hajer, M. and Verschoor, W. (2003), De politiek van het ontwerp; representativiteit en performance in de Nederlandse planningspraktijk. Amsterdam: rapport ASSR.

Hajer, M. (1995), *The Politics of Environmental Discourse*. Oxford: Clarendon Press.

—(2000), *Politiek als vormgeving*. Amsterdam: Vossius AUP.

—(2003), 'A frame in the fields: policy-making and the reinvention of politics', in M. Hajer and H. Wagenaar, eds, *Deliberative Policy Analysis. Understanding Governance in the Network Society*. Cambridge: Cambridge University Press.

—(2005), 'Setting the stage: a dramaturgy of policy deliberation', *Administration and Society*, 36(6), 624–47.

Hoggett, P. and Thompson, S. (2002), 'Toward a democracy of the emotions', *Constellations*, 9(1), 106–26.

Lewin, K. (1976), *Field Theory in Social Science; Selected Theoretical Papers*. Chicago: University of Chicago Press.

MacKuen, M. et al. (2010), 'Civic engagements: resolute partnership or reflective deliberation', *American Journal of Political Science*, 54(2), 440–58.

Marcus, G. (2002), *The Sentimental Citizen. Emotion in Democratic Politics*. University Park, PA: The Pennsylvania State University Press.

Miceli, M. and Castelfranchi, C. (2010), 'Hope: the power of wish and possibility', *Theory & Psychology*, 20(2), 251–76.

Pellizzoni, L. (2001), 'The myth of the best argument: power, deliberation and reason', *British Journal of Sociology*, 52(1), 59–86.

Poggi, I. (2007), 'Enthusiasm and its contagion: nature and function', *Affective Computing and Intelligent Interaction; Lecture Notes in Computer Science*, Vol. 4738, pp. 410–21.

Pratt, M. and Barnett, C. (1997), 'Emotions and unlearning in Amway recruiting techniques: promoting change trough "safe" ambivalence', *Management Learning*, 28(1), 65–88.

Richards, B. (2004), 'The emotional deficit in political communication', *Political Communication*, 21, 339–52.

Steenbergen, M. et al. (2004), *Toward a Political Psychology of Deliberation*. Florence: European University Institute.

Stokkom, B. van (1997), *Emotionele democratie. Over morele vooruitgang*. Amsterdam: Van Gennep.

—(2005), 'Deliberative group dynamics: power, status and affect in interactive policy making', *Policy & Politics*, 33(3), 387–409.

Sunstein, Cass R. (2003), 'The law of group polarization', in J. Fishkin and P. Laslett, eds, *Debating Deliberative Democracy*. Oxford: Blackwell, pp. 80–101.

Thompson, S. and Hoggett, P. (2001), 'The emotional dynamics of deliberative democracy', *Policy & Politics*, 29(3), 351–64.

Wagenaar, H. (1997), 'Beleid als fictie: over de rol van verhalen in de bestuurlijke praktijk', *Beleid en Maatschappij*, 1, 7–19.

Webb, D. (2007), 'Modes of hoping', *History of the Human Sciences*, 20(3), 65–83.

Weierter, Stuart J.M. (2001), 'The organization of charisma: promoting, creating and idealizing self', *Organization Studies*, 22(1), 91–115.

Wouters, C. (2007), *Informalization: Manners and Emotions Since 1890*. London: Sage.

Young, I.M. (2000), *Inclusion and Democracy*. Oxford: Oxford University Press.

PART TWO

Politics and fear

4

The liberalism of fear and the desire for peace

Michael Northcott

He needs must many fear whom many fear. Decimus Laberius
SENECA, 1995, p. 52

Perfect love casts out fear.
1 JN 4.18

The selling of the Iraq war in 2001 to the American people involved a highly sophisticated public relations campaign, managed by a White House public relations staffer, Carolyn Beers, who had previously managed the advertising account for major US brands such as Head and Shoulders Shampoo and Uncle Ben's Rice (Northcott, 2004, p. 2). The 'war on terror' was a brand the purpose of which was to sustain an atmosphere of fear in the United States, which was not hard to do following the terrorist attacks on the East Coast in 2001. The intent of the brand and its associated rhetoric was to justify a new set of foreign policy objectives and the creation of what William Pfaff calls a 'greater Middle East' and a new series of client states in Central Asia (Pfaff, 2007). And the brand sold very well and was propagated for free by most United States media outlets with zeal and without critical scrutiny for a period of at least three years (Altheide, 2006).

In addition to the discourse of fear, the Bush–Cheney administration invented a number of devices and rituals that heightened the popular sense of fear including the suspension of *habeas corpus*, the creation of the Guantanamo Bay concentration camp, and an extensive array of new forms of government surveillance under the Patriot Act and mostly administered by the new Department of Homeland Security.

The motive of the United States government in recreating the politics of fear, which it had earlier utilized in the cold war, may be identified in the speeches and strategy papers of the Bush administration. The terrorist attacks on America provided a 'moment of opportunity' for the United States to pursue a new geopolitical strategy which promoted American interests and values across the world against the enemies of 'freedom and democracy' (Bush, 2002). This strategy involved military intervention in many terrains if the United States was to protect its interests in the era of globalization, and to maintain its cultural and economic primacy as a superpower (National Security Strategy, 2002). And this strategy involved a new doctrine of 'preemptive defence' according to which military power was to be projected into regions and states anywhere on earth that were deemed to be developing a capacity to attack the United States or threaten its economic interests. The struggle had no territorial or temporal boundaries, and required the largest foreign mobilization of American military forces since the Vietnam War (Pierterse, 2005).

The brand the 'war on terror' creates the illusion that the United States is engaged in a global war with a range of enemies who include Islamists, anti-globalization activists, environmental and animal rights activists. The brand sustains a level of fear of the Islamist and even activist 'other' equivalent in cultural force to the fear of communist others which had legitimated the national security doctrines of the cold war era, and which sustained a shift in public spending from social to national security, and extensive overseas military interventions (Wolin, 2004, p. 521). The brand also assists in the continued subjugation of the citizenry, and the subversion of democratic participation, that the superpower state and its corporate sponsors and partners require (Wolin, 2004, p. 522).

The rationale for the adoption by the United States of a new doctrine of unilateral global power was various. In part there was the need of the corporate state, or what Eisenhower called the 'military industrial complex', to identify a new project of continual war to justify the levels of military spending required to sustain the superpower state and its corporate sponsors. But the new geopolitical strategy also had historical roots in accounts of America's 'manifest destiny', and of the providential spread of American dominion over its hemisphere. These beliefs, since Woodrow Wilson's intervention in the First World War, have increasingly taken on a global aspect and echoes of Wilsonianism are evident in the strategic agenda of the war on terror (Northcott, 2004, pp. 22–39).

What was more difficult to explain is the adoption of this same strategy, and of the associated politics of fear, by the government of Tony Blair. The library in which I researched this chapter in Edinburgh, the National Library of Scotland, informed its readers on a daily basis of the level of terror alert, with a large board at the entrance which displayed colours ranging from black through to red, and states of threat ranging from low to acute. In a recent speech to the Criminal Bar Association the head of the Crown Prosecution Service (CPS), Ken MacDonald QC, distanced British legal opinion from government adoption of this phrase as a description for state action to defend citizens against terrorists. MacDonald suggested that the CPS preferred recourse to conventional legal devices in its efforts to prevent terrorist attacks in Britain, and that stoking a climate of fear served only to add weight to the vanity of Islamist terrorists who claim in their videos that they are 'soldiers' in a holy war (Bannerman, 2007). However the language and the rhetoric of fear remained a significant element in the public speech of many New Labour politicians. In January 2007, the Home Secretary John Reid addressed the Scottish Labour Party and suggested that an independent Scotland would have weaker border controls against immigrants than those provided by the United Kingdom and that this would expose Scottish citizens to a greater risk of terrorist attack (Hutcheon, 2006). Reid also claimed that the United Kingdom was committed for at least a generation to the global war against Islamist terrorists, and that the level of threat to the United Kingdom was equivalent to that represented by the Second World War (BBC, 2007a).

We might say that the Blair government's willingness to accede to the new geopolitical strategy of the Bush administration was of a piece with Britain's 'special relationship' with the United States, reflecting as it did cultural, linguistic and economic ties. But given that resort to fear as a political driver is the conventional strategy of totalitarian states, and was a major feature in the rise of Nazism and anti-Semitism in Germany in the 1930s, it remains a paradox why New Labour, a liberal democratic government publicly committed to extending citizen engagement in politics, and to the recognition of human rights in British law, should resort to this most illiberal of political devices. It is also notable that the 'special relationship' did not motivate the Labour government of Harold Wilson to join the United States in its cold war interventionism in Southeast Asia in the 1960s.

The ostensible reason for the adoption of the politics of fear by the Blair government was the defence of the British people from terror attacks. But if this was the reason, it signally failed. Few outside of the British Cabinet believed that the war in Iraq was not a significant motivating factor in the terror attacks launched on Central London on 7 July 2005. And it is hard to believe that, had the British government not adopted the rhetoric and strategies of the American imperial push into the Middle East and the Caucasus since 2001, that British Islamists would be involved in the '30 terrorist conspiracies' that John Reid claimed were monitored by the security services in 2006 (Woodward, 2006). Even the Foreign Office came to believe that the rhetoric of the 'war on terror' had advanced Islamist hostility to Britain around the world and advised government ministers to avoid the term.

Far from reducing the risk of terrorist attacks, and fear of such attacks, the war on terror actually advanced both the fear and the reality of terror and violence, much of it sponsored by the war on terror itself, as exemplified by the incarceration without trial of Islamists as potential enemies of the state in places such as Belmarsh Prison and Guantanamo Bay (Heng, 2002). The Guantanamo regime of incarceration and interrogation was described by most observers as contrary to the Geneva Conventions governing the treatment of prisoners of war, and as amounting to torture, and although it was an extra-legal terrain, these practices and techniques infected the larger war on terror with the spread of torture and killing of detainees in Iraq and Afghanistan. This extra-legal and extra-territorial promotion of torture also infected government law officers in the 'homelands'. Both the Bush and Blair governments sponsored legal argument that evidence obtained from torture was permissible in courts of law because of the unique emergency said to be represented by Islamic terrorism (Starmer, 2006).

These developments bear troubling parallels with the rise of totalitarian regimes, and especially Nazism, which used the claimed emergency of Jewish originated threats to the prosperity and security of the German people to justify suspension of legal norms and the use of torture and terror against Jews and other enemies of the people (Milbank, 2002). As Sheldon Wolin suggests a state of fear was used by the architects of the war on terror to create compliance and political apathy in the general population and so sustain a willingness to sacrifice constitutional freedoms and the rule of law for the defence of national security (Wolin, 2004, pp. 559–63). Recall that after the terror attacks in 2001 Bush suggested that Americans should respond by uniting behind the government in its anti-terror laws and wars, and carry on flying and consuming (Wolin, 2001). This was no call to mobilize the citizenry in a renewal of threatened democratic values and freedoms. Instead the interests that are promoted by the extension of state power under the guise of the war on terror are those of the military and security services, and of the economic corporations who increasingly control the organs of state through their monetary power over political parties and the electoral process.

In a critique of the US government's response to the terrorist attacks, the Kentucky farmer and essayist Wendell Berry suggested the violence of the terrorists was a reflection of the violent nature of the global regime of international trade which the United States had promoted in the last 30 years. The use of destructive weapons against the United States was a by-product of a global corporate economy which accepts 'universal pollution and global warming as normal costs of doing business' (Berry, 2004, p. 19). It was also a reflection of the inequality implicit in the scale of American consumption of the earth's resources. American companies advance their wealth, and the culture of consumption, by advancing ecological and social collapse in other regions of the earth by their coercive harvesting of cheap labour, foods, fuel, metals, minerals and timber. The claim that American 'security' is advanced by the rhetoric of hate, the caricature of enemies and violent wars is at odds, Berry suggested, with the denials of freedom and the growth in political fear that have accompanied this claim. If peace and security are the true aims of government policy, then the means of realizing them is the recovery of meaningful local economic livelihood, political participation and the education of the people of the United States in the virtue of peaceableness:

> The key to peace is not violence but peaceableness, which is not passivity, but an alert, informed, practiced, and active state of being. We should recognize that while we have extravagantly subsidized the means of war, we have almost totally neglected the ways of peaceableness. (Berry, 2004, p. 20)

The reason the United States neglects peaceableness and advances violence is not only that war is profitable, which it is, but because the US federal government holds that 'it is possible to exploit and impoverish the poorer countries, while arming and instructing them in the newest means of war' (Berry, 2004, p. 19).

Berry suggested that Americans after 2001 faced a choice between an economic system dependent on worldwide sourcing of goods and services which would require a hugely expensive worldwide police force to secure it and restraints on freedom and civil rights at home, or a decentralized world economy whose aim would be to assure 'to every nation and region a *local* self-sufficiency in life-supporting goods' (Berry, 2004, p. 19). The virtues which underlie the recovery of a self-sufficient economy are those of 'thrift and care', 'saving and conserving', whereas 'an economy based on waste is inherently and hopelessly violent, and war is its inevitable by-product. We need a peaceable economy' (Berry, 2004, p. 22).

Berry's comments recall the claim of Ulrich Beck that globalization involves a condition of risk which is in many ways novel, linking people and societies through systems and technologies which involve the multiplication of risks between persons and organizations that are unknown to each another and places that are far distant from one another (Beck, 1992). A globalized world is an increasingly borderless world where viruses can cross national boundaries as easily as packets of drugs or plastic explosives. The side effect of global-ization is the emergence of a condition in which security in one country can no longer be assured when other countries with which goods or personnel are regularly exchanged are in states of insecurity or anarchy (Bauman, 2006, p. 96). Fear of violence from non-state actors is advanced by globalization as dependence on globally traded foods, fuels and fibres is combined with trade in weapons which sustain authoritarian elites in Third World countries whose populace are immiserated by the larceny of their lands, forests and oceans for corporate profit. For a superpower such as the United States this new global condition produces a situation in which no territory can any longer be said to be distinct from the project of global economic dominance if it contains actors or resources on which the United States has become economically dependent, or if it threatens the United States or its economic interests with violence (O'Keohane, 2002).

The logic of this position, as Benjamin Barber suggests, is that in order to sustain the global supremacy of its corporate interests it becomes necessary for the United States to advance its rule in every domain to the point where it is engaged in a unilateral war against all (Barber, 2003, p. 71). This seeming necessity produces a new cartographic view of the world in which terrains are identified by the United States as either connected and integrated into the global economic core or disconnected and isolated and hence threatening to the globalization project. And it is with the aid of this cartography that lists of rogue states are enumerated whose existence seems to require a pre-emptive military response (Barnett, 2004). This condition of war against all is a by-prod-uct of the superpower stance of the United States since the Second World War as first expressed in the cold war, and then in the strategic responses towards globalization, Islam and, increasingly, China under the administrations of Clinton, Bush and Obama. The imperial accumulation of surplus value with-out regard for ecological limits or social consequences produces a new and dangerous global condition, which Zygmunt Bauman characterises as 'liquid fear' (Bauman, 2006). While the Obama administration had been expected to initiate a change in direction in this respect, in reality, as Noam Chomsky argues, it has affirmed almost every element of the policies of its Democratic and Republican predecessors (Chomsky, 2011). War without end continues in Afghanistan, Iraq and Pakistan, and at the time of writing is extended to Libya while the US sustains over 800 military bases around the world. The rise of China as an economic and political superpower is also a key element in current US foreign and military policy. Competition with China for oil and influence is a key element in the strategic shift in military engagement and military bases into Central Asia – and away from Eastern Europe – that White House adminis-trations have initiated since the Clinton administration (Hoge, 2004).

The acknowledgement of the risks implicit in the neo-imperial form of economic globalization helps explain the commitment of the government of New Labour in Britain to the United States originated frame and rhetoric of the war on terror and the politics of fear. New Labour was also committed to developing a flexible and borderless economy which is uniquely open to world trade and investment and which welcomed the growing economic interdependence of nation states. Blair and Brown positioned their vision for Britain as an American–European hybrid in which British prosperity is built on open borders to goods and services, with the minimum of obstacles to the movement of labour and investment capital. Blair explicitly linked his support for military interventionism in places such as Iraq and Afghanistan with economic globalization: 'I think we live in a far more interdependent world where our self-interest cannot be pursued effectively unless we recognise that one part of the world affects another part of the world.' In such a world the only way to deal with threats to Britain's self-interest is 'to go out after the threat with others and deal with it.' And Blair saw this new interventionist strategy, much as Bush did, as a global struggle between a 'perversion of Islam' and the 'forces of progress' (BBC, 2007b).

This new strategy of neo-imperial military interventionism was not only a significant departure from the long-established tradition of non-intervention between nation states first promulgated by Hugo Grotius and at the Peace of Westphalia. It also deliberately downplayed the extent to which the forces which are destabilizing nation states in the developing world are imperial. If all the peoples of the world consumed as the beneficiaries of the consumer economy do there would be need for at least three planets (Bauman, 2006, p. 76). Pressures on natural resources and ecosystems, represented by the corporate-driven growth in the global consumer economy, destabilize governments and cause dramatic population movements. In this sense Islamic terrorism is a distraction, or a particular form of a much larger problem, as Darfur illustrates. The civil war in Darfur is usually presented in Western media as a conflict between Muslim Arabs and Christian Africans. But the civil war has arisen as a result of a large and involuntary movement of people, commonly identified as Arabs, from the drought plagued Sahel region into the 'black African' region of South Sudan (Pfaff, 2007). Scientific evidence indicates that the drought in the Sahel is a consequence of global warming whose effects are driving extreme climate events as a result of the dramatic growth in greenhouse gas emissions from the exponential increase in global trade in goods and services in the last 30 years (Zend, 2003).

The strategy of global military interventionism fails to recognize the ecological and social destruction created by growing global trade. Just as it is wreaking havoc in local and global commons, the public politics of developing countries are also frequently corrupted by trade arrangements with multinational companies. The areas of the world that are most politically unstable, and prone to civil unrest and terrorist violence, are precisely those areas where trade in high-value goods such as diamonds, precious metals, oil and gas, and tropical timber, is most prominent. Weapons and monies nefariously acquired through such arrangements are used by developing countries' elites to control local mass media, and to militarily subdue the protests of their own citizens at the sale and larceny of their natural resources (Christian Aid, 2005).

The strategy of military intervention as a way of patching up a politically imperious and ecologically dysfunctional global economy also completely misses the extent to which many of the risks posed by the increased global flows of goods and people are intrinsic to the global economic project. This was powerfully illustrated by the 2007 H5N1 bird flu outbreak at an English turkey factory, and by media and government reactions. Initially government vets identified the cause of the infection as wild bird movements. Subsequently it became clear that the infection came from the movement of infected turkey meat from a Hungarian slaughter house to a turkey factory and processing plant in Suffolk, where gulls and rats transferred the infection into the 'biosecure' turkey sheds (Elliott, 2007). Until this incident government and media consistently blamed the spread of avian flu on wild birds. But the poultry industry is the most globalized of all forms of intensive farming. Factories in Southeast Asia, and not wild birds, were the original source of the most deadly pathogen in the already chequered history of industrial farming. And movements of live and dead birds around the world are the cause of the international spread of avian flu from Vietnam to North Asia, India, Africa and now Europe. The regional movements of the disease in Asia are actually inconsistent with bird migratory patterns, as are its appearances in India and Africa, whereas they are entirely consistent with the movement by road and ship of industrially reared live and dead chicken. Furthermore, the vast majority of bird flu cases have been on factory farms. And in countries such as Nigeria, the Netherlands, India and now Britain factory farms are the only places where the pathogen has appeared (Nierenberger, 2007). And yet despite the evidence of the association of avian flu with intensive farming and the transnational trade in meat, governments, the mass media and even the UN Food and Agriculture Organization, continue to blame wild birds and the free range chickens of smallholders (Bleich, 2007).

This whole saga is a strong exemplar of the judgement that extreme global economic interdependence fosters insecurity and multiplies risk. But those who promote this interdependence in government and industry imagine that it is 'nature' which is the source of 'bio-insecurity' while the domination of nature by technological capitalism is said to render natural resources amenable and safe for efficient human use. As with the war on terror, the 'war' against avian flu is designed in such a way as to suggest that the policing of global flows of live and dead chickens under the regimen of global corporate capitalism, and their incarceration in systems which involve extensive electronic surveillance and technological control, will contain the problem and advance biosecurity while small farmers, rogue traders, wild birds, are identified as the source of threats to security.

Alongside the risks inherent in the global economy, Corey Robin suggests that inequality and fear of crime within the homeland play an equally significant role in promoting the return of the politics of fear, and in corroding a sense of peace and security: 'the kind of fear that arises from the social, political, and economic hierarchies that divide a people' is highly damaging to liberal politics (Robin, 2004). The outsourcing of millions of American manufacturing jobs to the developing world from the United States in the last 30 years has been accompanied by a dramatic increase in inequality which has created distrust and fear on the streets, and which is accompanied by a decline in political participation of those millions of Americans who find themselves in an underclass of low wages, poor educational opportunities and who live in violent, crime-ridden neighbourhoods. Neoconservative domestic and foreign policies are in effect delivering the United States to the Hobbesian condition of original violence in which men and women, and business corporations, are said only to contract together to form a state in order to protect their person and property from others who would violently attack them. For the neoconservatives who continue to dominate US politics with the recent rise of the 'tea party' movement, the neo-liberal state is only really good at one thing, and that is punishing wrongdoing both at home and overseas. It is no coincidence that prisons and military spending absorb so much of the budget of the United States under this ideology, while health and social services, and agencies for environmental protection and workplace safety are cut back under the budgets of both the Bush–Cheney and Obama administrations. In the neo-liberal perspective when the state tries to do other things that might be said to serve the common good – like regulating pollution or redistributing wealth or providing health care – it is said to be inefficient or even morally perverse (Northcott, 2004). The logic of a strong corporate economy and a weak state promotes ever more divisive social conditions at home and greater flows of goods and persons around the world, and so the global spread of the politics of fear becomes a self-fulfilling prophecy.

The origins of the modern politics of fear may be traced to Thomas Hobbes' *Leviathan* where he argues that fear is the natural state in which men enter into a social contract; from their 'natural condition' of individualism they look for a state to protect them and their property from their neighbours and from strangers. On Hobbes' account fear is *the* political emotion since it is only fear of the other which forces men to abandon their natural independence for certain purposes and join in society. For Hobbes men and women are intrinsically at odds with one another in their interests and in the goods they elect to pursue in their lives. Hobbes defines happiness as 'the continual progress of the desire, from one object to another, the attaining of the former being still but the way to the latter' (Hobbes, 1991, p. 69). The insatiable and incommensurable nature of individual and private desires requires that social power is monopolized by the state because the possibility of a shareable good is denied. For Hobbes politics is pursued on the basis of fear and not solidarity (Wolin, 2004, p. 249).

Hobbes' account of the politics of fear is prophetic since, as Wolin argues, it anticipates the extent to which modern political elites of all stripes have resorted to fear in order to justify their rule (Wolin, 2004, p. 293). This explains why modern intellectuals also resort to fear as a device for advancing solidaristic politics and the common good (Robin, 2004, p. 34). It was out of her experiences of the politics of fear in Nazi Germany that Judith Shklar developed her account of a 'liberalism of fear' in which she suggests that fear is anti-political and that freedom from fear is the first goal of politics. For Shklar the core task of liberal politics is to protect citizens 'against the fear of cruelty' (Shklar, 1998, p. 2). Shklar's 'liberalism of fear' seeks to counter Hobbesian fear with the claim that it is the core duty of the state to secure the political conditions such that 'every adult should be able to make as many effective decisions without fear or favour about as many aspects of his or her life as is compatible with the like freedom of every other adult' (Shklar, 1998, p. 3). This same liberalism of fear is also evident in Hannah Arendt's suggestion that fear of concentration camps and totalitarian terror could sustain a new political morality (Arendt, 1953).

The liberal account of politics as freedom from fear relies upon a crucial distinction between the political and the personal which Shklar and others suggest is also foundational to liberalism because this distinction sets limits to coercion 'with a prohibition on invading the private realm' (Shklar, 1998, p. 6). This is not to say that a liberal society does not have a normative shape, or that it does not depend on the development of moral character and conscience in its citizens. But the key thing about this character is that individuals are able to stand up for themselves and they are free to make independent and uncoerced moral choices. And this is why the eschewal of torture and fear is so foundational to liberalism. But with the rise of 'national warfare states' since 1914, torture is again widespread and personal freedoms are again threatened. The fear of fear returns with the return of widespread cruelty and it is against this fear that liberalism claims to be the true cosmopolitan political creed for 'systematic fear is the condition that makes freedom impossible, and it is aroused by the expectation of institutionalized cruelty as by nothing else' (Shklar, 1998, p. 6). And it is the capacity of the over-weaning state to make war, maim and kill which is the reason liberals protest against 'every extralegal, secret, and unauthorized act by public agents or their deputies' (Shklar, 1998, p. 6). Only the constant division and subdivision of state power, and the vigilance and vitality of voluntary agencies and legal process, can ensure that the state is kept within the bounds required by the liberalism of fear:

> where the instruments of coercion are at hand, whether it be through the use of economic power, chiefly to hire, pay, fire, and determine prices, or military might in its various manifestations, it is the task of a liberal citizenry to see that not one official or unofficial agent can intimidate anyone, except through the use of well-understood and accepted legal procedures. (Shklar, 1998, p. 12)

What is notable about Shklar's liberalism of fear is that, like Isaiah Berlin's account of negative liberty, or John Rawls' 'original condition', it fails to offer a positive account of politics in liberal societies. Instead it suggests that the best that can be hoped for after a twentieth century dominated by total war is a politics in which cruelty and coercion are kept at bay. But the paradox of the liberalism of fear is that it is actually more positive about the political significance of fear than its advocates at first claim, and in this sense is more Hobbesian than they imagine.

The dependence of liberals on the emotion of fear as a political driver in late modernity exposes some of the inherent weaknesses of liberal political theory, and in particular the inability of liberals to specify positive public political ends or practices. Law is described as a means for the restraint of wrong doing by the citizen and a restraint on the state, but it is not seen as capable of promoting a more positive vision of social life. Contrast this with the traditional western account, as held by the Dutch philosopher Hugo Grotius, according to which law is seen to be the fruit of community, and community and law are not means to an end – freedom of choice between diverse goods – but intrinsically good practices which sustain human flourishing (Grotius, 2005, pp. 85–91). The difficulty with liberalism is that it is so intrinsically consequentialist that it can ultimately offer no sure ground for the defence of something like community or even the rule of law against the over-weaning power of the state and the corporation other than the individual's right to choose. But as the state and the corporation become ever more successful in diverting this right into consumerism, political participation declines – and hence the resort to the politics of fear. Combined with the rising power of the state and the corporation, and their harnessing of science and technology in the extension of their powers, this produces a situation in which political fear again rears its ugly head in the form of what Wolin insightfully calls 'inverted totalitarianism' where it is not the state but the corporation which wields unchallenged power as even torture and war are privatized (Wolin, 2004, pp. 591–4). As Robin suggests, the liberal claim that fear, or the fear of fear, is a powerful political motivator is ultimately self-defeating because it legitimates the return to political fear as the justification of new state and corporate powers in response to global risk and terror (Robin, 2004, pp. 15–16).

The extent of the infection of the politics of fear in neo-liberal societies is evident in the turn even of some environmentalists and scientists to fear as motive in relation to the threat of global warming. In his novelistic debunking of global warming, *State of Fear*, Michael Crichton suggests that the hypothesis of anthropogenic global warming is being used to spread apocalyptic fear, and so enhance the powers of the state over the individual (Crichton, 2005). The science, Crichton suggests, is exaggerated because without this kind of global threat it is impossible for the nation state to justify its continuing centralization of powers over the lives of citizens, and its claims to govern and direct the goals and procedures of their lives. This is in an interesting suggestion when we consider that many of the leading advocates of state and collective action to respond to global warming also compare it to the threat of terrorism and nuclear war, including, for example, Sir John Houghton and Sir David King. They also believe that only fear of cataclysm, and representation of global warming as a kind of ultimate apocalyptic war with forces which threaten human security, will generate the kinds of shared purpose which will make collective action possible.

The politics of global warming, like the war on terror, reveals the paradoxical nature of the liberalism of fear, which rests upon an account of evil as 'real' and from which is derived the solidaristic potential of the fear of evil. Thus for Arendt the memory of the Holocaust provides the only sure way to resist a return to totalitarianism just as for Al Gore the fear of climate catastrophe offers the only sure way to remoralize the consumer society. But this is an essentially negative account of politics, which recalls the radical move in Western political theory made by Machiavelli, as well as Hobbes, towards a politics of interest and sovereign power, and away from a participative politics of active citizenship and a shared quest for the common good of people and planet (Wolin 2004, p. 211).

The question I will attempt to ask in conclusion is where we might find resources for the recovery of a more hopeful and peaceable vision of politics, and of participation in the political, not as a necessity for the restraint of evil but as an intrinsic aspect of a life worth living. If the innovators whose ideas are at the root of the politics of fear are Hobbes and Machiavelli, we might expect to find resources for repair in some of their predecessors in Western political thought. The Hobbesian division of personal interest and political power, which the liberalism of fear also sustains, contrasts significantly with the political thought of Augustine of Hippo who was the key architect of the tradition of political thought Hobbes inherited. For Augustine, the political is a far more complex interaction of soul and society. There is not one governing emotion – such as fear – which drives men and women to submit to sovereign power. Instead the possibility of the political arises from the concept of divine order which breaks into human history in the form of grace and which draws men and women towards participation in a good that is truly, and emotively, shared (Wolin, 2004, pp. 117–18).

In Augustine's definitive account of political emotions in *Civitatis Dei* he suggests that a commonwealth is a multitude of people who are bound together by their 'common objects of love' (2002, p. 20). The moral quality of a commonwealth therefore depends on the kinds of things that are loved. The supreme love is the love of God, and this love characterizes those who inhabit what Augustine calls the heavenly city or the Church. But there can also be worthy loves in an earthly city, even although in such a city there will not be so much common agreement about the love of worthy objects. And the love that is most widely held in the earthly city is the love of peace or the desire for security (Augustine, 1972, XIX, p. 17). Wherever men and women live together it is possible to discern that they will act together socially in order to bring about a state of affairs in which they can enjoy peace. This is because peace is that collective condition without which it is much harder to pursue such other worthy goals and ends as the nurture and education of the young or the contemplation of the eternal.

But if love of God, and love of peace, are the ordering loves of the heavenly and earthly cities, is there any need for other kinds of emotive political drivers? Well yes, Augustine suggests, there is, because despite the common desire for peace there are individuals, and groups of individuals who will still be drawn to, and may even love, violence. In such cases there is a need for another political emotion which is fear, for the wrong doer, in order to be sufficiently restrained in his wrongful desires, needs to fear the ability of the state to impose its laws and punish malefactors or else there will be no peace even for those who do love it. What motivates the law maker, the judge and those who punish crime is not anger or a desire for revenge but rather the understanding that they are representatives of God and of the commonwealth, and behind their actions is the judgement of God and it is this which ought to inspire fear of those whose job it is to enforce the law when people refuse to do what the law requires (Augustine, 2001).

To underscore the proposal that love is a superior political emotion to anger or fear, Augustine suggests that one of the best examples of judgement, from which all earthly judges and punishers should learn, is the story of the woman caught in adultery in the Gospel of John where Christ asks those about to stone her 'who among you is without sin? Let him be the first to cast a stone at her' (Jn 8.7). This also, Augustine suggests, is why people are generally happier to defend than to prosecute in a court of law for in interceding on behalf even of the guilty they act out of compassion and not from fear or a desire for vengeance. This does not mean that punishment is never appropriate, for sometimes punishment can itself be a form of mercy, saving the criminal from his own disordered desires, as well as protecting the innocent. But Augustine suggests that healing and redemption are what the sinner stands in need of, and mercy is far more likely to bring these about than fearful punishment.

Fear for Augustine is a secondary political emotion and it is a much more clearly negative and punitive emotion than it is for the advocates of the liberalism of fear. Fear is politically weak because it does not direct those who love the right things to love them any better. Nor does it educate the misdirected desires of those who do not love the right things so that they love what is worthy of love. Fear is at most a necessary political emotion that is only needful where the love of the right things is absent. On the other hand once having ensured that criminals right the wrongs they have committed in the way of theft by returning stolen goods, being 'conciliatory to those who are bad' is not to make them happy or keep them bad but 'because those who become good come from among them' and because 'self-sacrificial mercy pleases God' (Augustine, 2001, p. 88). This account is also consistent with Augustine's refusal of a doctrine of absolute evil. For Augustine evil is always defined as lack, a loss of being, rather than the kind of positive and even heroic force that moderns from Nietzsche onwards have conceived it.

In this perspective it may not be insignificant that the use of fear as a political emotion in the war on terror was accompanied by the preparedness of Bush, and Blair at times, to vilify those whom the war was said to oppose as 'evil' people devoted to evil ends. Bush in his speech in the national cathedral in Washington D.C. after the terror attacks suggested that since September 11 the United States faced radical evil. And in subsequent speeches he indicated that it would in turn need to resort to ambiguous means and that the struggle would require that the state and its agents were freed from some of the conventional restraints on its use of power and violence (Northcott, 2004).

As I have suggested elsewhere, there is something else going on here. After 2001 Bush, other members of the Republican party and the Bush–Cheney administration mobilized Protestant fundamentalist and apocalyptic rhetoric of the kind that distinguishes sharply between good and bad people in such a way as to suggest that the United States in the pursuit and defence of its superpower supremacy was advancing on the world stage 'the forces of light against the forces of darkness' (Northcott, 2005). The representation of the war on terror as an apocalyptic struggle in which the United States is realizing a divine mission to direct world history towards a certain end is also not inconsistent with earlier uses of providential and apocalyptic discourses in the history of the Republic. And it is consistent with cold war rhetoric in relation to which there has simply been a changing of the evil other from Communist to Islamist. Just as the battle with Communism could be represented as in part a moral and a religious struggle for freedom of conscience and faith, as well as for economic freedom, so the battle with Islamism can be represented as a struggle for Christian and Western values of democracy, liberty and the pursuit of wealth against Islamist forms of theocracy, and a counter to Islamist resistance to American cultural and economic influences.

Against the return to the politics of fear under the aegis of a perversion of apocalyptic Christianity, and its mirror image in a violent perversion of Islam, Augustine's account of the politics of mercy and peace may be said to have significant cultural power. It does not lend itself to the kinds of distinctions between good and evil people to which both Bush and Blair were prone. It opposes the politics of coercive punishment which the politics of fear promotes both at home and abroad. And it provides an account of the common good that does not require resort to fear to save the planet or to defend the nation state.

Augustine's account has one other crucial advantage over the liberalism of fear, for against the 'end of politics' that inverted totalitarianism involves it suggests that political participation is not epiphenomenal but essential to the functioning of a good society (Wolin, 2004, pp. 448–50). For Augustine, political participation is a good which is intrinsic to human life. And on this account demitting political power to autonomous procedures like markets or surveillance systems, or to corporate elites, is bound to advance a demoralized society, and a loss of hope in the political. Combating terrorism, like combating climate change, requires instead the engagement of citizens in positive projects of mercy and communitarian virtue. The kinds of projects needful to turn the imperious global economy from its collision course with the health of people and planet are careful, deliberative and embodied practices such as energy conservation, farmers' markets, fair trade and intercultural dialogue. These kinds of practices cannot be rolled out by private finance initiatives, central government directives or autonomous market procedures. They require instead active political participation, the recovery of local and eco-logical knowledges, and the remoralization of economic relationships. Such knowledge and practices generate security not because they are efficient but because they are peaceable, they rebuild local community and they care for the earth (Berry, 2004).

References

Altheide, D. (2006), 'Terrorism and the politics of fear', *Cultural Studies, Critical Methodologies*, 6(4), 415–39.

Arendt, H. (1953), 'Ideology and terror: a novel form of government', *The Review of Politics*, 15(3), 303–27.

Augustine (1972), *City of God*, trans. H. Bettensen. Hardmondsworth: Pelican.

—(2001), 'Letter 153: Augustine to Macedonius', in M. Atkins, ed., *Augustine: Political Writings*. Cambridge: Cambridge University Press, pp. 71–86.

Bannerman, L. (2007), 'There is no war on terror in the UK says DPP', *The Times*, 24 January.

Barber, B.R. (2003), *Fear's Empire: War, Terrorism and Democracy*. New York: Norton.

Barnett, T. (2004), *The Pentagon's New Map: War and Peace in the Twenty-First Century*. New York: Putnams.

Bauman, Z. (2006), *Liquid Fear*. Cambridge: Polity Press.

BBC (2007a), 'Terror war "to last generation"', *BBC News*, 15 January, Available at: http://news.bbc.co.uk/go/pr/fr/-/1/hi/uk_politics/6264597.stm.

—(2007b), 'Prime Minister Tony Blair, Interview with John Humphries', *Today Programme*, BBC Radio 4, 22 February.

Beck, U. (1992), *Risk Society: Towards a New Modernity*. London: Sage.

Berry, W. (2004), 'Thoughts in the presence of fear', in W. Berry, ed., *Citizenship Papers*. Washington, D.C.: Shoemaker and Hoard, pp. 17–22.

Bleich, E. (2006), 'Bird flu crisis: small farms are the solution not the problem', *Grain*, 24–28 July, Available at: http://www.grain.org/seedling_files/seed-06-07-11.pdf.

Bush, G. (2002), 'State of the Union Address 2002', Available at: http://edition.cnn.com/2002/ALLPOLITICS/01/29/bush.speech.txt/.

Chomsky, N. (2011), 'Noam Chomsky on Obama's foreign policy', *Democracy Now!* 15 March, Available at: http://www.democracynow.org/2010/3/15/noam_chomsky_on_obamas_foreign_policy visited on 28 April 2011.

Christian Aid (2005), *Fuelling Poverty: Oil, War and Corruption*. London: Christian Aid.

Crichton, M. (2005), *State of Fear*. London: Harper Collins.

Elliott, V. (2007), 'Bernard Matthews faces "illegal" imports inquiry', *The Times*, 9 February.

Grotius, H. (2005), *The Rights of War and Peace* Book 1 (ed. R. Tuck from the translation by Jean Barbeyrac). Indianapolis: Liberty Fund.

Heng, Y.-K. (2002), 'Unravelling the "war" on terrorism: a risk-management exercise in war clothing?' *Security Dialogue*, 33(2), 227–42.

Hobbes, T. (1991), *Leviathan*, ed. R. Tuck. Cambridge: Cambridge University Press.

Hoge, J.F. (2004), 'Global power shift in the making – is the United States ready?' *Foreign Affairs*, 83(4), 2–7.

Hutcheon, P. (2006), 'Reid says Scots state would be weak in the face of al-Qaeda', *Sunday Herald*, 2 December.

Milbank, J. (2002), *Being Reconciled: Ontology and Pardon*. London: Routledge.

National Security Strategy of the United States of America (2002), Washington, D.C.: The White House.

Nierenberger, D. (2007), 'A fowl plague', *World Watch Magazine* (January/February), Available at: http://www.worldwatch.org/node/4779.

Northcott, M. (2004), *An Angel Directs the Storm: Apocalyptic Religion and American Empire*. London: I.B. Tauris.

—(2005), 'Confessing Christ in the "War on Terror"', *Anvil*, 22, 119–24.

O'Keohane, R. (2002), 'The globalization of informal violence, theories of world politics, and the "liberalism of fear"', *Dialog-IO* (Spring), 29–43.

Pfaff, W. (2007), 'Manifest destiny: a new direction for America', *The New York Review of Books*, 54(2), Available at: http://www.nybooks.com/articles/archives/2007/feb/15/manifest-destiny-a-new-direction-for-america/.

Pierterse, J.N. (2005), 'Scenarios of power', in A. Cojas and R. Saull, eds, *The War on Terror and the American 'Empire' After the Cold War*. London: Routledge, pp. 180–93.

Robin, C. (2004), *Fear: The History of a Political Idea*. New York: Oxford University Press.

Seneca (1995), 'On anger', II. 11.4, in *Seneca: Moral and Political Essays,* trans. J.M. Cooper and J.F. Procope. Cambridge: Cambridge University Press.

Shklar, J. (1998), 'The liberalism of fear', in G. Kateb, ed., *Political Thought and Political Thinkers*. Chicago: Chicago University Press, pp. 3–20.

Starmer, K. (2006), 'Setting the record straight: human rights in an era of international terrorism', Legal Action Group Annual Lecture.

Wolin, S. (2001), 'Brave new world', *Theory and Event,* 5(4), Available at: http://muse.jhu.edu/journals/theory_and_event/toc/tae5.4.html.

—(2004), *Politics and Vision: Continuity and Innovation in Western Political Thought* (revised edn). Princeton, NJ: Princeton University Press.

Woodward, W. (2006), 'Reid: Christmas terror attempt highly likely', *The Guardian*, 11 December.

Zend, N. (2003), 'Drought in the Sahel', *Science,* 302, 999–1000.

5

Mobilizing fear
US politics before and after 9/11

Scott Lucas

The chief costs of terrorism derive not from the damage inflicted by the terrorists, but what those attacked do to themselves and others in response. That is, the harm of terrorism mostly arises from the fear and from the often hasty, ill-considered, and overwrought reaction (or overreaction) it characteristically, and often calculatedly, inspires in its victims. (Mueller, 2006)

In 2007 my mother, who for more than twenty years, has been concerned that I am cut off in Britain from what is going on in the United States, forwarded a letter to me that has been widely circulated on the Internet. Purportedly written by a Ms Pam Foster to a family member in Iraq but (no doubt unknown to my mother) composed in 2005 by a former speechwriter for Republican Party candidates, it countered allegations of abuse of prisoners held in Camp X-Ray at Guantanamo Bay with the refrain, 'I don't care!'. After all, the letter continued:

> Are we fighting a war on terror or aren't we? Was it or was it not started by Islamic people who brought it to our shores on September 11, 2001?
>
> Were people from all over the world, mostly Americans, not brutally murdered that day, in downtown Manhattan, across the Potomac from our nation's capitol and in a field in Pennsylvania?
>
> Did nearly three thousand men, women and children die a horrible, burning or crushing death that day, or didn't they?[1]

With its dismissal of 'I don't care' to incidents from the desecration of the Koran, the 'roughing up' and even shooting in the head of terrorist suspects, and the treatment of 'naked Iraqi prisoners' ('no more than a college-hazing incident'), the letter might seem to be founded on hatred. However, I doubt that the author, and I am certain that my mother, would agree. Instead, the letter's invocation of Americans decapitated by kidnappers, US soldiers slain by insurgents and innocents jailed for possession of the Bible converts the author's position into one of defence rather than aggression, based upon fear rather than animosity. Indeed, it is through that adoption of a defensive position that the author converts anger into an 'I do care' position to disseminate their views.

Whether or not my mother, or the author of the letter, recognized it, their thoughts fit into a discourse with a longer historical resonance. Moreover, although I have no evidence that either has ever worked with the US government, the sentiments and the manner in which they are expressed tap into a mobilizing of emotion by the state. This is a mobilization designed to serve political interests, objectives and strategies at home and abroad, all the time positioning those interests in the defensive language of national security rather than the offensive language of conquest and control. Put bluntly, it is the hypothesis of this essay that the projections of both 'radical Muslims', aided and abetted by the 'media', and the Americans – blown up, beheaded or simply overworked – who suffer at their hands are constructions of a far-from-benign 'culture of fear'.

There have been a series of valuable considerations of politics and the 'culture of fear' in the last decade. Barry Glassner (2000) brought the term to prominence in the United States with his book and then his appearance in Michael Moore's *Bowling for Columbine*.[2] Frank Furedi developed and dissected the concept, concluding that 'the absence of real choice is the message that is implicit in the many anxieties stimulated by society's obsession with risk', with governments 'treat[ing] their citizens as vulnerable subjects who tend not to know what is in their best of interest' (Furedi, 2002, p. 169; 2007, p. 142). David Altheide has examined the construction and projection of 'terrorism' as part of a 'politics of fear' (Altheide, 2006).

I think they can be applied effectively to the reconsideration of policy-making, specifically the making of US foreign policy, in both historical and contemporary cases. Although the 'culture of fear' was not specifically invoked, the concept underlay Richard Freedland's provocative study of the Truman Administration (Freedland, 1971). It is engrained in Herman and Chomsky's 'manufacturing consent' (1988) (which in turn builds upon Lippmann [1922] and Bernays [1955]) as well as Qualter's 'opinion control' in democracies (1985). Building upon this scholarship, I would suggest two general hypotheses:

1. Scholarly study of US foreign policy in the cold war has been so focused on objective explanations of strategy, geopolitics and, most important, 'national security' that it has ignored the subjective construction and projection of that policy. Provocatively stated, the Soviet Union served not so much as an actual nightmare than as a constructed nightmare to justify the projection of American power around the world.

2. Contemporary US foreign policy, like the political strategy of the 1950s, does not respond to fear with plans for 'security'; rather, it has sought to channel and even stoke fear to bolster implementation of a predetermined policy. Specifically and provocatively stated, the Bush administration did not stage the tragedy of 11 September 2001, but within hours of the event it began to consider how to use a war on terror to implement plans for regime change in Iraq.

Sixty years before my mother took advantage of the Internet to send her message, when the foes of America were not radical Islamists but Communists, President Harry Truman hosted a meeting with Congressional representatives. The Truman administration, having been told by Britain that London could no longer provide aid to Greece or Turkey, faced a challenge: how could it persuade the American public and Congress to send hundreds of millions of dollars to those two Mediterranean countries? The advice to the Democratic president from Arthur Vandenberg, the Republican leader in the Senate, was blunt: make a speech to 'scare the hell' out of the American people (Jones, 1955). Two weeks later, the president went before a joint session of Congress and issued what would become known as the Truman Doctrine: 'I believe that it must be the policy of the United States to support free peoples who are resisting attempted subjugation by armed minorities or by outside pressures' (Truman, 1947).

Truman's initiative was that of an 'official' executive political network, using the method of formal communication to justify policy rather than a private individual taking advantage of technological shift and acceleration to disseminate an urgent political message. Ironically, however, the role of the executive would be eclipsed in favour of a representation based on catalytic individuals whipping up a public fervour that overtook government policy.

On 9 February 1950 a then little-known senator from Wisconsin named Joseph McCarthy addressed a Republican women's club in Wheeling, West

Virginia, and declared that he had a list of 205 Communists who worked in the State Department (McCarthy, 1950). The number on the list fluctuated wildly, but McCarthy's persistent message of infiltration and subversion encouraged a climate of fear and domestic repression.

The problem with this storyline is that it inverts cause and effect. By the time McCarthy made his Wheeling speech, the US government was already well advanced in its projection mobilization of the threat within and without. Nine days after Truman set out his doctrine, the government issued an executive order requiring that any federal employee not only pass a security vetting but also sign a loyalty oath (Executive Order 9835, 1947). Truman issued other high-profile declarations about dangerous groups within American society, notably a speech on St. Patrick's Day in 1948 in which he asserted the following: 'I do not want and I will not accept the political support of Henry Wallace and his Communists. If joining them or permitting them to join me is the price of victory, I recommend defeat' (Truman, 1948).

The domestic mobilization of fear was connected to the government's foreign policy through its guidelines on 'US Objectives with Respect to the USSR to Counter Soviet Threats to US Security', first adopted in November 1948 (NSC 20/4, 1948). In its most famous incarnation, NSC 68 of April 1950, the policy sanctioned not only development of the hydrogen bomb but also substantial increases in conventional forces, economic and military aid to 'friendly' governments, information programs and covert operations. All of this depended upon congressional authorization of expenditure, however, and that in turn rested upon an intensive campaign to persuade the American public: 'The whole success of the proposed program hangs ultimately on recognition by this Government, the American people, and all free peoples, that the cold war is in fact a real war in which the survival of the free world is at stake' (NSC 68, 1950).

On 20 April 1950 President Truman, addressing the American Society of Newspaper Editors, launched the Campaign of Truth:

> We must pool our efforts with those of the other free peoples in a sustained, intensified program to promote the cause of freedom against the propaganda of slavery. We must make ourselves heard round the world in a great campaign of truth. (Truman, 1950; see also the *Times*, 1950)

Truman may have emphasized the 'positive' dimension of the American way of life but, in the Manichaean construction of the cold war, that political culture could only exist in tandem with the projection of the Soviet menace:

> Unwillingly our free society finds itself mortally challenged by the Soviet system. No other value system is so wholly irreconcilable with ours, so

implacable in its purpose to destroy ours, so capable of turning to its own uses the most dangerous and divisive trends in our own society, no other so skillfully and powerfully evokes the elements of irrationality in human nature everywhere, and no other has the support of a great and growing center of military power. (NSC 68, 1950)

Thus two months later, the incursion of North Korean troops across the 38th parallel marked a global showdown with Stalinist and Maoist Communism rather than a postcolonial civil war. And two years later, with that war turned into stalemate, the anti-Communist mobilization would rebound upon the Truman administration when presidential candidate Dwight Eisenhower accused the Democrats of 'the negative, futile, and immoral policy of "containment"' (Eisenhower, 1952).

It could be contended that, for all its damaging virulence, the climate of fear had receded by 1954. In an extensive national survey conducted by Samuel Stouffer that year, less than 1 per cent of Americans listed Communism as their primary concern. In contrast, more than 80 per cent cited 'personal and family problems', 43 per cent focusing on business or financial issues (Stouffer, 1992).

That, however, is too simple a reading. If the Communist menace was far from the explicit priority for most in the United States and if its most 'extreme' proponents such as McCarthy had fallen from grace, the threat could always be invoked. Thus, when the cold war moved beyond the European theatre to 'peripheries' such as Asia and Latin America, Chinese and Cuban evils circulated from White House press conferences to Hollywood films to weekly television series (e.g. MacDonald, 1985). The spectre of Communism would not be vanquished by military victory or by recognition of its 'realities' but by the collapse of political culture – at home and abroad – over Vietnam. Fear had not been met by a positive projection of 'freedom' but by tensions and even contradictions in the representation of that freedom, embodied in the famous (perhaps apocryphal) remark of an American officer in the aftermath of the Tet Offensive: 'It became necessary to destroy this village in order to save it' (Anonymous, 1971).

It would be foolish beyond simplicity to attribute fear solely to the machinations of government officials. Individual and community insecurity, be it fear of the known over what has occurred or fear of the unknown over what might happen, be it fear of the natural disaster or the man-made one, has a history long before 1945. The salient point is not that the US government manufactured fear. Rather, having just emerged from a period of global fear amidst war, genocide and turmoil, it could mobilize fear, using and contributing to the new structure of the 'national security state' and channelling anxieties in a public confrontation with Moscow.

What relevance does this historical background have when, for some, our dilemmas and challenges began on 11 September 2001? At one level, I would respond that the simplistic assertion that a society conditioned in part by the fear of the 'other', a fear re-stoked by Ronald Reagan's declaration in 1982 of the American confrontation with an 'evil empire', did not put that fear to rest just because the Berlin Wall fell and the Soviet Union collapsed (Reagan, 1982). To the contrary, other villains had emerged before and during those supposedly climactic events – Iran's 'mullahs', Nicaragua's Sandinistas, Libya's crazed Colonel Qaddafi in the mid-1980s, Panama's Manuel Noriega in 1989; and in 1990 Iraq's Saddam Hussein (complete with photographically altered Hitleresque moustache).[3]

More importantly, these worries were not just a context for political activity; they were stoked and used by the American executive pursuing its foreign policy agenda. To be sure, this was not a process that was always consistent – another lengthy essay would be needed to explain how the Reagan administration was trying to sell aircraft parts and missiles to the same ayatollahs that they were publicly denouncing[4] – but it was ever present. Furthermore in 1992, in an unprecedented effort, White House officials tried to link that mobilization to a new strategy seeking a 'preponderance of power' throughout the world. In a document innocuously called the Defense Planning Guidance, Assistant Secretary of Defense Paul Wolfowitz[5] proposed that the administration's

> first objective is to prevent the re-emergence of a new rival. This is a dominant consideration underlying the new regional defense strategy and requires that we endeavor to prevent any hostile power from dominating a region whose resources would, under consolidated control, be sufficient to generate global power. These regions include Western Europe, East Asia, the territory of the former Soviet Union, and Southwest Asia. (Defense Planning Guidance, 1982)

Pursuit of the strategy was deferred because of the defeat of the first President Bush by Bill Clinton, but it continued to colour American political discourse. Former government officials such as Wolfowitz, Dick Cheney, Donald Rumsfeld, Zalmay Khalilzad and Elliot Abrams (many of whom would later re-emerge in the current Bush administration) pressed their case for an American quest for 'preponderance of power' in think tanks and government commissions.[6] In one notable case, the Commission to Assess the Ballistic Missile Threat to the United States, chaired by Rumsfeld, dismissed intelligence from agencies like the CIA to declare that Iran, Iraq and North Korea would pose missile threats within the next five to ten years (Executive

Summary, 1998). Perhaps more important, the Clinton administration contributed to the ongoing projection of those threats with their identification of 'rogue states.' Consider, for example, the words of National Security Advisor Anthony Lake in 1994:

> Our policy must face the reality of recalcitrant and outlaw states that not only choose to remain outside the family but also assault its basic values. There are few 'backlash' states: Cuba, North Korea, Iran, Iraq and Libya. For now they lack the resources of a superpower, which would enable them to seriously threaten the democratic order being created around them. Nevertheless, their behavior is often aggressive and defiant. The ties between them are growing as they seek to thwart or quarantine themselves from a global trend to which they seem incapable of adapting. (Lake, 1994)

None of this is to suggest that 9/11 was a mere incident in a chain of events dating back to the start of the cold war (I hasten to add that I am not arguing that 9/11 was 'manufactured' to implement a plan for American dominance.) That tragedy, however, was not the *ab initio* foundation for a new US foreign policy or for a new construction of 'fear' in American culture. Rather, it acted upon – indeed, served as a catalyst for – both government planning and the context in which that planning was projected and developed.

On 31 January 2001, less than two weeks after the inauguration of George W. Bush, the president's National Security Council met for the first time. The lead item on the agenda was 'Regime Change in Iraq'. Secretary of Defense Rumsfeld asked his colleagues to 'imagine what the region would look like without Saddam and with a regime that is aligned with US interests. It would change everything in the region and beyond. It would demonstrate what US policy is all about' (quoted in Suskind, 2004). In effect, Iraq was going to be a demonstration case both of American power and the US quest for preponderance in the Middle East and beyond.

That quest was frustrated, in the short term, by other foreign policy issues and crises, such as the recurrence of violence in the Israeli–Palestinian dispute and the downing of an American reconnaissance plane by China in April 2001. The deferral of the quest did not mean, however, that the 'threat' had dissipated. Saddam continued to be held up as a menace to regional stability, and US warplanes periodically bombed Iraqi anti-aircraft positions. Other challenges to American 'security' were ever present, and indeed, in the aftermath of the incident with the US spy plane, there was the prospect of a showdown with the Chinese.

September 11, of course, was more than an abstract threat. It was a far too real, unprecedented illustration of how terrorism could be waged on the US mainland. Even more daunting, it was an act carried out not by an identifiable enemy state but by a transnational organization with no clear centre that could be attacked in response. So, on one level, the threat was met with the imagery of a 'War on Terror': the posters of Osama bin Laden – 'Wanted Dead or Alive' – and photographs of his acolytes, the institution of a colour-coded measure of the level of danger, the declarations that these enemies 'follow in the path of fascism, Nazism and totalitarianism' (Bush, 2001). At another, however, the challenge had to be made tangible by giving the United States someone or something to attack – in this case, the Taliban regime of Afghanistan that was allegedly giving shelter to bin Laden.[7]

But September 11 was far more than a manifestation of how 'fear' would be met by an ongoing battle for 'security.' What it offered to the Bush administration, tragically, was the opportunity to reframe that battle in the service of its long-term foreign policy goals. National Security Advisor Condoleezza Rice asked her staff, 'How do we capitalize on these opportunities [presented by 9/11]?' (quoted in Lemann, 2002). Secretary of Defense Rumsfeld offered the answer in instructions to his staff: 'Best info fast. Judge whether good enough hit S.H. [Saddam Hussein] at same time. Not only UBL [Osama bin Laden]. Go massive. Sweep it all up. Things related and not' (*CBS News*, 2002). While Bush and his advisors deferred an immediate attack on Iraq, which some in the administration supported, notably Undersecretary of Defense Paul Wolfowitz, the president made it clear that 'if we could prove that we could be successful in [the Afghanistan] theater, then the rest of the task would be easier' (quoted in Woodward, 2002, p. 84).

This is not to deny that the upsurge in fear, accompanied by grief, anger and displays of patriotism, was not heartfelt. The government, however, did not stand aside from those emotions. To the contrary, the mobilization of those emotions could defer if not resolve, tensions and contradictions raised by the implementation of long-standing government plans. Fear, rather than evidence, could offer the foundation for the Bush Administration to move from Kabul to other targets.

Consider, for example, the 'Campaign for Freedom' of the Advertising Council – the non-profit service organization through which ad agencies produce government campaigns. In one television spot, a young man attempts to check out a book from a local library. His request is not only met by hostility by the librarian; as he turns, with some trepidation, from the counter, he is met by two dark-suited gentlemen who escort him from the building. Those who saw the commercial, run through the autumn and winter of 2001/02, may have been unaware of the irony that at that time the FBI was demanding that librarians hand over lists of readers who had checked out books on subjects such as Islam (or that more than 1,000 people in the United States had been detained without charge after 9/11).[8]

Consider, in the 'foreign policy' complement to this domestic projection, the mistaken but persistent linkage of Saddam Hussein with Al Qa'eda and 9/11 by a majority of the American public and the encouragement of that linkage by government statements, including those by President Bush.[9] Consider the 'public diplomacy' effort in which, as Vice President Cheney was proposing to Tony Blair in March 2002 that planning a move from Afghanistan towards an invasion of Iraq, his wife was opening at the Museum of London an exhibit of twenty-eight photographs of 9/11's 'Ground Zero' by Joel Meyerowitz. (To heighten the message, the photographs were displayed in the room next to the permanent exhibit on the Blitz of the Second World War.)[10]

It can now be argued that, far from fulfilling the global blueprint set out by the Bush administration with the president standing on US warships declaring, 'Mission Accomplished' (Bumiller, 2003), the venture in Iraq clearly marked the downfall of the quest for a 'preponderance of power'. Perhaps more provocatively, it could be contended that there has been an assimilation of 'fear' similar to that of the mid-1950s, a duality holding together the menace of the 'other' with the immediately relevant challenges of family, finance and well-being. Even after the end of the Bush administration, the threat level continuously scrolled at 'Elevated: Orange' on Fox's news ticker, hundreds of detainees remained in Camp X-Ray and other prisons around the world, Osama bin Laden sat (probably in the northwest frontier of Pakistan) beyond the reach of American forces, and Saddam's execution faded before other day-to-day political and economic tensions. President Obama stands accused of continuing rather than challenging the Bush approach to secrecy, invoking it 'to quash legal inquiries into secret illegalities more often than any predecessor', compiling the 'worst record in history for persecuting, prosecuting, and jailing government whistle-blowers and truth-tellers', and 'maintaining the power to secretly kidnap, imprison, rendition, or torture'.[11]

These issues, however, are no longer quite as prominent in American discourse, be it Page 1 of the *New York Times* or (more cogently) *The Huntsville (Alabama) Times*. If you can forgive a personal assertion for this point, my mother may send me e-mails such as the one that I used to open this chapter, but her concerns – and those of my father, my sisters and other relatives in the United States – are usually closer to the bank balance than they are to the purported 'clash of civilizations'.

Still, as in the cold war, fear may be re-mobilized against new enemies or old enemies restored. It remains to be seen whether the current denunciations of Iran will lead to military action or whether we have reached a 'tipping point' where the images cannot be translated into another campaign. It remains to be seen whether another theatre of conflict – for example, Israel–Palestine or Israel–Lebanon – becomes a stage for wider intervention, whether there is a re-configuration of the old tensions with Russia or China, or whether another unexpected 'terrorist' atrocity turns the international kaleidoscope once more. For, unlike the cold war, there is no symbolic marker – no fall of the Wall, no end to an enemy system such as Communism – that can offer long-term absolution of the fear that has been cultivated in past generations and, in particular, in the first years of this century.

Notes

1 The letter originally appeared on the website www.gopusa.com on 6 June 2005 and can be seen in its entirety at http://www.americandaily.com/article/8987. The version from 'Ms Foster' omitted the first three paragraphs, converting it from specific responses to *Newsweek*'s expose of the desecration of prisoners' Korans at Camp X-Ray into a general reaction to accusations of misbehaviour by the US military.

2 See also the earlier examination by Freeland, 1971.

3 The *New Republic*'s cover of 3 September 1990 put the altered image of Saddam above the giant caption 'Fuhrer in the Gulf'.

4 In the 'Iran-contra' episode, exposed in 1986, the Reagan Administration tried to fund the efforts of the Nicaraguan contras to overthrow the Sandinista government through revenues from the sale of arms to the Iranian government, then fighting a protracted war against Iraq.

5 The document was written by Wolfowitz's aide Zalmay Khalilzad, who would become George W. Bush's Ambassador to Afghanistan after the fall of the Taliban, Ambassador to Iraq after the toppling of Saddam Hussein, and Ambassador to the United Nations.

6 For one now well-known example, see the documents of the Project for a New American Century at http://www.newamericancentury.org.

7 I deliberately use the modifier 'allegedly' for, on 20 September 2001 and again on 13 October 2001, the Taliban offered to negotiate the handover of Osama bin Laden for trial in an Islamic court. See Burns, 2001;Anonymous, 2001.

8 The 'Campaign for Freedom' no longer survives on the Advertising Council's website (www.adcouncil.org), although a related campaign, 'I am an American', can be found at http://www.adcouncil.org/default.aspx?id=61. A good summary of the Campaign for Freedom, including the contradictions of the 'Library' spot, is in Norman, 2002. On the detentions after 11 September, see Gumbel, 2001.

9 Consider, for example, Bush's speech of 1 May 2003: 'The battle of Iraq is one victory in a war on terror that began on September the 11th, 2001' (Bush, 2003). Two years after 9/11, almost 70 per cent of Americans still believed that 'Saddam Hussein was personally involved in the Sept. 11 attacks' (Associated Press, 2003).

10 The photographs are exhibited at 'After September 11: Images from Ground Zero', http://www.911exhibit.state.gov. See also Kennedy, 2003.

11 Letter from 24 former government officials, 'Rescind President Obama's Transparency Award Now', The Guardian, 14 June 2011, http://www.guardian. co.uk/commentisfree/cifamerica/2011/jun/14/rescind-barack-obama-obama-transparency-award.

References

Altheide, D. (2006), Terrorism and the Politics of Fear. Walnut Creek, CA: Rowman Altamira.

Anonymous (1971), 'Beginning of the end'. Time, 8 November.

—(2001), 'Bush rejects Taliban offer to hand Bin Laden over', The Guardian, 13 October, Available at: http://www.guardian.co.uk/world/2001/oct/14/afghanistan.terrorism5.

Associated Press (2003), 7 September, quoted in '69% of Americans Believe Saddam Linked to 9/11: Poll', Arab News, 7 September 2003, Available at: http://www.arabnews.com/?page=4&section=0&article=31530&d=7&m=9&y=2003.

Bernays, E. (1955), The Engineering of Consent. Norman, OK: University of Oklahoma Press.

Bumiller, E. (2003), 'Keepers of Bush image lift stagecraft to new heights', New York Times, 16 May, Reprinted at: http://edition.cnn.com/2003/US/05/16/nyt.bumiller/.

Burns, J. (2001), 'Afghans coaxing Bin Laden, but US rejects bid', New York Times, 21 September, Available at: http://query.nytimes.com/gst/fullpage.html?res=9400E5DC1E3BF932A1575AC0A9679C8B63&scp=2&sq=+bin+laden&st=nyt.

Bush, G. (2001), 'Speech to Congress', 21 September, Transcript at: http://edition.cnn.com/2001/US/09/20/gen.bush.transcript.

—(2003), 'Bush makes historic speech aboard warship', Available at: http://edition.cnn.com/2003/US/05/01/bush.transcript.

CBS News (2002), 'Plans for attack began on 9/11', CBS News, 4 September, Available at: http://www.cbsnews.com/stories/2002/09/04/september11/main520830.shtml.

Defense Planning Guidance (1982), 'Excerpts at Public Broadcasting System, Frontline: The War Behind Closed Doors', Available at: http://www.pbs.org/wgbh/pages/frontline/shows/iraq/etc/wolf.html.

Eisenhower, D. (1952), 'Republican Party platform', reprinted at The American Presidency Project, http://www.presidency.ucsb.edu/showplatforms. php?platindex=R1952.

Executive Order 9835 (1947), 21 March, Reprinted at: http://tucnak.fsv.cuni. cz/~calda/Documents/1940s/Truman%20Loyalty%20Oath,%201947.html.

Executive Summary (1998), Commission to assess the ballistic missile threat to the United States, 15 July, Reprinted at: http://www.fas.org/irp/threat/missile/ rumsfeld/.

Foster, P. (2005), 'I don't care!', 6 June, Available at: http://www.americandaily. com/article/8987.

Freeland, R. (1971), *The Truman Doctrine and the Origins of McCarthyism*. New York: Knopf.

Furedi, F. (2002), *The Culture of Fear*. London: Continuum.

—(2007), *The Politics of Fear*. London: Continuum.

Glassner, B. (2000), *The Culture of Fear: Why Americans are Afraid of the Wrong Things*. New York: Basic.

Gumbel, A. (2001), 'US detaining foreign nationals without charge and legal advice', *The Independent,* 12 November, Available at: http://news.independent.co.uk/ world/americas/article143675.ece.

Herman, E. and Chomsky, N. (1988), *Manufacturing Consent: The Political Economy of the Mass Media*. New York: Pantheon.

Jones, J. (1955), *The Fifteen Weeks*. New York: Harcourt, Brace, and World.

Kennedy, L. (2003), 'Remembering September 11: photography as cultural diplomacy', *International Affairs*, 79(2), 315–26.

Lake, A. (1994), 'Confronting backlash states', *Foreign Affairs*, March/April, Available at: http://www.foreignaffairs.org/19940301faessay5095/anthony-lake/confronting-backlash-states.html.

Lemann, N. (2002), 'The next world order', *The New Yorker,* 1 April.

Lippmann, W. (1922), *Public Opinion*. New York: Macmillan.

MacDonald, J.F. (1985), *Television and the Red Menace*. New York: Praeger.

McCarthy, J. (1950), 'Speech of Joseph McCarthy, wheeling, West Virginia', Available at: *History Matters*, http://historymatters.gmu.edu/d/6456.

Mueller, J. (2006), *Overblown: How Politicians and the Terrorism Industry Inflate National Security Threats, and Why We Believe Them*. New York: Free Press.

Norman, P. (2002), 'The Ad Council's campaign for freedom', *Flak Magazine*, 9 July, Available at: http://www.flakmag.com/tv/freedom.html.

NSC 20/4 (1948), 'US objectives with respect to the USSR to counter soviet threats to US security', 23 November, Available at: http://www.mtholyoke. edu/acad/intrel/coldwar/nsc20-4.htm.

NSC 68 (1950), 'United States objectives and programs for national security', 14 April, Available at: http://www.fas.org/irp/offdocs/nsc-hst/nsc-68.htm.

Qualter, T. (1985), *Opinion Control in the Democracies*. New York: Macmillan.

Reagan, R. (1982), 'Speech to British House of Commons', 8 June, Transcript at: http://www.cfif.org/htdocs/freedomline/current/america/ronald_reagan_evil_ empire.htm

Stouffer, S. (1992 [1954]), *Communism, Conformity, and Civil Liberties*. New Brunswick, NJ: Transaction.

Suskind, R. (2004), *The Price of Loyalty: George W. Bush, The White House, and the Education of Paul O'Neill.* New York: Simon and Schuster.

Truman, H. (1947), 'Speech to Congress', 12 March, Transcript at: http://www.yale.edu/lawweb/avalon/trudoc.htm.

—(1948), 'Address to the friendly sons of St. Patrick', *New York City*, 17 March, Transcript at: http://teachingamericanhistory.org/library/index.asp?document=1452.

—(1950), 'Speech to American Society of Newspaper Editors', 20 April, cited in 'Truth as a weapon in Cold War', *The Times*, 21 April 1950.

Woodward, B. (2002), *Bush at War.* New York: Simon and Schuster.

PART THREE

The affective dimension of political mobilization

6

Political despair

Deborah B. Gould

This chapter grows out of an observation about the affective landscape of the early twenty-first century United States: I posit a pervasive, if variably experienced, political despair – that is, feelings of political inefficacy and hopelessness, the sense that nothing will ever change, no matter what some imagined collective 'we' does to try to bring change.[1] In my view, scholars and activists must grapple with this constellation of negative political affects if we want to better understand the sources of political action and inaction. Three decades ago Doug McAdam developed the concept of *cognitive liberation*, arguing that for people to form and participate in social movements and other forms of protest, they need to believe that something is 'both unjust and *subject to change*' (McAdam, 1999, p. 34; emphasis his). Following from McAdam's insight but with terminology that adds emotion into the mix and signals that the experience of 'cognitive liberation' may in practice be more akin to a vague sensation rather than a lucid, coherent thought, my questions in this chapter revolve around senses of political possibility and impossibility. Characterizations of the 2011 popular revolution in Egypt that describe its unthinkability just days before its outbreak dramatically illustrate the need to explore how a pervasive sense of political hopelessness can be transformed, seemingly overnight, into a widely circulating sense of political possibility accompanied by strong feelings of collective agency and motivation to act on them.[2] Along with the question of how the unthinkable becomes thinkable, and how those who once felt hopeless come to see themselves instead as political protagonists able to act on the historical stage, we also need to consider how senses of political *impossibility* emerge and take hold, and how and the extent to which they preclude action and demobilize movements.

In this chapter I draw from my research about and experiences in the direct-action AIDS movement in the United States, ACT UP, to analyse political despair: how it operates in activist contexts, the unconscious processes it can set in motion, activist norms regarding it, its different temporalities, and, most generally, its effects on social movements and their participants. After providing a detailed account of the workings of despair in ACT UP, I turn at the end to a discussion, perhaps surprisingly, of the generative political potential of despair.

Despair's emergence

Feelings always arise and play out in contexts, and their workings and effects are conditioned by those contexts. The task, then, is to approach political feelings with a historical perspective, rejecting any *a priori* claims that would posit a necessary relationship between a specific emotion – say, political despair – and a given response – say, political demobilization. Universalizing claims like 'hope is necessary for movements', 'despair is depoliticizing', and 'anger leads people to the streets' may be useful in providing direction to inquiries about the role of emotion in contentious politics, but the particulars of any given situation often require pushing up against such claims in order to see how relationships between feelings and action work in practice. I begin, then, with a discussion of ACT UP's changing affective landscape and an exploration of why, how and with what effects despair emerged within the direct-action AIDS movement.

From its start in 1987 through 1989, ACT UP's activism provided an enormous sense of empowerment and political efficacy for participants, due in large part to the dramatic victories that activists achieved early on. During this period, the scientific-medical establishment, pharmaceutical companies and numerous government bodies responded to ACT UP's demands, and, in a context where research studies about different AIDS drugs appeared promising, activists felt optimistic.[3] Our victories corroborated and bolstered a newly emergent sense that we could force the powers that be to listen to and respond to us, that we could force change, that we could, and *would*, save lives. Activists' enactments of anger and hope in the streets helped to produce those very sentiments, warding off and submerging the gloom that had preceded ACT UP and that threatened to return in the face of continuing deaths. Additionally, the direct-action AIDS movement was receiving a lot of press, both mainstream and in lesbian and gay communities across the country, and was growing rapidly in response. Although some more establishment-oriented lesbians and gay men criticized the movement's militancy, a pervasive sentiment during this period was hope-filled optimism that street activism would change the course of the AIDS epidemic, prolonging and potentially saving the lives of countless gay and bisexual men. Looking back on that period, ACT UP/New York's Theo Smart remarked on activists' optimism: 'We believed that we could indeed win the battle against AIDS' (Smart, 1992, p. 43).

That optimism began to fade in ACT UP's later years. Concrete activist victories that prolonged the lives of people with AIDS continued into the early 1990s, but the deaths continued to accumulate, and movement on the AIDS treatment front stalled.[4] Despondency about the accumulating deaths and pessimism about the movement's ability to save lives began to circulate and, as I describe later, proved difficult to navigate. A growing despair among activists was apparent in a comment from ACT UP/NY member Robin Haueter in October 1990: 'The feeling we have is that for all we've done, we haven't done enough. People are still dying' (Camia, 1990, p. 7A). People *were* still dying, in ever-growing numbers, and no promising drugs were on the way. Theo Smart suggests that among some activists in late 1991, 'the conviction that a cure would not be found in their lifetime began to take root' (Smart, 1992, p. 44). Meanwhile, the deaths were relentless. ACT UP/Los Angeles member Mark Kostopoulos acknowledged his frustration: 'We've worked for three years . . . but all our successes haven't changed the fact that people continue to die' (Barker, 1991). In 1992, British gay/AIDS activist and writer Simon Watney described the gay world as 'a community approaching despair' (Watney, 1992, p. 18). In a list that explained reasons why and cited evidence supporting the contention itself, Watney wrote, 'Ninety-seven thousand gay men . . . have already died in the U.S. At least 50 per cent of gay men in New York are thought to be HIV-positive. . . . The suicide rate amongst HIV-*negative* gay men is alarmingly high' (Watney, 1992, p. 18; emphasis in original).

Pessimism and despair intensified in April 1993 when European AIDS researchers released their Concorde study, the longest study of the anti-AIDS drug AZT conducted thus far, which found that early intervention with AZT did not prolong patients' lives (Epstein 1996, pp. 300–05). The news out of the Ninth International Conference on AIDS, held in June 1993 in Berlin, was even more devastating. Member of ACT UP/Chicago and ACT UP/Los Angeles, Ferd Eggan, recalled the Berlin conference as 'the downest time . . . the worst'.

Essentially, the reports were that there was nothing that was working and that there was no hope to be had whatsoever. And everybody *was* dying. I mean, all the people who had gone on AZT and had been healthy for awhile all started dying. And so I think there was a feeling of futility, a feeling that we had done a lot, and maybe stretched it as far as we could, you know, the Ryan White Care Act was paying for care for people, the government had finally begun to respond, but at the same time, there was no cure; there was no treatment; there was no nothing. (Eggan, 1999, emphasis his)

The situation was equally bleak through 1994 and 1995.

Feeling despair

We can begin to explore despair's workings and effects by considering what happens to a movement when deaths of its members and of people in the surrounding community accumulate, one after another, an endless amassing of dead bodies. The unceasing AIDS deaths generated despair in ACT UP in two interrelated ways. First, the stream of illnesses and deaths, and the sense that the deaths would not cease or even slow down anytime soon, generated a physical and emotional exhaustion among many members of ACT UP that was fertile ground for despair. Second, the accumulating deaths, with no end in sight, shattered ACT UP's hopeful vision that its street activism would save lives.

The word exhaustion evokes being emptied, drained, depleted. Consider the daily lives of ACT UP members during the early 1990s. Along with planning and executing numerous demonstrations, AIDS activists visited friends and fellow activists in the hospital; changed diapers and cleaned bed sores; drove friends to doctor's appointments; watched lovers be reduced to needing help to eat and go to the bathroom; feared seroconverting and getting sick; felt guilty about being unable to stand the thought of visiting yet another friend in the hospital; learned how to hook up a catheter; helped friends move into hospice; learned about more friends testing HIV-positive; listened as loved ones said they had decided to stop taking their meds; went to memorial service after memorial service; stopped knowing what to say or how to help; helped lovers and friends kill themselves.

If you had HIV/AIDS, daily life also entailed gagging on pills that eventually were revealed to be ineffective; fearing every flu and cold; incessant nausea; loss of appetite and weight; constant fatigue; witnessing your body become unrecognizable to you; consoling (or not) friends who were freaking out about your visible deterioration, angry at you for succumbing, unable to face your approaching death, who no longer could stand to be near you; denying or acknowledging your impending death; losing your independence; considering whether to enter hospice care; planning your memorial service; watching your body fail the latest pill regimen; experiencing excruciating pain; deciding whether to hold onto life until the bitter end or to kill yourself, and, if the latter, how to do so.[5]

In the late 1980s and early 1990s, hope tantalized us, holding out the possibility that *someone* would get better, would beat this horror, would survive. But as the deaths within LGBT communities and within our own ranks accumulated, the hope that your friend, lover or comrade might be able to hang on for a little longer, until the next medical 'miracle' was available, became more difficult to hold onto. Any hopes we might have had were demolished, and people became increasingly tired of false hopes, indeed, worn out by them.

In describing why she eventually left ACT UP/New York, Jean Carlomusto acknowledged the role played by the never-ending deaths and her consequent exhaustion: 'I just got really burnt out and sort of withdrew from life in general for a period of time. A lot of that was about the cumulative amounts of deaths that happened' (Carlomusto, 2002, p. 42). ACT UP was quick-paced and all-consuming; caretaking, which many of us were involved in to one degree or another, was similarly absorbing. The pace allowed little time to pause and almost no space for an interior life.

For everyone living so close to AIDS in that period, daily life was physically and emotionally draining. ACT UP/New York member Marion Banzhaf points to the amassing of deaths as being particularly traumatic: 'It got to be too much. You can't sustain that level of loss without becoming traumatized by it' (Banzhaf, 2002). ACT UP/Chicago member Jeanne Kracher had a similar analysis about the toll that the accumulating deaths was taking on people in ACT UP. 'I think people were exhausted. . . . How did we manage all the grief, how can you manage that? I mean, how does anybody manage?' (Kracher, 2000). In this climate of utter exhaustion, surrounded by unrelenting death and illness, with no end in sight and no good prospects on the treatment front, despair easily edged out hope.

As if that wasn't enough, daily life for many AIDS activists during the early 1990s also included political despair, intimately connected to the unending illnesses and deaths. No matter what we did, no matter our astonishing victories, people continued to die. They started to live longer, but then they died anyway. ACT UP/New York member Dudley Saunders recalls,

> ACT UP had all these incredible successes so quickly. New York still has the best insurance laws in America. It's incredible, the things we got done. We'd won all these battles, but the war – we were all still dying. There really was no hope. It was horrible. (Saunders, 2003)

Tim Miller from ACT UP/Chicago also juxtaposes the victories and the deaths:

> Even if we had a success every day it might not have been enough success. Because people were still getting sick. And in Chicago, I think people were

relatively healthy for a great period of time. And then all of a sudden, a lot of people started getting ill. A lot of people started dying. And that's demoralizing. (Miller, 1999)

Social movements offer a vision of a different future and a way to get there. As ACT UP's hopeful vision of activism leading to a cure faltered, a vision of unremitting illness and suffering, of early deaths of lovers, friends and fellow activists, of decimated queer communities, of continuing societal neglect and attacks from the right, and of an ever-exploding crisis took over. We had no other vision to offer; every imaginable future seemed bleak. Political despair, then, arrived on the heels of ACT UP's hopeful but receding vision, and as despair took hold, it depleted many ACT UP members' activist energy, replacing their rousing desire and forward momentum, sometimes even their anger, with frustration, exhaustion and immobility.

If an empty hole is what remains after someone dies (Brown, 1994, p. 157), then that hole grew immense in ACT UP during the early 1990s. Unconsciously, we tried to fill it with demonstrations and fact sheets; with pithy and poignant agit-prop, angry chants and campy humour; with flirtation, sex and another angry action.[6] Still, no matter how much we all tried, the hole became more gaping, more devastating and the growing despair became harder to cover over. A sense of political efficacy and optimism initially helped us to navigate the daily toll of the AIDS epidemic. But it is hard to hold onto the hope that through your action you will be able to save lives when all your actions, even those that are unqualified successes, feel entirely inadequate to the task. As ACT UP/Chicago member Jeff Edwards noted, after years of 'intensive, all-consuming political involvement in which ACT UP had exploited every tactic short of violence, people were still dying, with no end in sight; maybe, some were coming to think, political action was fruitless' (Edwards, 2000, p. 493). As the deaths continued unabated, it became harder to believe our own hopeful rhetoric that action equalled life, as one ACT UP catchphrase put it. Many ACT UP activists felt we had reached the limits of activism, which sapped our hope and generated an even more absolute despair.

Despair has different tempos for different individuals, and although despair was prevalent in the early 1990s, not everyone in ACT UP felt it. I remember feeling anger, only anger. Grief and despair about the deaths and about our seeming political inefficacy emerged for me only in 1994, during ACT UP/ Chicago's last year. Soon after, especially as I began my research about the movement, I was flooded with those feelings, a deluge that suggested to me the extent of my previous denial, a psychic process that I return to below. Prior to that point, I was mainly aware of my anger: about the AIDS crisis, about government negligence, about the right wing's use of AIDS to advance

its homophobic agenda, about the illnesses and deaths of friends and comrades, about the disappearance of a vital world. But while it is true that activists felt despair to different degrees and at different intensities, the evidence
indicates its pervasiveness during the direct-action AIDS movement's period
of decline.

The workings of despair

Indeed, despair contributed mightily to ACT UP's undoing. Two factors help
to explain why and how despair did its destructive work. First, the unconscious processes that it set in motion had extraordinary force and were difficult for individuals and the movement to navigate. Second, and related, ACT
UP's *emotional habitus* – a term I use to describe the collective, largely nonconscious, emotional dispositions within a social group along with members'
embodied, axiomatic attitudes and norms about feelings and their expression – provided no means for activists to address the growing despair except
through denial.[7]

Despair and unconscious processes

In a 1993 speech ACT UP/New York member and cultural theorist Douglas
Crimp posed the question 'Why do we despair' and offered the following
answer:

> Surely because we seem no closer now than we did when ACT UP was
> formed in 1987 to being able to save our lives. And unlike that moment,
> when the very fact of our growing activism afforded the hope that we could
> save ourselves, very few of us still truly believe that the lives of those now
> infected can be saved by what we do. (Crimp, 2002, pp. 227–8)

Our street activism was exhausted, no longer offering hope. Crimp continued, 'Without hope for ourselves and our friends many of us now turn away
from these battles' (Crimp, 2002, pp. 227–8).

Understanding despair through a more or less cognitive lens, we might
expect a growing hopelessness about AIDS and AIDS activism to lead some
to a conscious, even rational, decision to leave ACT UP; its activism seemed
to be no longer working, so why continue? That may be true to an extent,
but, because what made the despair especially powerful were the unconscious forces it set in play, I think a more affective rendering of emotion that

takes nonconscious and non-rational processes seriously offers a more fruitful approach.[8] Revolving around despair were immense grief and a devastating feeling of helplessness, a sense that the AIDS crisis would not end
soon, that AIDS deaths would continue no matter what activists did. We can
imagine why AIDS activists might want to disavow such a psychically painful
constellation of feelings. In Crimp's words, 'It should come as little surprise
to us that we might now find AIDS an idea that has become unbearable and
against which we might wish to defend' (Crimp, 2002, p. 227) and that we
might also require 'a psychic defense against our despair about AIDS' (Crimp,
2002, p. 228). That is, AIDS activists might want to defend against the pain of
grief and of despair; against the tremendous shame and guilt that in despairing you were giving up on ACT UP and the potential it once had signalled, that
you were somehow giving ground to and even worse, becoming complicit
with those who wanted to see gay men dead, that you were deserting your
own people and thus in some sense abandoning your gay and perhaps HIV-
positive self as well.

Given that constellation of painful feelings associated with the growing
despair, AIDS activists might turn away from AIDS and AIDS activism, perhaps feeling exhausted and numb but not necessarily even aware of their
own despair. They might turn towards activism that was emphasizing healthy
gay bodies rather than dying ones, fighting to lift the ban on gays in the military, for example (Crimp, 2002, p. 228). Alternatively, they might turn away
from activism altogether, overwhelmed by the deaths and consequent grief,
demoralized by a sense of political inefficacy, wracked by guilt both about surviving and about giving up, and simply unable to feel activist rage any longer.

Or, in a contrary way, and I am again drawing from Crimp here, the pain
of despair, the shame at feeling yourself giving up, might have encouraged
some to disavow those sentiments via a moralistic deploring of *other* activists
who were ostensibly abandoning the fight. Reacting to a shift in focus in lesbian and gay politics away from AIDS and towards issues like the ban against
gays in the military, some AIDS activists demanded of former comrades and
of others in the lesbian and gay community, 'Where's your anger?!' alongside
exhortations to 'feel your rage' and 'remember AIDS'. For Crimp, this moralistic 'hectoring' by some remaining AIDS activists indicated the direct-action
AIDS movement's disavowal of despair, our collective failure to assess and
confront its depths (Crimp, 2002, pp. 222, 227, 244).

The force of these unconscious processes significantly shaped how the
movement navigated the painful feelings associated with despair. We ignored
it, denied it, repressed it, projected it onto others who we berated for succumbing to it. Despair was in the room with us, but it found no route other
than denial.

Forbidding despair

The psychic and the social buttressed one another in this case in the sense that ACT UP's emotional habitus disallowed despair. And that is the second way in which despair contributed to ACT UP's undoing.[9] In offering street activism as a response to despondency about the horrors of the AIDS crisis and to the sense of political impotency that was widespread in the early and mid-1980s, ACT UP fashioned itself as an antidote to despair, a place to 'turn your grief into anger'. Despair, then, was verboten in ACT UP, the constitutive outside of the movement's emotional habitus. ACT UP/New York member David Barr points out that ACT UP 'didn't have a discourse about emotions other than anger', but, even so, 'they were all there' (Barr, 2002). There, but unacknowledged. Barr's sense was that ACT UP's emotional habitus required feelings like grief and despair to be submerged for fear that permitting their expression somehow would destroy the organization; the ethos, he suggested, was as follows: 'We just better not stop being angry, because that will open up all this other stuff and then we're really in trouble' (Barr, 2002). So, while despair and its companions were banned, anger was required, as was the optimistic belief, even faith, that ACT UP's collective action would save lives, especially the lives of people with AIDS *in the room*. AIDS activism entailed an assertion of heroic agency: never mind the enormous barriers standing in our way, we *would* save our lives and the lives of our lovers, friends and comrades. In this context, there was no space for despair, which, following feminist philosopher Alison Jaggar, might best be described as an 'outlaw emotion' (1989).

Operating beneath conscious awareness, a social group's emotional habitus provides members with an emotional disposition, with a sense of what and how to feel, with labels for their feelings, with schemas about what feelings are and what they mean, with ways of figuring out and understanding what they are feeling. An emotional habitus contains an emotional pedagogy, a template for what and how to feel, in part by conferring on some feelings and modes of expression an axiomatic, natural quality and making other feeling states unintelligible within its terms and thus in a sense unfeelable and inexpressible. ACT UP's emotional habitus made despair largely unintelligible and intensely difficult to feel and express.[10]

What lay behind the proscription against despair in some ways differed for HIV-negative and HIV-positive participants. HIV-negatives demonstrated solidarity with HIV-positives by expressing anger about the crisis, by indicating their faith in and commitment to activism, by putting their bodies on the line, by holding onto hope for a cure. Therefore, despairing of the crisis ever ending, of being able to save the lives of those now infected, might flood one with shame about failing to be a properly hopeful AIDS activist as well as guilt about giving up on the struggle and thereby in some sense abandoning people with AIDS. It was thus difficult to admit, even to yourself, that you were despairing of an end to the crisis, that you were feeling both helpless and hopeless.

Anxiety about betraying people with AIDS might propel you to disavow your despair and fight all the harder. And, indeed, as I suggested above, many of us were so steeped in ACT UP's emotional habitus that all we felt was anger and conviction that our activism would succeed; it was hard to acknowledge or even to recognize sentiments of despair. But others quietly left the movement, overwhelmed by the deaths and consequent grief, demoralized by a sense of political inefficacy and helplessness, wracked by guilt both about surviving and about giving up, wanting to avoid being in the room with desperate people with AIDS who needed your help and somehow were holding onto hope when you were no longer able to, wishing to avoid seeing yourself as someone who was betraying people with AIDS as well as abandoning the movement when it most needed more troops.

Addressed by ACT UP/New York member Gregg Bordowitz in his video *Fast Trip, Long Drop* (1993), people with AIDS within the movement shouldered an additional burden. They had to assume the role of the hopeful, persevering person with AIDS, heroically determined to fight the virus and survive the crisis. To preserve the vision that ACT UP's activism was saving lives, to inspire the uninfected to keep fighting on their behalf, they had to cloak their own dying as well as any despair they might feel. For both HIV-negatives and HIV-positives, then, to despair was to breach one's proper role as an AIDS activist and thereby *affectively* ditch the movement and (other) people with HIV/AIDS.

That was the ethos against despair, but in the early 1990s, many in the movement did start to feel it. The unrelenting deaths anesthetized many members' feelings of anger and overwhelmed their hope that activism would be able to stop the dying. Rather than attend to this growing despair, ACT UP members were more likely to ignore its depths, disavow its prevalence, and badger people because they were 'succumbing' to it, none of which helped people overcome despair (Crimp, 2002, p. 227). ACT UP's emotional habitus, born in a moment of despair and consequently oriented towards dealing with despair by overcoming it, offered no other response and, indeed, under the pressure of growing despair, itself began to unravel. Activists continued to elevate and authorize anger, but the force of the despair began to numb people to anger, lessening the effectiveness of activists' emotion work (Hochschild, 1979, 1983).

Ferd Eggan recalled the shift in his own feeling states. While in ACT UP/ Chicago, 'the anger about people dying sustained [him]'. But by the summer of 1990, when he moved to Los Angeles and began working in an AIDS service organization, everything 'had become too complex and too human to just be angry'. He recalls,

> It was easier when the government wasn't doing anything. Then the government was doing something, but the something was inadequate. Then ultimately it wasn't just the question of whether it was *quantitatively* inadequate; it was *qualitatively* inadequate. 'Cause there was no resolution to the crisis, because there was no medication, there was no treatment, there was no cure. (Eggan, 1999; emphases his)

The complexity of AIDS, the unending deaths, and the lack of positive prospects on the treatment front overtook Eggan's anger. He continued, 'Kevin Farrell [from ACT UP/L.A.] and I and a couple other people just said, "Well, you know, mainly we just feel *bad*. We don't feel fiery demandful for something, because there isn't any *something*"' (Eggan, 1999; emphases his). For Eggan, the death in 1992 of a close friend in ACT UP/Los Angeles Mark Kostopoulos, marked the moment when ACT UP's emotional habitus seemed exhausted.

> All of these ACT UP veterans got together, [Mark's] friends, people who had been in ACT UP for years, and we wanted to have a political funeral down the street. But at the same time . . . a lot of us just wanted to feel sad. We didn't particularly want to have a political funeral. We just wanted to feel sad, to mourn. I mean, we had just sort of reached the end of righteous indignation. (Eggan, 1999)

Eggan notes that 'others were still very much full of anger' (1999), but for some, sadness, grief and despair were now overwhelming anger.

Because the movement's emotional habitus prohibited despair, it was unable to provide helpful tools for navigating that affective state when it arose despite efforts to exile it. It was a shameful secret not to be divulged to anyone. In that context, despair emerged in a way that individualized and depoliticized the feeling. Anger, in contrast, had united us, forming an important part of our collective self-definition. Even if our anger often had different sources and targets, there was a sharedness about the feeling, and it seemed like we all could relate to one another through our collective anger about the AIDS crisis.[11]

Whereas anger had been collectivizing, despair was individuating, particularly insofar as it violated ACT UP's emotion norms and, in part as a result, went largely unacknowledged. With no collective space carved out for its expression, participants who felt despair had no way of interjecting it into their activist lives. As a result, it remained illegible to the room at large, an unacknowledged presence, but one that was nevertheless *felt* by many. But to feel it placed one outside of ACT UP's culture. It created a feeling chasm that seemed impossible to bridge: How does despair legibly speak to anger? How does anger speak to despair, except by demanding 'Where's your anger?' As the movement declined, that question was asked over and over during ACT UP meetings, 'as if checking other people for I.D.,' in the words of ACT UP/New York member John Weir. Where 'rage bestow[ed] authenticity' (Weir, 1995, p. 11), despair only created alienation from fellow activists and from ACT UP itself. Where anger had made participants feel like they were part of something vibrant and larger than themselves, despair made people feel alone, guilt-ridden, sad and bad, and inclined to leave the movement.

Along with unconscious processes, then, the movement's ethos against despair contributed to its inability to attend to it when it did emerge. What is notable here is both the power of ACT UP's emotional habitus to structure its members' affects and emotional expressions – effectively submerging despair – as well as the limits of that power – the movement's emotional habitus did not rid people of the negative affect itself. In light of more total-izing usages of the habitus concept, let me use this empirical finding of vari-ability of feeling and contestations of emotional norms within a collectivity to make a conceptual point: while the axiomatic and nonconscious qualities of an emotional habitus give it a force that *shapes* how members of a social group feel, emote, label and understand their feelings, habitus are nonde-terministic. As systems of dispositions, habitus are not exact blueprints but consist of 'virtualities, potentialities, eventualities' whose actualization is con-tingent (Bourdieu and Wacquant, 1992, p. 135). With no established prac-tices for navigating feelings of despair, once it developed among a number of participants, it affected the organization as a whole, draining many people's energies and effectively (and affectively) depleting the ranks.

Despair and activism?

Are there alternate routes for political despair? Scholars and activists alike tend to put movement and hope in one basket and demobilization and despair in another. But the following brief discussion of a very different moment in AIDS activism, the period when the direct-action AIDS movement emerged, challenges the presumption that despair and its companion feelings inevitably deactivate, revealing instead that the effects of despair, like any individual or collective feeling, are contingent.[12]

Despair helped to destroy the direct-action AIDS movement but it played a role in its emergence as well, in the second half of 1986, when the number of recorded AIDS cases was approximately 25,000 and the total number of known deaths from AIDS-related conditions was more than 15,000 (Centers for Disease Control and Prevention, 1986, p. 5). In 1981, the year marking the official start of the epidemic, about 250 people died from AIDS-related complications. By mid-1986, when direct-action AIDS groups began to emerge, the number of deaths per year had surpassed 7,000, a 2,700 per cent increase over the first year (Centers for Disease Control and Prevention, 1987, p. 5). By January 1987, half a year later and just months before the founding of ACT UP/ New York, the number of deaths per year was closer to 12,000 (Centers for Disease Control and Prevention, 1989, p. 17). When ACT UP/New York held its first meeting on 12 March 1987, the numbers of diagnoses and deaths per year were rising exponentially, and there were no FDA-approved drugs to treat AIDS.[13] As well, the lesbian and gay community's activism to fight the crisis, primarily lobbying and occasional candlelight vigils, was failing to move the government and scientific-medical establishment to respond. Lesbians' and gay men's powerlessness vis-à-vis all levels of government – and the deadly consequences of that powerlessness – were clear, and yet more confrontational activism was outside of most AIDS and lesbian and gay activists' political imagination. In that context, as thousands of gay and bisexual men died while the government aggressively ignored the epidemic, people became increasingly pessimistic about saving the lives of people with AIDS. The period just prior to the emergence of direct-action AIDS activism, then, was a period of horror, grief, desperation and despair, a time of 'deepening gloom' in lesbian and gay communities, in Epstein's words (Epstein, 1996, p. 117).

How did those feelings influence lesbian and gay political responses to AIDS? While it certainly is true that despair sometimes flattens political possibilities, exacerbating a sense of inefficacy and hopelessness and generating political withdrawal, it also sometimes works to open new political horizons, alternative visions of what is to be done and how to do it.[14] In this case, feelings of hopelessness and desperation, rather than foreclosing political activism, spurred lesbian and gay support for confrontational tactics that had long been abandoned by the mainstream, establishment-oriented gay movement. As Epstein contends, 'One response to these difficult times was a rebirth of activism, epitomized by the actions of groups like ACT UP' (Epstein, 1996, p. 117). In a context where existing forms of AIDS activism were coming up largely empty, people's despair acted as a goad, inspiring creative risk-taking and an abandonment of the tried and true (but evidently ineffective) path in order to strike out in new, untested activist directions. Despair, in other words, helped to wrench open the existing political horizon. Amid an escalating epidemic, government negligence in addressing the crisis, widespread clamouring by politicians and pundits for repressive legislation including quarantine for people with AIDS, and more general attacks on lesbian and gay rights, activists effectively tapped into sentiments of despondency, desperation and despair about the AIDS crisis and offered street AIDS activism – oppositional, self-consciously confrontational, uncompromising, indecorous – as a legitimate and necessary route to save lives. Activists altered the affective experience of despair by coding it to mean 'having nothing left to lose', and rather than paralysing, despair became freeing.[15] Activists collectivized and politicized despair, conjoined it with anger, and channelled those feelings into militant street-based AIDS activism. Counterintuitively, then, the despair of this period helped to launch a movement.

Given a widespread view that hope is necessary to activism,[16] my claim about the prevalence of despair in the moment of ACT UP's emergence might seem implausible. Despair connotes utter hopelessness, a sense that nothing can be done to change oppressive circumstances; despairing people, we might presume, do not act up. That may frequently be true, but the directionality of political feelings, where they take us, and the sorts of behaviour they motivate, cannot be established in an *a priori* fashion. Aspects of their nature, especially their nonstatic, combinatory and indeterminate qualities, suggest why. *Nonstatic*: emotion, etymologically related to motion, suggests movement and flow rather than stasis. Even feelings of complete hopelessness oscillate and change, sometimes due to a momentous event – a Supreme Court ruling, a successful people's revolution elsewhere – sometimes due to the engagements of everyday life – gathering with people, having a conversation, viewing a work of art, reading history, listening to music, seeing graffiti on the street. *Combinatory*: feelings come bundled together, and they do not always form a coherent package. Antonio Gramsci's famous dictum referencing pessimism of the intellect along with optimism of the will suggests the possibility of feeling despair and hope simultaneously. Despair can coexist not only with grief and sadness, as it did in ACT UP's later years, but also with an activating anger, as it did in the 1986–1987 period. How despair combines with or gets tethered to other feeling states affects its political potential. *Indeterminate*: feelings are not deterministic, and they do not produce invariant effects; despair *can* demobilize, and that may be its most probable direction and effect, but such an outcome is contingent rather than necessary or inevitable. Along with being conceptual, my insistence here is political: despair need not be the end of the story in an activist context; *how activists contend with that negative affective state matters*.

Despair's potential

With the indeterminacy of political feelings in mind, then, I'll conclude with a brief discussion of activists' ethos about and navigations of despair. To understand why and how despair contributed to ACT UP's undoing, we need to return to the movement's emotional habitus and to the emotion work that generated it. Given the emotional habitus and political horizon that prevailed in the early 1980s, prior to the emergence of ACT UP, direct-action AIDS activists understandably engaged in emotion work that harnessed grief to anger, channelled both into direct action, and thereby attempted to bury the despair circulating in lesbian and gay communities in that moment. Despair is not necessarily depoliticizing, but it seemed to be in the early and mid-1980s, and it also was painful to feel. As a result, AIDS activists tried to submerge it, in themselves and in others, and their authorizations of anger and incitements to feel faith in direct action succeeded for a number of years.

That emotion work was crucial for ACT UP's emergence and growth, but the emotional habitus that we generated and that shaped our activism did not provide us with ways to deal with the despair that eventually took hold within the movement. In the context of accumulating deaths and a growing sense of our inability to save lives, exhortations to anger and to keep the faith lost their resonance, no longer collectivizing and activating as they once had, nor offering a route out of despair.

Could it have been otherwise? Given the course of the AIDS epidemic in the early 1990s and how overwhelming feelings of hopelessness and helplessness were in that context, I am not sure whether efforts to deal with despair in ways other than through denial would have lessened its destructive impact on the movement. Even so, given the occasional prevalence of despair in the contemporary political landscape, it is worth considering whether activists can respond to such bad feelings in ways other than by denying or defending against them.

ACT UP wasn't alone in disavowing despair. The political left in the United States more generally similarly prohibits despair; we tend to deny its existence, moralize against it and attempt to convert it into proper, acceptable activist feelings, à la 'don't mourn, organize'.[17] But not acknowledging bad feelings and continual exhortations to feel outrage leave the politically depressed feeling unaddressed, or worse. Why go to a meeting or action only to be made to feel bad that you feel bad? Rather than requiring outrage and optimism, perhaps we should recognize that people feel multiple complex feelings regarding the state of the world. What might be the political potential of working *with* despair rather than denying it or trying to convert it into the ostensibly requisite hope? What might happen if we acknowledged despair, addressed it, collectivized it and even politicized it and mobilized on that basis?

On May Day, 2003, a little over a month after the start of the United States' war in Iraq, Feel Tank Chicago – an art/activism/research collaborative group interested in political emotion – held the First Annual Parade of the Politically Depressed.[18] Wearing bathrobes and slippers, ten people stood in front of the State of Illinois Building in downtown Chicago holding signs with messages like 'Depressed? It Might Be Political,' 'Shocked, Awed, and Seriously Depressed', and 'Don't Just Medicate, Agitate!' Feel Tank held the Second Annual Parade one year later and then skipped the next two years, 'too depressed to get out of bed'. We held the Fifth Annual Parade on 4 July 2007 with as many as 60 people participating. We paraded through the streets of downtown Chicago amid tourists and Fourth of July revellers. Posters again referenced feelings of political despair, dissatisfaction, frustration and exhaustion, and linked them to the possibility of active resistance. Some passersby stopped to wonder about this perhaps surprising event where people proclaiming political depression were, nevertheless, marching in the streets. Many asked what it was all about. Some joined in, perhaps relieved to find other political depressives interested in collectivizing their bad feelings. Cab drivers honked their approval. The Parade of the Politically Depressed evidently struck a chord.

The route for despair is not fixed, and while some circumstances, like those facing direct-action AIDS activists in the early 1990s, make despair extremely difficult to address, how we do shapes the effects it will have. Most importantly, we can recognize the political nature of our senses of possibility and impossibility, and find ways to move forward with both.

Notes

1 This chapter draws from Gould (2009, ch. 7). I wish to thank my collaborators in Feel Tank Chicago for our ongoing conversations about political hope and despair.

2 Charles Kurzman's study of the 1979 Iranian revolution (2004) illustrates a dramatic instance where widespread feelings of political impossibility were rapidly replaced by a new sense of possibility and belief in collective agency.

3 The conventional wisdom that emerged at the Fifth International Conference on AIDS in Montreal in June 1989 was that 'HIV infection might soon become a chronic manageable illness' (Epstein, 1996, p. 237).

4 The class of drugs that have helped people to live longer, protease inhibitors, did not emerge until 1995–1996. ACT UP's activism was a crucial factor in the development of these drugs, but that extraordinary success was not

yet known in the early 1990s when more pessimism emerged and ACT UP began to decline.

5 When I first began writing about despair in ACT UP, I reread Douglas Crimp's important essay from 1989 about AIDS activists' difficulties in mourning the deaths and devastation wrought by AIDS in queer communities – 'Mourning and Militancy'. Crimp also created a list of daily activities, a list 'of the problems we face', as a way to convey the psychic enormity of what gay men were facing (Crimp, 1989, pp. 15–16). The coincidence made me consider why one might turn to the genre of the list to convey what daily life amid the AIDS epidemic was like. A list seems particularly apt for conveying the sheer immensity and horror of a crisis like AIDS: it can indicate the scale and scope of a crisis, as well as the complex relationships of differently positioned people to it. A list can also suggest its own incompleteness and thus create a sense of enormity and vastness.

6 What I am saying here should not be read as suggesting that ACT UP's street activism and other activities are reducible to the fulfillment of psychic needs. We can recognize the political nature of activism even while pointing to the role that unconscious processes often play.

7 I first encountered the term *emotional habitus* in Kane 2001 (particularly pp. 253–4), who derives it from the work of Norbert Elias, Pierre Bourdieu and Thomas Scheff. I say more about the concept below. See also Gould (2009, especially pp. 32–6).

8 See Gould (2009, 2010) where I argue for the utility of the concept of *affect* for prying open a conceptual space to explore those aspects of human motivation that are nonconscious, non-rational, nonlinguistic and noncoherent, a conceptual space that has shrunk considerably with the rise of rational-actor theories in the social sciences and has been difficult to inhabit in light of the important claims of the cultural and linguistic turns about the centrality of linguistic meaning-making practices in social life. My intent is to challenge an overly cognitivized and rationalized view of political emotion.

9 See Holmes (this volume) for a discussion of how forbidden feelings affected second-wave feminist movements.

10 One reason that I like the term *habitus* for thinking about feelings is that it locates feelings within social relations and practices, thereby pointing towards their conventionality and countering a standard understanding of feelings as wholly interior to the individual. I am especially drawn to the concept because it forces us to consider *together* phenomena that are often opposed to one another: the social and conventional aspects of emotion, on the one hand, along with the nonconscious and bodily components, on the other. Indeed, an emotional habitus has force precisely because its bodily and axiomatic qualities obscure the social, conventional nature of feelings and generate the sense that what one is feeling is entirely one's own. I prefer the term *emotional habitus* to a concept from the sociology of emotions literature that on its face might appear similar – *emotion culture* (Gordon, 1989) – because the former, by emphasizing *practices*, especially those that are nonconscious and noncognitive, offers an account of why and how specific feelings become widespread within a collectivity and why and how they sometimes change.

11 Peter Lyman has described anger as 'the essential political emotion' (Lyman, 1981, p. 61). See the special issue of the *European Journal of Social Theory* (vol. 7, no. 2, 2004) that explores anger through this lens.

12 For analyses that explore the generative and creative political potential of loss (of bodies, ideals, places), see Eng and Kazanjian, 2003. See also the work of Feel Tank Chicago: www.feeltankchicago.net.

13 One week later, on 19 March 1987, the FDA announced that it had licensed the pharmaceutical company Burroughs Wellcome to produce AZT, the first antiviral (and highly toxic) AIDS therapy. Burroughs Wellcome set the price at $10,000 annually, making AZT the most expensive drug in history. See Crimp and Rolston (1990, pp. 27–9).

14 Solnit (2004) makes a similar point.

15 Insofar as street vendor Mohamed Bouazizi's act of self-immolation in December 2010 suggests feelings of despair on his part and perhaps more widely among Tunisians, it would be interesting to explore whether and how activists contended with that apparent despair and whether and how such feelings, perhaps widespread, helped launch the Tunisian Revolution of 2011.

16 See, for example, McAdam (1999, p. 34) and Aminzade and McAdam (2001, pp. 31–2).

17 Solnit argues precisely the opposite, that audible elements of the left only focus on the 'bad news' of the world, thus bolstering an identity that is 'masculine, stern, disillusioned, tough enough to face facts' (2004, pp. 15–16). I agree that the left tends towards apocalyptic narratives about the world, but I also think that the emotional demand of those narratives is to be outraged and to not give in to despair (corroborating Solnit's point about the left's masculinism).

18 Full disclosure: I helped to plan this event and participated in it, along with others described below. Photos from Feel Tank Chicago's Parades of the Politically Depressed are available at www.feeltankchicago.net.

References

Aminzade, R. and McAdam, D. (2001), 'Emotions and contentious politics', in R. Aminzade, J. Goldstone, D. McAdam, E. Perry, W. Sewell, Jr., S. Tarrow and C. Tilly, eds, *Silence and Voice in the Study of Contentious Politics*, Cambridge: Cambridge University Press, pp. 14–50.

Banzhaf, M. (2002), Interview conducted by Deborah Gould, 12 September, New York. Interview housed in my personal ACT UP archive.

Barker, K. (1991), 'Taking AIDS battle to Capitol Hill', *Washington Post*, 29 September, B4.

Barr, D. (2002), Interview conducted by Deborah Gould, 11 September, New York. Interview housed in my personal ACT UP archive.

Bourdieu, P. and Wacquant, L. (1992), *An Invitation to Reflexive Sociology*. Chicago: University of Chicago Press.

Brown, R. (1994), *Gifts of the Body*. New York: HarperCollins.

Camia, C. (1990), ''90s AIDS outlook grim, experts say, but medical advances deemed likely', *Dallas Morning News*, 29 October.

Carlomusto, J. (2002), Interview conducted by ACT UP Oral History Project. Available at: www.actuporalhistory.org.

Centers for Disease Control and Prevention (1986), *AIDS Weekly Surveillance*, 29 December, 1–5.

—(1987), *AIDS Weekly Surveillance*, 28 December, 1–5.

—(1989), *HIV/AIDS Surveillance, Year End Edition*, January 1990, 1–22.

Crimp, D. (1989), 'Mourning and militancy', *October*, 51(Winter), 3–18.

—(2002), *Melancholia and Moralism: Essays on AIDS and Queer Politics*. Cambridge, MA: MIT Press.

Crimp, D. and Rolston, A. (1990), *AIDS Demo Graphics*. Seattle, WA: Bay Press.

Edwards, J. (2000), 'AIDS, race, and the rise and decline of a militant oppositional lesbian and gay politics in the U.S'. *New Political Science*, 22(4), 485–506.

Eggan, F. (1999), Interview conducted by Deborah Gould, 30 October, Chicago. Interview housed in my personal ACT UP archive.

Eng, David L. and Kazanjian, D. (2003), *Loss: The Politics of Mourning*. Berkeley and Los Angeles: University of California Press.

Epstein, S. (1996), *Impure Science: AIDS, Activism, and the Politics of Knowledge*. Berkeley and Los Angeles: University of California Press.

Gordon, S.L. (1989), 'Institutional and impulsive orientations in selectively appropriating emotions to self', in David D. Franks and E. Doyle McCarthy, eds, *The Sociology of Emotions: Original Essays and Research Papers*, Greenwich, CT: JAI Press, pp. 115–36.

Gould, D. (2009), *Moving Politics: Emotion and ACT UP's Fight against AIDS*. Chicago: University of Chicago Press.

—(2010), 'On affect and protest', in A. Cvetkovich, A. Reynolds and J. Staiger, eds, *Political Emotions*, New York: Routledge, pp. 18–44.

Hochschild, A. (1979), 'Emotion work, feeling rules, and social structure', *American Journal of Sociology*, 85(3), 551–75.

—(1983), *The Managed Heart*. Berkeley and Los Angeles: University of California Press.

Jaggar, A. (1989), 'Love and knowledge: emotion in feminist epistemology', in A. Jaggar and S. Bordo, eds, *Gender/Body/Knowledge*, New Brunswick, NJ: Rutgers University Press, pp. 145–71.

Kane, A. (2001), 'Finding emotion in social movement processes: Irish land movement metaphors and narratives', in J. Goodwin, J. Jasper and F. Polletta, eds, *Passionate Politics: Emotions and Social Movements*, Chicago: University of Chicago Press, pp. 251–66.

Kracher, J. (2000), Interview conducted by Deborah Gould, 15 February, Chicago. Interview housed in my personal ACT UP archive.

Kurzman, C. (2004), *The Unthinkable Revolution in Iran*. Cambridge, MA: Harvard University Press.

Lyman, P. (1981), 'The politics of anger: on silence, ressentiment and political speech', *Socialist Review*, 11(3), 55–74.

McAdam, D. (1999), *Political Process and the Development of Black Insurgency, 1930–1970*. 2nd edn, Chicago: University of Chicago Press.

Miller, T. (1999), Interview conducted by Deborah Gould, 13 July, San Francisco. Interview housed in my personal ACT UP archive.
Saunders, D. (2003), Interview conducted by ACT UP Oral History Project. Available at: www.actuporalhistory.org.
Smart, T. (1992), 'This side of despair', *QW*, 13 September, 43–44.
Solnit, R. (2004), *Hope in the Dark: Untold Histories, Wild Possibilities*. New York: Nation Books.
Watney, S. (1992), 'Political funeral', *Village Voice*, 20 October, 18.
Weir, J. (1995), 'Rage, rage', *New Republic*, 13 February, 11–12.

7

'Building On A Firm Foundation Of Tolerance And Love?'

Emotional reflexivity in feminist political processes

Mary Holmes

Introduction

Academics and activists have often assumed that emotions can be used to protest against domination, but emotions are not inevitably subversive of the rational ordering of power. The relationship between emotions and social movements is complex (see e.g. Aminzade et al. 2001; Flam and King, 2005; Goodwin et al. 2001; Groves, 1995). Feminism as a social movement exemplifies this complexity well. While some emotions, particularly anger (Holmes, 2004), may be central to feminist movement, a wide range of emotions play a part in all social movement activity (Gould, in this volume). Exerting positive political change depends partly on emotional practices and styles which are socio-historically located. These practices and styles can usefully be defined as cohering into various types of emotionality, or ways of being emotional. Emotionality differs from emotionology, which describes emotional norms (Pupavac, 2004, p. 151; Stearn and Stearn, 1986, p. 14). This chapter explores and critically celebrates feminist emotionality within the second wave of feminism. The term 'second wave' may misrepresent what has been a long, ongoing struggle by women against oppression (e.g. Mitchell, 1966), but it is convenient shorthand for the surge of activity that occurred in the 1960s and into the 1980s. The terms 'feminist' and 'women's liberation' are interchanged in this chapter, although women's liberation usually had a more radical flavour. Most of the collectives and individuals discussed identified as women's liberationists, but the term feminists is also used to include the broad range of women involved in second wave struggles.

Emotionality in feminist movement can best be understood with the help of theorizing about the emotionalization of reflexivity (Holmes, 2010). This theorizing is briefly outlined in the first section of the chapter. The second section explores how second wave feminism used emotions in challenging the very way politics was done. The second wave feminist movement in Aotearoa/New Zealand is taken as representative of such movements in most Western nations, as established by referring to literature on other countries. The particularities of the movement in Aotearoa are also considered. Knowledge of it is drawn from a textual analysis of self-produced feminist writings in New Zealand between 1970 and 1984, the methodological details of which are discussed elsewhere (Holmes, 2008). Feminist writings included feminist magazines such as the long-running *Broadsheet,* the less well-known *Bitches, Witches and Dykes (BWD),* and the lesbian magazine *Circle,* as well as reports from feminist gatherings such as the four United Women's Conventions (UWC) in the 1970s. The analysis is furthered in the third section of the chapter by looking at how feminists represented themselves as political subjects around the core valuing of unity and emotional commitment. Finally, emotional practices within feminism are dissected. This will illuminate how feminist political processes involved emotions in ways that were not inevitably subversive, but in some cases could move political change and overcome patterns of dominance. Such a view stresses the importance of emotional reflexivity in navigating a complex contemporary world and especially in using political means to try and change that world.

Emotional reflexivity in politics

Reflexive modernity requires individuals to increasingly draw on their feelings to guide their thoughts and actions within a range of social spheres including politics. The complexity of late modernity can be difficult to deal with emotionally, as traditional practices fade. Behavioural and emotional alternatives expand, although emotions may sometimes overwhelm attempts to manage them. People must reflexively engage with emotions as they relate to others within various and often unfamiliar contexts (Holmes, 2010; Mills and Kleinman, 1988). Emotions are practiced within these interactions but feeling rules (Hochschild, 1983) are not always followed because those rules may be rapidly changing and may not always be clear. An individual's feelings can also often conflict with the rules, due to the relationships between the people in particular settings (Burkitt, 1997; 2002, p. 49). Emotions are produced by and produce subjects, but emotional practices are used to distinguish and reinforce social status. As Burkitt (1997) notes:

> The self and emotions are not just a question of positionings within discourses, stories and narratives: instead emotion is to do with flesh and blood selves, actively bound in power relations and interdependencies whose embodied expressions and feelings are to do primarily with the relationships between them. This is the matrix in which emotions appear and can be properly understood. (pp. 53–4)

Although there are theories of emotions as relational, most remain overly cognitive (e.g. Denzin, 1984; Kemper, 1978). Combining such approaches with theories of reflexivity (e.g. Archer, 2003, 2007; Beck et al. 1994) can produce a more emotionalized theory of reflexivity (Holmes, 2010). From this it is possible to make sense of the empirical data on feminism and to what extent it demonstrates emotional reflexivity.

People draw on feelings when acting politically, and they do so according to their relation to others. Ian Burkitt (2005) has applied a relational view of emotions to an analysis of political mobilization, but this can be extended. In his analysis he seeks to illustrate the crucial part that emotions play in governing and resisting governments. He examines the London peace march in 2003 and the Madrid train bombings in 2004 to illustrate how governments try to use emotions to control populations, but with unpredictable results. People are incited, induced and seduced towards supporting a government's agenda – in this case to go to war with Iraq. However, resistance can emerge rather than support because emotions are ambivalent and unpredictable. Those who marched in London in 2003 were angry not about Saddam Hussein, but about Tony Blair not listening to their opposition to the war. In Madrid, the popular government tried to gain re-election by using people's anger against local terrorists after the bombings. It emerged however that not ETA, but an Islamist group was responsible. This ignited fury against the government for taking Spain into the Iraq war and they lost the election (Burkitt, 2005). This relational understanding of the shifting of power can be used to analyse resistance not just as something enacted against governments.

Social movement resistance, for example, often questions the very nature of political processes; emotions play a complex part in this challenge.

Emotions are not revolutionary in themselves because they are ambivalent. Ambivalence can refer to the simultaneous experiencing of contradictory emotions such as pride and shame (Gould, 2007), but it can also refer to the uncertain impact of emotions on relations to others. Homi Bhabha (1994) establishes the uncertainty implicit within emotionally laden political resistance occurring in postcolonial societies. For Bhabha, the colonized's mimicry of their colonizers is subversive in highlighting that the dominant colonial identity is not 'natural'. However, the inevitable subversion this appears to involve is undermined by the colonized becoming like the oppressor. This might be helpful in analysing movements to overcome women's oppression within Aotearoa/New Zealand's postcolonial context, but has limitations. Anne McClintock (1995, pp. 64–5), while broadly in sympathy with Bhabha, is concerned about 'the politics of agency implicit in the mimetic schema' (McClintock, 1995, p. 63). Being like the oppressor is an ambivalent form of resistance, but it is not the only kind. Bhabha's concern with form does not explain resistance more broadly because it does not effectively understand social and economic power as gendered and located.

The ambivalence of emotions presents a challenge for reflecting and acting based on feelings and this needs analysing within particular contexts such as the second wave feminist movement in Aotearoa/New Zealand. Second wave feminist movement was part of late twentieth century challenges to liberal democracy, which included criticism of its supposedly rational underpinnings. New social movements stressed aspects of life excluded from formal politics such as selfhood, knowledge production, sexuality, bodies and emotions (Seidman, 1994). Like other movements of the time, feminism involved *ressentiment,* which maintains the pain of domination as central to identity (Brown, 1995, p. 74). However, a position as victim of oppression is not the only possibility feminism offers. Rather than discuss Brown's (1995) proposed politics of desire as a solution, I turn to the sociology of emotions, especially that which relates to symbolic interactionism, for its potential to explain the connections between emotions and a relational reflexivity (Holmes, 2010). Although the social process logically and temporally pre-exists the self-conscious individual, the individual also contributes to that social process (Mead, 1962, p. 186). This means that emotions are not only produced and organized by social relations (Kemper, 1978, 2002), but emotions also produce social relations. Actors sometimes 'do' emotions in relation to rules or norms (Hochschild, 1983), but emotions are messier and sometimes more overwhelming than this (Mills and Kleinman, 1988). Emotional practices are often bound more by the ambivalence of relations with others than by clear rules. Those relations take particular forms according to their cultural and socio-historical location. To what extent emotions are culturally specific is debateable (see Davetian, 2005; Heelas, 1996), but there is evidence of the negative consequences of imposing dominant Anglo-American emotion norms onto others. Conflict can be pathologized and emotional imperialism fails to recognize differences in emotionality in ways which can depoliticize and disempower (Pupavac, 2004; West-Newman, 2004). In this case differences in emotionality need to be placed within a socio-political view of the second wave feminist movement in Aotearoa/New Zealand.

Challenging rational politics

A distinguishing feature of second wave feminism was its efforts to do politics in more expressive, participatory ways and while the particularities of New Zealand feminism are important it was broadly representative of Western feminist challenges to liberal, 'rational', hierarchical political processes (Holmes, 2008). The second wave was a surge in feminist activity that in Aotearoa/New Zealand was noticeable by 1970 (Dann, 1985). Although reformist feminist groups such as the National Council of Women were important at this time, they followed established political practices (Cassell, 1989; Else, 1993) and will not be covered. This chapter is about a feminist political mobilization which centred around efforts to do politics differently. Feminists left detailed accounts of their processes in their writings. Conventional 'male' political processes were criticized with women's liberationists instead privileging participation and forming collectives (Holmes, 2008).

Feminists were initially reflexive about their processes in rather 'rational' ways. Consciousness raising (CR) groups were frequently the first step in forming collectives,[1] but as their name implies were rather shy of emotions, especially as a factor in ongoing political action. In CR groups, political analysis was gradually pieced together from women's sharing of their personal experiences. This was intended to highlight women's common cause and to establish the particulars of their shared oppression in order to act to overcome it. Turn taking and a non-judgemental atmosphere were important (*Auckland University Women's Liberation Group Newsletter*, March 1974, p. 3),[2] but the primary purpose of it all was analysis, not emotional bonding. This is clear in the comments of one of the most prominent feminists, Sandra Coney:

> Where some women's experiences seem to conflict these can be examined to find common roots for the seeming differences. This process helps us to see the political nature of our lives; it enables us to build a

theory of women based on the truth; it ensures that our political actions will be radical and effective since they will be based on a sound analysis of our situation. (*Broadsheet* 71, July/August 1979, pp. 28–9)

The highly emotional business of dealing with large and small humiliations constituting women's oppression was treated as something to motivate political analysis and action, and then be left behind. CR groups acknowledged the importance of emotions by departing from the feminist principle of openness. After the first meeting CR groups were usually closed to promote trust and acceptance (*Auckland University Women's Liberation Group Newsletter*, March 1974, p. 3). However, groups 'finished' their consciousness raising and then became open to other women as they started to direct their political action outwards. Only in rare cases was it proposed that CR be ongoing, as emotional support. Yet this could provide a kind of regular training in emotional reflexivity that has been more recently valued by activists (King, 2006). The Juno collective, was one of the few proposing that continuing CR could better link personal change and political activity (*Juno*, Special Issue, January 1977, p. 5). They were sceptical of feminist political methods based on grossly simplified beliefs that women were emotionally nurturing: compassionate, honest, loving. To them, an acrimonious split within the Broadsheet collective (discussed later) was sufficient evidence 'that women carry the shit from "out in society" into the movement with them'. CR relied on '[f]eeling and intuition [which] are two of the few things traditionally considered part of the woman's domain'. It was recommended that women should use this intuition and feeling, thought to have developed over centuries, to their advantage (*Broadsheet* 54, November 1977, p. 26), but it was unclear what those feelings might be and how they could be used to overcome 'the shit from "out in society"'. This was especially problematic given the commitment to reaching consensus.

Consensus decision-making was core to feminist processes within collectives (Dann, 1985, pp. 29–30) but it relied on a reflexive ability to interpret one's own and others' emotions that was not well defined. Feminists rejected the cold rationality traditionally associated with political decision-making in favour of more (emotionally) expressive participatory models. This is one interpretation of the iconic feminist slogan 'the personal is political' (for others, see Barrie, 1987; Pateman, 1989, p. 131). Highly tiered power structures and formal meeting procedures, including deciding by majority vote, were judged inadequate. Feminists focused on radical change rather than reform were usually adamant that the conventional 'male' political processes must be rejected, but Julie Thompson thought that appropriate feminist structures had evolved that went beyond reacting against 'male structures' (*Broadsheet* 39, May 1976, p. 5). Organizing collectively meant promoting consensus, openness and structurelessness (the avoidance of hierarchies). However, there were varying ideas about what these meant and how to put them into practice. For instance, the Working Women's Alliance, described its organization as 'under constant review' (*Working Women*, July 1975, p. 1). Despite such reviews the basic principles of collective organizing remained largely intact. Trish Spinster's definition of a feminist collective was typical: they were a group of women with a particular purpose for meeting and who made decisions through consensus (*BWD*, August 1982, p. 4). Consensus decision-making supposedly avoided confrontational debating. Whether providing services for women (Vanderpyl, 2004), or engaging in political activism, collectives were committed to consensus. As Spinster explained, consensus had 'something to do with agreeing. It is when everyone agrees on a decision . . . the idea is to talk about it and work it out until a consensus can be reached' (*BWD*, August 1982, p. 4). Consensus decision-making challenged patriarchal individualism, eschewing the liberal democratic model of individual voices competing (Young, 1991) in favour of striving for agreement. In practice, women did not always think or feel the same way about issues and strong feelings could not always be overcome by discussion. Consensus was supposed to create inclusive and participatory decision-making and thus overcome power hierarchies. Thus, structurelessness was another central principle of feminist collective organizing.

Principles of structurelessness implicitly assumed that women's liberationists would feel united as sisters, but emotions arose from interactions, they did not just determine them. Leaders and hierarchies were rejected in favour of working together more fluidly. The reality was full of contradictions (Cassell, 1989; Freeman, 1972; Hayward, 1993).[3] There were contradictions between not wanting leaders and yet needing them, between 'an ideal of individual self-realisation and a principle of radical egalitarianism' (Cassell, 1989, p. 133), and between the ideal of avoiding structures and the reality of informal ones developing. Some understanding of these contradictions can come from Alberto Melucci's (1989) argument that new social movements express their ends through their means. Avoiding structures was both ends and means for feminist collectives. It could allow women to develop their abilities and have greater self-confidence. It could also prevent groups falling apart if one key leader left. However, structurelessness could prevent groups from fulfilling their aims (Cassell, 1989, p. 146). The reliance of structurelessness and other feminist processes on the reification of unity, disavowed the more troublesome emotions involved within women's liberation organizing.

Political subjects: unity and emotional commitment

Feminist political processes both assumed and required a reflexive unity of purpose and shared feelings about women's oppression, but the ambivalence of emotions was neglected and feminists struggled to acknowledge dissent. Once consciousness raising had been employed in order to establish the nature of women's oppression and the common political interests it was believed to generate, then collectives could be formed to enact the political vision. Hierarchies would not be necessary because all women would be equal in finding the way forward. Trish Spinster noted the typical belief, 'that we are all in this together – are all on about the same thing – i.e. Women's Liberation – and so we must and should be able to work together. The differences between us can be worked out, and we can reach a consensus about what we are doing and how. That we should reach agreement' (*BWD*, August 1982, p. 4). Such agreement both symbolized and enacted a repudiation of women's supposed distrust and animosity towards each other, but it became heavily loaded with expectations that women would feel a sisterly sympathy that would enable them to move forward politically. In practice consensus was difficult to achieve, partly due to the ambivalence of emotions. Feminists might experience both feelings of belonging and of exclusion. These could be aggravated by the processes employed. True consensus supposedly involved reaching a common understanding, but this understanding was often impossible in a group with varying political views, particularly when there was 'a job to get done' (*BWD*, August 1982, p. 5). The problem individual dissent, especially angry dissent, posed for feminist politics was well documented at the time (Holmes, 2004). In many respects unity was an illusion maintained only by excluding or silencing dissenters. Voicing a different opinion could upset unity, but if not expressed it also undermined unity because the supposedly consensual decision did not really represent the entire group. Collective members who continually disagreed usually left. Collectives thus tended towards homogeneity, as a shared outlook was crucial to move quickly onto 'subtler issues' (*Woman*, 28, June 1973, p. 1). Feminist gatherings were one site where dissatisfaction emerged because of the impasse between 'those wanting to further already advanced ideas; and those wanting to acquire a basic understanding of [the] issue at stake' (Meikle, 1976, p. 152). It was prophesized that 'this dilemma of level of debate is going to recur in future [United Women's] conventions, particularly as more women become involved in the Women's Movement' (Meikle, 1976, p. 153). Consensus decision-making was especially prone to becoming a 'politics of coersion (sic) for instance, not being able to register our dissent on the basic premise that all emn (sic - men) oppress all women' (*WWRC Newsletter*, August 1982, p. 6). Structurelessness sheltered coercion and even sometimes 'tyranny'. Alison Laurie argued that some lesbian groups working without formal structures were exclusionary, employing 'a mystical and wooly (sic) notion' of how the group operates, invoking 'this great group-thing, but it doesn't work when *she's* there' (*Circle*, March 1975, p. 6). This was not a problem limited to lesbian groups, as Nancy Peterson illustrates in explaining why she left the *BWD* Collective:

> [w]e have thrown out hierarchical meeting procedures; we have thrown out voting as a decision making tool (because it represents a tyranny of the majority); and we have replaced all this with something we call consensus decision making. We have thrown out one kind of structure to replace it with another kind, about whose dynamics we are quite vague. (*BWD*, June 1982, p. 10)

The vagueness surrounding alternative processes did not prevent them being deemed central to women's liberation, because they were considered fundamental to the discovery of women's 'true' identity and true emotions. Feminist processes would bring properly feeling feminist subjects into being. As a course introducing Women's Liberation noted such 'male' hierarchical ways of working must be rejected for women to find out what 'they themselves truly are' (Dunedin Collective for Woman, 1972, p. 2). With reflection and action women could think, feel and act in new ways. It was assumed that this would foster unity in the cause and differences between women were neglected by many feminists. Those who felt marginalized within the movement articulated the limitations of unity and shared feelings. In sociological terms, different groups of women learned different feeling rules (Hochschild, 1983) and perhaps had varying emotional capital (Nowotny, 1981). There are problems with the notion of emotional capital because it sees emotionality as resting on the habitus, on routine ways of being and doing emotions that are hard to maintain within the uncertainty of reflexive modernity (Holmes, 2010, p. 146). However, emotional practices and styles do vary in patterned ways among different social groups. For example, some working-class feminists thought that 'women's ways' of organizing were just middle-class ways. The Working Women's Alliance, for example, criticized structurelessness and not having leaders for being a 'muddled approach' that was highly frustrating for working women (*Working Women*, June/July 1976, no page number). Lesbian feminists, however, thought that many of their sisters in the movement had not gone far enough in doing politics differently. When lesbians involved with the magazine *Circle* were accused of disrupting the 1977 United Women's Convention they responded that their accusers did not seem to understand 'that lesbians actually CARE about other women, that we deal openly and unmatronisingly with them, and that it is male-oriented women who have adopted the male political practice of secret wheeling and dealing' (*Circle*, Autumn/Winter 1977, p. 11). This echoes an old binary: good caring woman/ bad power-hungry man. A nurturing emotional view of women is called upon as key to feminist politics, yet this is the very emotionality thought to make women unfit for the rational decision-making defined as politics (Pateman, 1989). The answer was to reform that politics, exchanging its basis on power for a grounding in knowledge, work and love. There would be no more leaders, hierarchies or authoritarianism (*Broadsheet,* 42, September 1976, p. 28).

Expectations were that feminist emotionality would be power free. Visions of a loving, unified feminist politics contrasted ideals of women's 'real' nurturing identity to negative definitions of power as 'power over' (*Broadsheet,* 70, June 1979, p. 22; Curthoys, 1997; Yeatman, 1994). This reflects the common tendency of 1960s and 1970s politics to denounce power as it existed among one's adversaries (Foucault, 1980, p. 116). Men and other dominant groups *had* power (Curthoys, 1997; Yeatman, 1994).[4] Comments on a split in the Broadsheet collective exemplify this view. The split involved, among other things, a falling out over a proposed sharing of office space with the Women's Art Collective. One of the latter collective's members thought that the events exemplified 'the abuse of power which can occur when proceedings become institutionalised and under the control of a faction within a group' (*Circle*, Winter 1978, p. 84). Power was seen as held by people or groups and usually described as 'a resource or a relationship which enables the holder to control or manipulate the environment or other people' (*Juno*, 2, 1978, p. 1). There was little sense of any positive potentiality of power as a resource or relationship. Power was typified a 'bad' and this had significant consequences for feminist emotionality.

Feminist emotionality

In reflecting and acting on emotions feminists seldom acknowledged that power could be exercised and constructive conflict occur in ways that might move issues and relations forward, even if often upsetting (Holmes, 2004). Instead:

> Those who dissent are seen as a negative, ungrateful element who can do nothing but unjustifiably attack – or is it trash? In theory we are not supposed to have women in power in the Movement. This, of course, is

an illusion. Non-hierarchical as the Movement may be, we do have women who, relatively, hold a lot of power. Power, and especially power amongst us, is a taboo subject. . . . This notion of united power [promoted by the concept of sisterhood] is based on the false belief that the mere fact of being women is a binding enough characteristic to create instantaneous sisterhood above political and unequal power distribution. (*BWD*, May 1981, p. 5)

Emotional reflexivity could produce positive, if not necessarily conflict free, forms of emotionality for feminists. More informal ways of doing politics, did bring joy and could build the emotional stamina of feminists and help attract new women to the cause (see King, 2005; Summers-Effler, 2005). The advantages of collective processes were that they built emotional and practical skills that contributed to women's self-confidence and to their political success. A 'Herstory of the Convention Committee' in the 1979 UWC booklet argued that consensus decision-making had 'encouraged flexible, natural leadership for different leaders emerged for different purposes . . .'. The 'development of individual strengths and also the acceptance of individual differences' was deemed to have been encouraged by the open structure (United Women's Convention Committee, 1979, p. 90). Conflict did occur, especially around writing a statement of feminist perspective for the booklet (United Women's Convention Committee, 1979, p. 89).[5] However, what principally emerged was 'a strong collective identity, a source of support and sisterhood' (United Women's Convention Committee, 1979, p. 89; also *Broadsheet*, 65, December 1978, p. 18; Russell, 1979, p. 21). This participatory good will was hoped to extend to the convention (*Broadsheet*, 24, November 1974, p. 3). Efforts to make feminist processes work were thought by many to be 'a meaningful political experience', in which the nurturing energy gained could be 'turned outward to reflect social change' (*WWW Newsletter*, 17, January 1974, p. 4). Some attention to emotional reflexivity for activists could help ensure good experiences (King, 2006). In one of the workshops at UWC 1979, Juliet Seule reported that '[t]here was no leader, but women's experiences with leaderless groups made itself felt. There were enough women present who could make active suggestions, ask leading questions and display their own listening skills, for the group dynamics to work' (*Broadsheet*, 70, June 1979, p. 20). In a second workshop Seule said the convenor stated that 'she wasn't there as an "expert" to teach us about anger', rather that they as participants were the workshop – their 'experiences' and their ideas. The 'politics of her approach' were commended (*Broadsheet*, 70, June 1979, p. 20). That *some* women were making 'active suggestions' and asking 'leading questions', suggests they were experienced in thinking about and working with emotions.

The ordering and analysis of the 'experiences' discussed still fell largely to the convenor, and her attempts seem to have been successful in producing feelings of unity. This did not always happen.

Feminists were reflexive about the limitations of their processes, not always expecting them to be easy and feel good, but feminist ways of being emotional were often linked to wider goals. The Wellington Women's Liberation Front were committed to structurelessness, for better and for worse. Freedom to discuss issues was achieved but not everyone contributed equally, and issues could become confused and decisions difficult. The Front nevertheless continued to try to avoid hierarchy and work at these participatory processes. Feminist groups recognized '"the process/product" conflict. For feminists how you work is critically important; our work processes should embody our political belief' (cited in Brownlie, 1970, p. 26). It was part of those processes to work at 'dealing with conflicts and tensions amongst us and of showing support and caring for individual people to guard against "burn-out" from overwork' (*Broadsheet*, 81, July/August 1980, p. 15). However, where there were deadlines, it was hard to find the time for the caring and support. Broadsheet, for instance had a magazine to put out each month and found it 'hard to find the time to devote to the process of working' (*Broadsheet*, 81, July/August 1980, p. 15). The Juno collective claimed they avoided discussing group processes, eschewing this radical politics in order to get the magazine out (*Juno*, Special Issue, January 1977, p. 11). Yet feminists generally maintained critical examination of the processes that they employed, often indicating their emotional nature. In 1983 *Broadsheet* published an article called 'Collectively Speaking'. Appreciating the irony, they said it had 'taken months for this issue on collectives to come together. Many of the reasons for this illustrate some of the difficulties in working collectively – reaching consensus, the slow process of decision-making, who takes responsibility' (*Broadsheet*, 108, April 1983, p. 28). The New Plymouth's Women's Centre's contribution to this article acknowledged that '[e]veryone found consensus decisions hard to deal with at first, coming from a background of voting or having no say'. They 'often spent half an hour deciding on something, then scrapped it in the last five minutes'. Or they would decide something because they were 'too tired to discuss it any more'. (*Broadsheet*, 135, December 1985, p. 13). Groups that were able to navigate such struggles successfully were usually less diverse, small, supportive and based on existing friendships (cf. Freeman, 1972). Dunedin Collective for Woman, for example, credited their success to strong friendships formed through CR groups, to the maximum participation which having small groups allowed, and to the way the collective acted as a support group. This was a general collective, engaging in a range of projects rather than having one central aim. Having no manifesto helped the collective be flexible. Controversial projects could be eschewed in favour of more unifying enterprises and with different projects happening women could offer different skills each time and hierarchies were less likely to become entrenched. All this no doubt made avoiding arguments easier. The members also recognized that Dunedin was a small and rather conservative town, this facilitated frequent meeting, but also made unity necessary for survival (*Broadsheet*, 108, April 1983, p. 33). Personalized attacks on other women were prohibited and strong bonds of support encouraged the resolution of any conflicts that did arise.

Generally feminists struggled to find constructive ways to incorporate criticism and conflict into ways of being emotional. Attempts at emotional reflexivity continued to value feelings of unity. Unity verged on a sacred article (*Circle*, March 1975, p. 8; *Broadsheet*, 63, October 1978, p. 6). The title of the hugely popular *United* Women's conventions said it all about the aims for which they strove (see Coney, 1973, p. 74). Prior to the 1977 convention, Sandi Hall warned that '[o]ne of the worst things that could happen to the feminist movement would be a division of women from women. . . . To gain our goals we must be wise enough, tolerant enough, strong enough to see that unless we set our own house in order, building on a firm foundation of tolerance and love, we cannot succeed as we hope to succeed' (*Broadsheet*, 47, March 1977, p. 39). This reflects the pathologization of certain emotions as 'negative' which has occurred in other spheres such as psychiatry and even international relations (Horowitz and Wakefield, 2007; Pupavac, 2004). Criticizing other feminists could be seen as an act of betrayal, from which it was almost impossible to move forward. This seems to be what happened with the split in the Broadsheet collective. One of the things that allegedly contributed to that split (*Circle*, Winter 1978) was a *Broadsheet* editorial on 'The State of the Movement' in which Christine Dann tried to articulate the problems of criticizing other feminists. She argued that women attacked each other because the lack of structure within collectives made other resolution so hard. This seemed to her an expression of how the difficulty of attacking the oppressor makes the oppressed learn to turn on each other. Criticism, she felt had also become one-sided because some groups were putting themselves beyond criticism (*Broadsheet*, 61, July 1978, p. 7).[6] The response was explosive, and the split became an emotional vortex which bruised many feminists in its whorl.

Experiences such as acrimonious splits in collectives made it unsurprising that conflict between women was generally portrayed as an evil to be avoided, but there were those who recognized that working through disagreements might be politically important even if emotionally difficult (Holmes, 2004). Maori feminists were more likely to view conflict as an important part of political process given their engagement with nationalist as well as feminist struggles (see Mohanram, 1996). Finding ways through conflict between diverse Iwi (tribes) were key to Maori survival, and drew on Maori principles for working through disagreements. Such principles were later made famous as the basis for a youth justice system (see Jackson, 1988) that was influential in many nations (Maxwell and Morris, 1993). While the exact nature of those principles and the degree of their indigeneity may be debated (see Daly, 2002) (albeit sometimes in slightly dubious searches for authenticity), it was certainly the case that Maori feminists were realistic about the problems of feeling unity with each other, or other non-white women, let alone Pakeha (non-Maori, usually meaning white Europeans). The First National Hui[7] (meeting) of Black Women[8] was held in Otara in September 1980. At this hui Rebecca Evans pointed out to black women working with white men or women, 'many of the political contradictions and difficulties of these enforced unholy alliances' (*BWD*, December 1980, p. 13). Independence from both men and whites was stressed at the second hui where one Ama Rauhihi said: '. . . "Don't let any man tell you how to live. Don't let any white tell you how to live. . . ."' (*BWD*, November 1981, p. 17). Unity tended to be viewed more as a strategic necessity to be worked at, rather than a feeling that would obviously attend feminist activism. Ngahuia Te Awekotuku (1993) reinforced the need for Maori women to work together and free themselves from male and white definitions in her paper to the 1978 Piha congress. She noted that it has been difficult for Maori women to speak out for themselves as they were accused of doing things 'the pakeha way' if they did (p. 190). The first national hui nevertheless 'pointed out the necessity for united action and . . .[t]he theme of [the] Second (sic) Hui became "UNITY FOR SURVIVAL"' (*BWD*, November 1981, p. 17). This referred usually to unity among black women. That black feminists remained largely separate from the predominantly pakeha groups, indicates a lack of confidence in the ability of the latter to adequately represent Maori and other women of colour. Some pakeha feminists did attempt to engage positively with Maori and other black feminists. The reports on the hui above come from *BWD* because the mainly pakeha collective handed over a portion of the magazine to black feminists to operate as a 'black forum'. However, this in itself led to some only partially documented problems within the collective and between them and other black feminists (see Holmes, 2008, p. 145, n. 106). More successful seem to have been changes to the Women's Studies Conferences, which instituted caucuses for marginalized groups such as Maori, Pacific Island and lesbian feminists (Holmes, 2008, p. 110). Also important were the radical ideas of Maori feminist activist Donna Awatere, as expressed in a series of *Broadsheet* articles on Maori Sovereignty, which were later issued as a book (see Awatere, 1984). A group of pakeha feminists who wanted to constructively engage with Awatrere formed calling themselves Women for Aotearoa (the Maori name for New Zealand). Their response to Awatere was respectful and non-confrontational. However they tended to talk about how they were respectful of the differences in each other's ideas rather than the importance of being respectful of her ideas. They noted that the article they wrote was not forced into a collectively written piece, but compiled various elements of their responses to Awatere's ideas. They wanted to 'allow [their] idiosyncrasies and disagreements to show through'. Not all wrote, but all contributed to the working through of ideas (*Broadsheet*, 110, June 1983, p. 16). Such efforts involved trust, which was not always easy to summon, as the 1979 UWC convention committee noted. Delegating work was a matter of trusting other women and that worked well apart from some breakdowns in communication. Elsewhere they found they 'did not trust some women's behaviour' so they did not give up control of the microphone and they 'did not trust the other women present to have controlled (sic) the situation'; nor that 'whatever happened at the convention was OK and part of the process. This breakdown in trust was highly stressful for the committee' (United Women's Convention Committee, 1979, p. 95), but they acknowledged that they had perhaps made it hard for women at the convention to trust them because '[t]he committee intentionally avoided the "star" syndrome and kept in the background as a group'. Women therefore knew little about them and did not know whether they were trustworthy, having to rely mainly on the gossip going around (United Women's Convention Committee, 1979, pp. 95–6). This also made it hard for complaints and criticisms to be channelled to them in any organized way. Conflict and dissent were therefore sacrificed to a desire to control the convention rather than accept what might happen as part of the process. Avoiding conflict was emotionally easier but often problematic for making political progress.

Those with political experience were better able to exercise emotional reflexivity in ways that produced productive forms of emotionality. They could navigate the emotional and practical difficulties of feminist processes and use them to achieve political goals. The different levels of knowledge, experience and commitment among women in the movement were difficult to manage within the structurelessness advocated and '[t]he strongest voice and loudest is often heard and those who are less articulate and less confident are more often not heard, though their opinions be just as valid' (*Woman*, 96, 31 January 1977, p. 3). An article by Alison Laurie on lesbian feminist groups critically examines some of these problems. Practically, those lesbian activists who had come to politics through radical feminism had a lack of experience of working in diverse groups. Those lesbian groups that emerged via the gay movement were, she claimed, more experienced in this respect and more tolerant of group members' eccentricities. She saw a difference in focus so that gay movement lesbians were more interested in widespread social and political change for lesbians, compared to feminist movement lesbians centred on dealing emotionally and politically with their own lesbianism (*Circle*, March 1975, pp. 1–2). The lack of structure in lesbian groups was a major problem because of the diversity of those groups. In the place of structure, powerful emotional dynamics became core to group functioning. Any structure was seen as a 'male' way of doing things and therefore negative, but in its absence a charismatic group of women then set the standards of the group and '[d]eviants and non-conformists are not tolerated. Banishment from the group is the result'. Those banished formed new groups, which soon had the same problems (*Circle*, March 1975, p. 3). Other lesbian feminists noted similar problems (*Circle*, November 1982, pp. 1–3), and indeed they were common to all feminist groups (Holmes, 2004, 2008).

An emotional commitment to women's liberation was supposedly all that the sisterhood required, but the participatory political processes were more easily controlled by experienced and knowledgeable women. Sarah Calvert claimed that commitment was the 'primary (and often only) resource' of the women's movement (*Broadsheet*, 90, June 1981, p. 32). Commitment had to have been demonstrated, rather than simply declared, and therefore those with a history of feminist involvement were soon favoured. Two well-known feminists Sandra Coney and Sharyn Cederman represented 'knowledge' and 'commitment' as desirable capital for women to bring to the feminist decision-making process. Those with 'less' knowledge and 'less' commitment (presumably of and to feminism) were regarded as less 'developed' and less qualified to have their views represented (see *Broadsheet*, 31, July 1975, p. 32; *Broadsheet*, 81, August 1978, p. 15). Feminist movement could not be solely based on strong (shared) feelings of commitment to a cause.

The more doubt that arose about feminists sharing a unity of feeling and purpose, the more feminist processes were liable to change. Principles of openness were sacrificed, although not swiftly. The Broadsheet Collective remained open from 1972 until 1980, when it became 'a closed collective which means there has to be a unanimous decision to invite a new person onto the collective and that person must be a radical feminist who's shown a commitment to the magazine and who's worked on it for a while'. This differed from the early days when anyone involved with the magazine in any way could be on the collective (*Broadsheet*, 81, July/August 1980, p. 15). Arguments against openness began to appear in the later 1970s. For instance, organizers of the UWC 1979 saw a conflict between 'the ideal of flexibility and the necessity of efficiency' when previous decisions were challenged at later meetings (United Women's Convention Committee, 1979, p. 90). The

Wellington BWD collective dispensed with openness when it assembled women of similar political background who knew they could work together, seeing 'no reason to set our group aside in favour of another group' and denying responsibility for making the group open (*BWD*, August 1982, p. 4). Giving up openness could of course make it easier for those collectives with tasks to perform to get the job done using feminist processes. In short, structurelessness and openness were often negotiated together, in ways illustrating that emotionality had varying forms that could undermine or enrich feminist struggles for change.

Conclusion

Reflexivity requires drawing on emotions in a rapidly changing world, especially where individuals are striving to change that world politically. Feminist writings demonstrate this emotional reflexivity in operation and how it privileged certain ways of being emotional within feminist movement.

The political struggles for women's liberation involved reflecting and acting in opposition to existing political processes, because of their hierarchical structures and reification of reason. However, emotional reflexivity required interpreting one's own and others' emotions and this was not always easy. Feminists worked to be more participatory in their processes, assuming that they would find common cause through shared feelings about liberation and the best means to achieve it. CR was the first step, but focused on 'rational' analysis of women's experiences, rather than emotional bonding – which was usually expected to arise 'naturally'. Such bonding was expected to facilitate consensus decision-making and permit structurelessness. These pillars of the collective process did not magically operate whenever women gathered to change their world, and indeed some feminists did not imagine that they would. Nevertheless, emotions proved to be rather more ambivalent within political processes than was bargained for by those feminists enthusiastic to throw off the constraints of reason. Feminists felt excluded from, as well as at home within, collectives, but collective processes were adhered to in the belief that they would help women find authentic forms of emotionality on which to found and enact liberation. The dominant feminist belief was that such emotionality would leave behind conflict and power over others. In practice this vision of emotionality usually denied the validity of 'negative' emotions, despite some efforts to recognize the emotion work involved in diverse women finding agreement on complex and often emotive issues (cf. Gould, in this volume). There was the hard grind of long and difficult collective meetings, but there was joy in learning to do new things and to do them with other women. This could include learning about emotions within and through new ways of interacting with women. There were also many emotionally painful experiences (see Cahill and Dann, 1991). Trust was important in avoiding or surviving these, but whereas processes were trusted, women's ability to resolve conflicts or find ways forward despite differences was not. Generally, those with more political experience within feminism and other social movements were better able to find a form of emotionality that was workable within a diverse movement trying to make political progress. Experience helped some feminists find emotional styles and practices that worked for them rather than against them, and many were able to turn their undoubted emotional commitment to women's interests to impressive political effect. For some collectives this involved alterations to feminist political processes, the most common being trading open participation for groups of like-minded women that had or could develop strong relationships. While this could be problematic for working across differences, like-minded did not inevitably mean alike. Many feminist groups that endured and had some impact were based not on 'natural', joyful unity but on a trust that relied on past experiences of showing respect for any differences and on being able to agree. Thus emotional practices worked for feminists when emotionality was oriented around respectful relations, and sometimes these could deal with difference. This required ongoing interactions in which shared feelings were not assumed but reflected and acted on as part of a shared history as a group. It was under these conditions that emotional reflexivity helped feminists change the world.

Notes

1 For instance Megan Fidler, a previous co-editor of *Broadsheet*, states that the magazine grew out of the consciousness raising groups of the 1970s (Unpublished seminar notes 1991, p. 1). Also, the Wellington Collective which produced the August 1982 issue of *BWD* was formed from an established and closed political discussion group, as they explain in that issue. Dunedin Collective for Women also 'started back in 1971, before even *Broadsheet* was born, as one small group of eight women . . . who began a consciousness-raising process among themselves, 'and also started ways of reaching out to the Dunedin community' (*Broadsheet*, 108, April 1983, p. 32).

2 Due to the large number of sources used in this textual analysis, references to the issue of the feminist periodical are given in the text and the periodical listed as one item in the references.

3 The Freeman piece was available earlier, probably in pamphlet form, as part of a feminist collection, or in feminist newsletters or journals for feminists

to read. Hayward (1993) writes specifically about how the experience of the women's movement in New Zealand illustrates some of the problems with participatory democracy.

4 This was not the only way in which feminists conceptualized power, there were also references to power as protection and power as capacity (see Yeatman, 1994), although the former was more evident in challenges to divisions between public and private (see Holmes, 2008) and the latter not particularly common in second wave feminism, although perhaps implicit in discussions about responsibility. Also, Curthoys (1997, pp. 6–7) argues that feminism as a liberation movement opposed all 'power over', not just the power of men over women. To an extent I agree, but power was represented as something to be avoided almost always by associating it with 'maleness', because they were the adversaries in feminism.

5 The organizers made an interesting distinction, saying that in the policymaking stage consensus worked well, but the more 'organisational orientation' of the second year led to problems. The distinction between policy and non-policy (where consensus was not thought necessary) decisions was blurry and 'too many trivial issues' were brought forward for consensus. This took up too much time and was too taxing (United Women's Convention Committee, 1979, pp. 89–90).

6 The Broadsheet split revolved around various complex disputes which are a little difficult to decipher from the accounts available, but was largely a split between heterosexual and lesbian members of the collective. The disputes involved disagreements about the relationship of sexuality to feminist politics, and tended to reveal heterosexual feminists struggling or even refusing to recognize that their sexuality was politically relevant (see Holmes, 2008, pp. 66–7, 95). Dann's mention of 'some groups' is a reference to the lesbian feminists who split from the collective.

7 I do not italicize Maori words that are routinely used as part of New Zealand English.

8 The term 'black' was regarded at this time as a politically correct way to refer to non-white women (and men) in order to emphasize their common political interests.

References

Aminzade, R.R., Goldstone, J.A., McAdam, D., Perry, E.J., Sewell, W.H. Jr., Tarrow, S. et al. (2001), *Silence and Voice in the Study of Contentious Politics*. Cambridge: Cambridge University Press.

Archer, M.S. (2003), *Structure, Agency and the Internal Conversation*. Cambridge: Cambridge University Press.

—(2007), *Making Our Way through the World: Human Reflexivity and Social Mobility*. Cambridge: Cambridge University Press.

Auckland University Women's Liberation Group Newsletter (1974), March–August, Auckland University Women's Liberation Group: Auckland.

Awatere, D. (1984), *Maori Sovereignty*. Auckland: Broadsheet.

Barrie, L. (1987), 'The personal is a cultural construction', *Sites*, 15, 68–75.

Beck, U., Giddens, A. and Lash, S. (1994), *Reflexive Modernisation: Politics, Tradition and Aesthetics in the Modern Social Order*. Cambridge: Polity Press.

Bhabha, H.K. (1994), 'Of mimicry and man: the ambivalence of colonial discourse', in H.K. Bhabha, ed., *The Location of Culture*. London: Routledge, pp. 121–31.

Broadsheet (1972–1984), Broadsheet Collective: Auckland.

Brown, W. (1995), *States of Injury: Power and Freedom in Late Modernity*. Princeton, NJ: Princeton University Press.

Brownlie, C. (1970), 'Are you going to burn your bra?', *Thursday*, 1 October, 4–6, 26.

Burkitt, I. (1997), 'Social relationships and emotions', *Sociology*, 31(1), 37–55.

—(2002), 'Complex emotions: relations, feelings and images in emotional experience', in J. Barbalet, ed., *Emotions and Sociology*. Oxford: Blackwell/ The Sociological Review, pp. 151–67.

—(2005), 'Powerful emotions: power, government and opposition in the "war on terror"', *Sociology*, 39(4), 679–95.

BWD (Bitches Witches and Dykes), (1980–1982), BWD Collective: Auckland and Wellington (August 1982 issue only).

Cahill, M. and Dann, C. eds (1991), *Changing Our Lives*. Wellington: Bridget Williams Books.

Cassell, J. (1989), *A Group Called Women*. Prospect Heights, IL: Waveland Press.

Circle (1973–1984), Circle Collective: Wellington.

Coney, S. (1973), *United Women's Convention*, Auckland: United Women's Convention Book Committee/WEA.

Curthoys, J. (1997), *Feminist Amnesia: The Wake of Women's Liberation*. London: Routledge.

Daly, K. (2002), 'Restorative justice: the real story', *Punishment and Society*, 4(1), 55–79.

Dann, C. (1985), *Up From Under: Women and Liberation in New Zealand 1970–1985*. Wellington: Allen and Unwin.

Davetian, B. (2005), 'Towards an emotionally conscious social theory', *Sociological Research Online*, 10(2), Available at: http://www.socresonline.org.uk/10/2/davetian.html.

Denzin, N.K. (1984), *On Understanding Emotion*. San Francisco, CA: Jossey-Bass.

Dunedin Collective for Woman (1972), *An Introduction to Women's Liberation*. Dunedin Collective for Woman: Dunedin.

Else, A. ed. (1993), *Women Together: A History of Women's Organisations in New Zealand: Nga ropu wahine o te motu*. Wellington: New Zealand Historical Branch, Department of Internal Affairs and Daphne Brasell Associates Press.

Flam, H. and King, D. (2005), *Emotions and Social Movements*. London: Routledge.

Foucault, M. (1980), *Power/Knowledge: Selected Interviews and Other Writings, 1972–1977*. New York: Pantheon.

Freeman, J. (1972), 'The tyranny of structurelessness', *Berkeley Journal of Sociology*, 17, 151–64.

Goodwin, J., Jasper, J.M. and Poletta, F. eds (2001), *Passionate Politics: Emotions and Social Movements*. Chicago: University of Chicago Press.

Gould, D. (2007), 'On feeling bad and acting up: despair in activism', Paper presented at the ESRC Seminar: 'The Affective Dimension of Political Mobilization', University of the West of England, Bristol, Wednesday 20 June.

Groves, J.M. (1995), 'Learning to feel: the neglected sociology of social movements', *Sociological Review*, 43(3), 435–61.

Hayward, B. (1993), 'Participatory democracy: questions raised by feminist involvement with practice and theory', in H. Catt and E. McLeay, eds, *Women and Politics in New Zealand*. Wellington: Political Science and Victoria University Press, pp. 27–40.

Heelas, P. (1996), 'Emotion talk across cultures', in R. Harre and W.G. Parrott, eds, *The Emotions: Social, Cultural and Biological Dimensions*. London: Sage, pp. 171–99.

Hochschild, A.R. (1983), *The Managed Heart: Commercialization of Human Feeling*. Berkeley, CA: University of California Press.

Holmes, M. (2004), 'Feeling beyond rules: politicising the sociology of emotion and anger in feminist politics', *European Journal of Social Theory*, 7(2), 209–27.

—(2008), *The Representation of Feminists as Political Actors: Challenging Liberal Democracy*. Saarbrücken: VDM Publishers.

—(2010), 'The emotionalization of reflexivity', *Sociology*, 44(1),139–54.

Horowitz, A.V. and Wakefield, J.C. (2007), *The Loss of Sadness: How Psychiatry Transformed Normal Sorrow into Depressive Disorder*. New York: Oxford University Press.

Jackson, M. (1988), *Maori and the Criminal Justice System: He Whaipaanga Hou: A New Perspective*, Parts 1 and 2. Department of Justice: Wellington.

Juno (1977–1978), Juno Collective: Auckland. Note: 6 issues produced. Numbers 2, 3 and special issue January 1977 cited.

Kemper, T.D. (1978), *A Social Interactional Theory of Emotions*. New York: John Wiley.

—(2002), 'Predicting emotions in groups: some lessons from September 11', in J. Barbalet, ed., *Emotions and Sociology*. Oxford: Blackwell/The Sociological Review.

King, D.S. (2005), 'Sustaining activism through emotional reflexivity', in H. Flam and D. King, eds, *Emotions and Social Movements*. London: Routledge, pp. 150–69.

—(2006), 'Activists and emotional reflexivity: towards Touraine's subject as social movement', *Sociology*, 40(5), 873–91.

Meikle, P. ed. (1976), *United Women's Convention 1975*, June, Wellington.

Mitchell, J. (1966), 'Women: the longest revolution', *New Left Review*, 40, 11–37.

McClintock, A. (1995), *Imperial Leather: Race, Gender and Sexuality in the Colonial Contest*. London: Routledge.

Maxwell, G.M. and Morris, A. (1993), *Families, Victims and Culture: Youth Justice in New Zealand*. Wellington: Department of Social Welfare and Institute of Criminology.

Mead, G.H. (1962), *Mind, Self, and Society: From the Standpoint of a Social Behaviourist*. Chicago: University of Chicago Press.

Melucci, A. (1989), *Nomads of the Present: Social Movements and Individual Needs in Contemporary Society*. London: Hutchinson Radius.

Mills, T. and Kleinman, S. (1988), 'Emotions, reflexivity and action: an interactionist analysis', *Social Forces*, 66(4), 1009–27.

Mohanram, R. (1996), 'The construction of place: Maori feminism and nationalism in Aotearoa/New Zealand', *NWSA Journal*, 8(1), 50–69.

Nowotny, H. (1981), 'Women in public life in Austria', in C. Fuchs Epstein and R. Laub Coser, eds, *Access to Power: Cross-National Studies of Women and Elites*. London: George Allen & Unwin, pp. 147–56.

Pateman, C. (1989), *The Disorder of Women: Democracy, Feminism and Political Theory*. Cambridge: Polity Press.

Pupavac, V. (2004), 'War on the couch: the emotionology of the new international security paradigm', *European Journal of Social Theory*, 7(2), pp. 149–70.

Russell, M. (1979), 'United women's convention: no bed of bread and roses', *Listener*, 91(2048), 20–21.

Seidman, S. (1994), *Contested Knowledge: Social Theory in the Postmodern Era*. Oxford: Blackwell.

Stearns, C.Z. and Stearns, P.N. (1986) *Anger: The Struggle for Emotional Control in America's History*. Chicago and London: University of Chicago.

Summers-Effler, E. (2005), 'The emotional significance of solidarity for social movement communities: sustaining Catholic worker community and service', in H. Flam and D. King, eds, *Emotions and Social Movements*. London: Routledge, pp. 135–49.

Te Awekotuku, N. (1993), 'Some ideas for Maori women', in C. MacDonald, ed., *The Vote, the Pill and the Demon Drink: A History of Feminist Writing in New Zealand, 1869–1993*. Wellington: Bridget Williams Books, pp. 189–90.

United Women's Convention Committee (1979), *United Women's Convention: Easter 1979; University of Waikato*. Hamilton: University of Waikato.

Vanderpyl, J. (2004), Aspiring for unity and equality: dynamics of conflict and change in the 'by women for women' feminist service groups, Aotearoa/New Zealand (1970–1999). Unpublished PhD Thesis, University of Auckland.

West-Newman, C.L. (2004) 'Anger in legacies of empire: Indigenous peoples and settler states', *European Journal of Social Theory* 7(2), 189–208.

Woman (1972–1980), Dunedin Collective for Woman: Dunedin.

Working Women (1975, 1976–1978), Issues 2 and 6–19. Wellington: Working Women's Alliance.

WWRC Newsletter (1980–1982), WWRC (Wellington Women's Resource Centre): Wellington.

WWW Newsletter (1973–1974), WWW (Wellington Women's Workshop): Wellington.

Yeatman, A. (1994), 'Feminism and power', *Women's Studies Journal (NZ)*, 10(1), 70–100.

Young, I.M. (1991), *Justice and the Politics of Difference*. New Jersey: Princeton University Press.

PART FOUR

The politics of reparation

8

The apology in politics

Michael Cunningham

Introduction

Until approximately the early 1990s the apology was a phenomenon largely connected to the private sphere and that of interpersonal relations, often between individuals and occasionally between groups. Correspondingly, most of the academic literature considering the apology came from other disciplines including sociolinguistics and psychology. In the period since the early 1990s demands for, and the granting of, apologies have become much more frequent in the public sphere. Indeed, the contemporary period has been described as the 'age of apology' (Brooks, 1999a), one in which we have witnessed an 'epidemic of apology' (Thompson, 2002, p. viii).

This has been marked by an increase in the academic literature reviewing and critiquing aspects of the apology as a political phenomenon. The majority of academic work on the apology in politics and related disciplines is favourable to the use of the apology and makes a defence of it. By 'defence' I mean that the apology in politics is seen as both intellectually defensible and can have a utility in addressing issues of recognition for previously marginalized groups or helping to foster reconciliation between groups.

After a more detailed consideration of the types of apology that have emerged in the period in question this chapter will pursue five broad themes; first, the relationship between the apology and emotions, secondly, why the apology has emerged into the public sphere, thirdly what philosophical or conceptual questions are raised by the apology in politics, fourthly the relationship between the apology, ideological traditions and political responses to the apology and finally whether the apology has a utility in domestic or international politics.[1]

Various typologies of the apology could be constructed and defended. I would argue that an important primary distinction and two subsidiary distinctions can be usefully borne in mind. The primary distinction is between apologies offered by state and non-state actors. A cursory review of the apology will reveal numerous made by states (or state representatives) and numerous others offered by non-state actors including NGOs, religious and commercial organizations. This distinction is important for two reasons. First, if one is discussing the 'apology in politics' or the 'political apology' one might reasonably restrict discussion to apologies, or related expressions of regret or other linguistic formulations, to those given by state actors. However, of course, if one were considering the 'politics of apology' then one might cast the net much wider to include issues relating to non-state actors. Second, the distinction is potentially important as political traditions and political commentators frequently claim that the actions or responsibilities of state and non-state actors raise different questions since the former are often classified as political actors in the way that the latter are not. This is not to argue that empirically the actions of the two categories may not be connected or intertwined; the point is that one may analyse them in conceptually different ways.

The emphasis in this chapter is going to be upon the questions raised by state actors engaging with the apology so, in that sense, it is about the 'apology in politics' rather than the 'politics of apology' which would also focus on other actors in civil society.

With the focus upon state actors, the two subsidiary categories come into play. Apologies by states (or state actors) can be divided into interstate and intra-state apologies and again into those made to specific, identifiable groups of individuals and those made to collectives or indeterminate groups. Therefore, the 'apology in politics' as defined above can be allocated, with few or no exceptions, into one of four categories along the two axes indicated. This categorization is useful because it offers a way to classify and sort the huge amount of apologies that have occurred over the last two decades or so and also because the critiques made of the apology may be more relevant to some of these categories than to others. This will be illustrated further in the following section relating to philosophical and conceptual critiques.

The apology and emotions

It will be argued here that the defence of the apology comes from two different traditions in politics and an interesting aspect of the apology is that it can be justified on two differing grounds and the following section will relate this to the theme of emotion and politics. It is clear that a variety of emotions are, or can be, related to the apology. By way of example, and not an exhaustive list, five emotions can be identified as common to many cases of the apology. Three emotions, guilt, shame and remorse may be features of the apologizing party and hurt and anger may be features of the party seeking or being granted an apology. If we extrapolate from an interpersonal apology it would seem implausible that all of these five would be missing from the combinations of speech acts, rituals or interaction that constitute an apology.

The apology given in 2008 by the Australian administration led by Kevin Rudd to the aboriginal peoples can be used to illustrate the point. The argument by Honneth (1995) that hurt and anger are motivations for recognition and serve politically to mobilize groups and their supporters is a useful way to consider the aboriginal campaign and the culmination of this mobilization was the apology which can be understood as the Australian people, or their most senior representative, expressing regret for, and shame about, the state-endorsed discriminatory practices of recent Australian history.

As a generalization, the eruption of these emotions and related ones into the political sphere has been welcomed by those who see the apology and the implicit and explicit emotions related to it as representing advances both in the way we think about and define politics and in the political and cultural recognition of marginalized groups. I would contend that this 'camp' views the emergence of emotions in politics as legitimate and providing a challenge to more conventional views of politics which included, for example, the tendency to focus upon power and interests or to consider ideas about justice or other normative issues through a focus on reason and universalism which marginalized emotion as an area of investigation. As Clarke et al. (2006, pp. 7–8) have noted, politics as a discipline has been slow in treating seriously the role of emotions.

The following claim is rather speculative; however, there is value in trying to locate those who support the apology in politics and the associated emotions within a tradition of critique and critical thinking which believes that, for example, Enlightenment traditions of reason or liberal conceptions of justice are inadequate both in providing an ethical framework for politics and capturing the fullness and diversity of human identity and experience. That traditional political discourse is ill suited to an exposition and endorsement of the emotional content of the apology is underlined by the fact that some authors writing about the public apology have pointed out that practices and emotions sometimes associated with the apology (e.g. repentance, shame, forgiveness) and their collective and public expression have echoes of theological practices and this tradition and 'way of thinking' can give fruitful insights into the practice of apology (see Auerbach, 2005; Celermajer, 2009; Shriver,

1995; Weiner, 2005). Psychology is another discipline that has informed writing on the apology undertaken from a broadly political perspective, here ideas of trauma, healing and 'closure', whether used in specific or more general senses, feature in texts on apology (see Lazare, 2004; Olick, 2007). To summarize this position, the presence of emotions in the political apology are not problematic in the sense that emotions have a legitimate role and place in political mobilization, interaction and discourse and the fact that emotions (e.g. the shame or regret of the apologizer) make explicit a moral dimension to state and institutional activity is to be commended.

However, there is a second way to think about the apology which, while endorsing its potential value, plays down the role of emotion. One of the most contentious issues in the discussion of apology is whether emotions can be attributed to a collective or are always and only attributes of the individual agent. This is not an issue to be resolved here; suffice to say that methodological individualists would claim that the idea of collective shame or collective anger is meaningless. For those who contest the applicability of emotions in politics or deny the logic of the collective emotion the apology can be defended, in the two senses outlined above, in the following way. The apology can be viewed as an institutional response to an injustice. Let Tony Blair's oft-cited apology in 1997 for the Irish Famine stand as an example. It is consistent to argue that Blair could meaningfully apologize as he is the current representative of an institution (the British state) that has an institutional continuity with the administration of the 1840s that committed an injustice by failing to do more to avert the famine. This would depend upon a concept of political responsibility that crosses administrations; however, it would not logically require either Tony Blair or any current British citizens to feel shame or guilt about the injustice or, conversely, that the emotion of hurt or anger is particularly strong among contemporary Irish citizens. The crucial point in this construction is that the apology is by an *institution* and for an *injustice*. By using these two terms, the emotional content can be downplayed or eliminated. Govier and Verwoerd argue that institutions and collectives can meaningfully apologize but argue that the emotional content is likely to be diminished in institutional cases (2002, p. 74). Thompson makes a similar point in endorsing the apology because the state has trans-generational responsibilities but arguing that the statesperson making the apology need not personally show or feel remorse (2008, p. 36).

While what constituted an historical injustice or who decides this may be contentious, by moving justice centre stage the terminology is closer to the traditional concerns of normative political theory and further from the more recent manifestations of critical thinking mentioned above. It follows, I would argue, that the apology, or certainly particular apologies, could be endorsed by those who are sceptical of the idea of collectively held emotions and supportive of methodological individualism.

The emergence of the apology

There appears to be no single reason for the emergence of the apology in the mid-1990s. More empirical work needs to be done to see if particular factors can be isolated; however, it may be that this would be too methodologically complex and it may be difficult to get beyond generalities about multi-causality. Bearing this in mind, some observations can be made. In a recent text Fette outlined seven possible reasons for the emergence of the apology but interestingly did not offer further commentary on the relative weight or significance of these, possibly for the reason just mentioned (Fette, 2009, pp. 135–6). With the codicil that it would repay more empirical investigation, it will be argued here that it is useful to consider the emergence of the apology in relation to three factors which may interconnect to produce a successful claim for an apology. The first relates to intellectual and political developments at a macro level, the second to structural political changes and the third to contingencies often related to the role of individuals.

First, the macro-level developments. The rise of the apology needs to be understood in the context of wider intellectual and political currents of the contemporary period. Many of the claims for the apology are claims for recognition (in some form) of groups or collectives and this is related, implicitly at least, to two developments. One is a critique of, and dissatisfaction with, perceived overly narrow liberal conceptions of recognition, rights and justice. These are the types of critique loosely associated with communitarian ideas. In roughly the same period, the left internationally became more interested in identity politics and the sensitivities of previously marginalized ethnic or other groupings, in part at least because of the decline in the efficacy of class politics and the retreat of the politics of the material. The codification of human rights following the Second World War provided a framework within which activists and intellectuals could press for an application, or extension, of these rights to groups and collectives (Negash, 2006).

Secondly, structural political changes refer to the political space in which these broader intellectual currents or ideas could be made manifest. The collapse of the Soviet Union and Warsaw Pact regimes and the transition from military dictatorships in Latin America allowed the interrogation of past wrongs and the writings of other histories. There is some evidence that campaigns by human rights or other groups in one area or country can act as a network of support or advice to others so that something of a 'snowball' effect relating to the apology takes place as it is easier for states to apologize if others are so doing (Yamazaki, 2006, p. 113).

The third factor is the contingent one often related to specific individuals. Without the broad intellectual developments sketched above it is unlikely that these interventions would have materialized; however, in certain countries particular politicians (usually prime ministers or presidents) became personally involved with the question of apology and some marked a change of political tone from their predecessors. Examples include Kevin Rudd in Australia, Bill Clinton in the United States, Jacques Chirac in France, Tony Blair in the United Kingdom and Tomiichi Murayama in Japan: all of whom either apologized or showed some contrition for their states' past actions and thus represented a more self-reflexive trend in the political morality of states.

Philosophical and conceptual questions

The aim of this section is to highlight six of the problems that have been raised by the pursuit or use of the apology in the public sphere and possible ways to respond to them. Where relevant, these issues and problems will be illustrated by examples from case-studies to try to clarify the point and demonstrate the link between the conceptual or philosophical point and the concrete reality of the politics of apology.

The first two points are similar and related since they claim that the apology is, in general, not a concept relevant to politics. I shall term these the category mistake objection and the realist objection. The other four objections – the contingent or pragmatic objection, the responsibility objection, the indeterminacy objection and the 'statute of limitations' objection – are of a different order in that they do not disqualify the apology from the political sphere *in toto* but raise questions about its applicability to particular cases.

The category mistake objection is particularly pertinent in a book about politics and the emotions since it would emphasize that the political sphere is one where emotions should be excluded. The objection raised is that the apology is, or should be, best understood as an act between individuals and an important feature of this exchange is a sense of guilt in the apologizer. (This is reflected in the fact that much of the literature concerning apology which predates the political texts came from sociolinguistics or a theological tradition concerned with repentance and forgiveness between individual actors). Therefore, the 'move' of the apology into the political sphere is either unacceptable or problematic on the grounds that it has no relevance to this sphere.

As indicated in the section above on emotions and politics, one way to respond to this is to decouple the apology from guilt in the public or political sphere. One can be consistent in arguing, following Arendt, that collective guilt is inappropriate in the political sphere but that the apology can represent an acceptance of collective political responsibility (Schaap, 2001). Therefore, while guilt is not a meaningful attribute for the polity, or the citizens which constitute it, the concept of responsibility is meaningful.

The second objection draws on the realist tradition in politics. This Machiavellian tradition maintains that 'doing' politics is not dealing with problems and issues on the basis of abstracted notions of justice nor is it to derive courses of action from normative principles. Rather, attempts to deal with contemporary conflicts or tensions within or between states will reflect power relations and contingent negotiation and the 'messiness' inherent in these. Politics is a sphere in which the application of normative principles, or certainly abstract normative principles (e.g. 'we should apologise because it is just'), is largely irrelevant.

Now let us turn to those objections which do not rule out the use of the apology in the political sphere but offer critiques which might limit the extent of its applicability. The first of these has some similarities with the second objection above but is conceptually different. Rather than object to the use of normative values as a guide to political action, the position would be that the pursuit of the apology, which may be just or crucial to the promotion or realization of recognition, would have to be balanced against the likely costs or disbenefits of such a course of action. Two examples of this will be given. First, there is the potential (and, in real life, actual) problem of the 'backlash' which will be considered further below. In simple terms, if the promotion of a good (i.e. an apology as an element of justice) provokes disharmony among different groups, should it still be pursued? This has elements of a consequentialist argument and is open to the objection that one could not reasonably estimate the likelihood or extent of a backlash before promoting a specific apology or apologies more generally. Second, there is the concern that the apology, and other symbols, practices and institutions which emphasize the identity or recognition of minority ethnic groups will encourage or reinforce non-state or non-national identities that will weaken the polity by undermining or downplaying a commonality of identity or the universality of citizenship. This is a concern that has been voiced by both conservatives, who fear the dissolving of a common national history and identity, and liberals concerned by an erosion of universalism. (Some of these themes will be explored further below in the sections on political responses and the utility of the apology).

The second objection in this group is that one cannot logically apologize for something for which one is not responsible and, therefore, individuals cannot apologize for injustices or transgressions which predated their existence. This is a particularly common objection found in popular discourse about apologies. There are, broadly, two ways to counter this objection. First, with relation to the political apology, it can be argued that a representative of the state (the president or prime minister) or a state institution (e.g. the US Congress, the Japanese Diet, the UK House of Commons) can meaningfully apologize for events which predated the existence of the current office-holders because they have an institutional continuity with those of the earlier period. An analogy may be drawn with the role of treaties between countries; most countries will honour treaties drawn up by predecessors and consider them binding so accepting a continuity in the need to address an injustice need not appear strange.

Alternatively or additionally, one can draw on aspects of a communitarian tradition or a Burkean one which argues that what constitutes one as a citizen or member of a polity is necessarily linked to previous generations and responsibilities flow from this. Therefore, injustice and its rectification are, or should be, trans-generational concerns. Examples of related and more specific objections are, for example, that as a member of the working class I have not benefited from the past injustice that materially disadvantaged (or disadvantages) certain minority groups or that, as the child of recent immigrants, I have no connection to, or responsibility for, the injustices committed by previous generations. Weiner has countered these objections by arguing that the sense of responsibility should be rooted in one's political identity as a citizen and thus one cannot, or should not, be allowed an 'opt out' on the basis of class or the recent arrival of one's family in the country (Weiner, 2005, p. 18).

In some cases of apology, such as the one made to Japanese-Americans interned in the Second World War in the United States, records allow an uncontroversial identification of the victims of injustice. However, this is often not the case. The third objection in this group is what may be termed the 'indeterminacy' objection focusing on the fact that in many cases it is difficult to identify the victims of the injustice. A simple example is that of slavery. There have been repeated calls for an apology to African-Americans by the US state for the policy of slavery. Yet to whom would the apology be made? Are the victims of slavery those who were slaves, or does it include their descendants as well? It may be impossible to argue that contemporary African-Americans are the victims of slavery, and thus deserve an apology for the injustice, in a manner comparable to that of slaves. However, it is not implausible to argue either that many individual contemporary African-Americans are economically or socially disadvantaged due to the legacy of slavery or that collectively African-Americans bear psychological scars from the legacy of institutionalized racism and thus an apology would be meaningful and justified. An additional issue is this: if the apology is being sought for an ethnic grouping it is not always clear who exactly is a member or on what grounds membership is either claimed or granted. It is not a facetious point to note that if compensation of some form constituted part of the apology, or followed from it, it would be rational to claim to be part of the group.

Fourthly, there is the 'statute of limitations' objection. This may overlap with the one directly above but it is conceptually different. That an injustice happened a long time ago may mean it is hard to identify the specific victims; however, even if they can be identified (and an injustice can be specified) it has been argued that the passage of time and the changing circumstances that will have occurred renders the need for rectification less pressing (see Waldron, 1992). This is intuitively appealing since an injustice (or any injustice?) that happened thousands of years ago does not have the same resonance as one that happened a year ago. But how is one to judge when is too long ago? The problem is, as Weiner (2005, pp. 19–23) has observed, that what constitutes time (or a 'long time') differs in different spheres of human activity and the frameworks associated with them. Therefore, for example, those examining or contesting an apology from a legalistic or juridical perspective may construct time differently from those employing a therapeutic or theological framework.

Ideology and the political response to the apology

The previous section has indicated some of the problems that are commonly raised in the academic literature about the applicability of the apology to the political sphere. As indicated above, the majority of academic texts about the apology in politics are generally favourable to the idea and supportive of the idea that trans-generational conceptions of justice make the apology a coherent project.

The aim of this section is to offer some reflections upon the wider political response to the emergence of the apology. It should be noted that this is not an exhaustive review of case-studies as the sheer number would preclude this but an attempt to offer some general points about politics and the apology beyond the academy and academic considerations.

It is my argument that there is a seeming paradox in the politics of the apology though it is one that is explicable. This paradox is that the apology is broadly compatible with the political traditions and ideology of conservatism; however, in practice people of a conservative disposition are frequently opposed to the apology. In general terms, much of the academic and some of the more popular discourse supportive of the apology emphasizes the intellectual coherence or importance of trans-generational responsibility and a conceptualization of responsibility that transcends the idea of individual responsibility. This discourse also supports the making of restitution (the apology) to indeterminate groups or collectives. Additionally, the importance of communal identity and the importance of history in the construction of this identity are prominent features. These are compatible with most strands of conservative thought and, from this perspective, it is possible to critique the 'narrowness' of a liberal conception of justice which focuses upon legal redress and is often premised on individual or corporate responsibility and the identification of specific individuals as victims of the injustice.

Conversely, parties, groups and individuals of the 'liberal left' are more likely to support the apology in general or be politically mobilized to support specific groups seeking one. However the 'conservative' aspects of the apology outlined above, and the fact that the apology can be seen as a 'backward looking' phenomenon with its emphasis on what has happened, can be in tension with aspects of both liberal and leftist traditions.

To turn to the liberal tradition. It can be argued that important strands of the liberal tradition sit uneasily with the concept of apology. The liberal focus on the individual and individual autonomy, both ontologically and politically, renders the idea of collective responsibility problematic. This is particularly a problem if responsibility over generations is considered in national collective terms since much of liberalism would recoil at the idea that autonomous individuals could be held responsible for that which they had not done.

A second way in which an emphasis on individualism can make the apology problematic or incoherent is related to the indeterminacy question raised above. In many of the high-profile cases of apology, claimed or given, it is difficult to identify without controversy who are the victims of injustice. The injustices associated with slavery and the treatment of aboriginal groupings stand as examples that include people, as members of collectives, who had radically different experiences and people who are far removed in time, space or circumstance from the worst or original injustice. If the concept of justice, like that of responsibility, is closely connected to identifiable people suffering specific acts as in the tradition of liberal jurisprudence, the indeterminacy of victims of injustice renders some apologies intellectually dubious. That these 'wider' conceptualizations of justice are incompatible with liberalism chimes with Celermajer's claims that the rise of the apology is related to conceptualizations that have 'defied the logic of liberalism's justice' (Celermajer, 2009, p. 2).

Although it is a diverse school of thought, a leftist or socialist tradition also has ideological elements which sit uneasily with the notion of apology. Three will be briefly outlined here. First, socialism is a 'forward looking' ideology based on the (re)construction of society on rational and Enlightenment principles. As Torpey states, 'efforts to rectify past wrongs have . . . jostled with, and perhaps to some degree supplanted, expansive visions of an alternative human future of the kind that animated the socialist and civil rights movements of the preceding century' (2009, p. 28). The tendency to look back and to make history and memory central to the political project, as the apology often does, can mark a retreat or turning away from the construction of the new society. However, it should be noted that recognition of injustices and the dealing with the emotions of fear and distrust often linked to them may in certain cases be useful or necessary in people 'moving forward' to construct a new society or mend relations in a fractured polity (see the chapter by Rigby and Kaindaneh in this collection).

Secondly, and perhaps related to the previous point, socialism is a tradition of universalism. Through revolution or state intervention or decentralizing power, depending on the subset of the tradition, society could be recast for the benefit of all. This universalism is, potentially at least, challenged or breached by forms of politics which focus on difference. It may be argued that this is not necessarily true of the 'politics of apology'; however, many cases do involve recognition of a group or community as different and may underpin a form of politics, or political arrangements and structures, which sit uneasily with universalism.

Third, some socialist traditions are rooted in the material. Although the apology may be linked to, or be followed by, material forms of compensation or reparation it can be conceptually and practically separate and thus the apology itself lies in the symbolic sphere of politics. There may be more than one socialist conceptualization of justice but most are much more likely to favour a material-related conceptualization related to collective ownership, reconstituted property relations or redistributive policies than to the arena of the symbolic.

To return to the apparent paradox mentioned above. Empirical work would suggest that it is the 'right' broadly defined which opposes the apology. For example, in well-documented studies of opposition to an apology to aboriginal peoples in Australia, for slavery in the United States, to various victims of the Japanese in the Second World War and for British involvement in the slave trade (and other examples would replicate this), it is conservative groupings which oppose the apology. The form of opposition may vary or be disparate and include political party opposition, paramilitary-style direct action and pressure groups through to websites, bloggers, 'op. eds' and letter writers. However the crucial factor is that this opposition is, explicitly or implicitly, set against what is seen as an attack on the integrity of the nation or an attack on the representation of its history, whether the apology is to other states or nations or to groupings within the state. Although I have argued conservatives should not have an intellectual problem with the underpinnings of the apology this opposition does not often appear to be to the apology *per se* but to those that are seen to denigrate the critic's nation. Given that nationalism is often a component of popular conservatism (and an important element of its ideological heritage), it provides the political and ideological linkage between conservative tendencies and opposition to the apology.

It has been argued above that the ideologies of liberalism and socialism sit uneasily with some of the features and implications of the apology, yet it is the 'liberal left' which generally is supportive of the principle and the practice of the apology. This would seem to be the result of intellectual and political developments over roughly the last 40 years. Both liberalism and socialism of the variants outlined above have been subject to the critique that their conceptualization of the citizen and their universalism were inadequate to capture what constituted people's identities. These critiques, which are often subsumed under the 'communitarian' label, fed into an intellectual and political concern with what could loosely be called 'the politics of identity' and 'the politics of recognition'. Following Torpey (2009), these trends may have their roots in, or reflect, the decline on the left of a confidence in the progressive potential of class-based activity and alternatives to capitalism. Although not all apologies claimed or granted have the same features or characteristics, the 'age of apology' marks a concern with the symbolic rather than the material and with group identity rather than individual rights. Thus, developments in the field of what may be loosely termed 'progressive' politics render the apology a phenomenon which can be endorsed.

The utility of the apology

Some thoughts will be offered concerning the utility of the apology. After two decades or more in the public arena can anything be said about the utility of the apology. Two questions may be distinguished: 'what is it for?' and 'does it work?'

A simple question but one that is not always addressed explicitly is what is the apology for; what is its purpose? Different apologies may have different geneses and different ends; however, a general pattern would be that those who seek them are looking for an acknowledgement or recognition of an injustice. In the case of minority groups in intra-state apologies, this is often linked to the idea that an apology will validate an historical narrative which has previously been suppressed or marginalized. Those who are offering a sincere apology would typically have two motivations; to recognize that an injustice of some form has been committed and the desire that the recognition would help to integrate the marginalized group into the polity from which it was excluded. Therefore, successful apologies will, or can, acknowledge or rectify an injustice and provide recognition, in the form of cultural or political inclusion or validation, for previously marginalized groups. If these are achieved then most commentators would see a value in the process of apology.

However if one reviews the literature on apologies and considers the case-studies there are three categories of factors which militate against the successful apology or bring into question its utility. It should be made clear here that an identification of these practical, or political, problems can be compatible with a defence *in principle* of the apology in the political sphere.

The first category can be termed the operational one. Some writers have identified a list of factors which make for a successful apology and the absence of one or more may derail the process (see Gibney and Roxstrom, 2001, pp. 926–37, for criteria governing interstate apologies). Even when a government is prepared to make an apology it is by no means certain that it will be deemed adequate by the intended recipient. Problems may include the wording of the apology (it may appear insincere, qualified, partial or self-serving), the deliverer (whether it should be, for example, the head of state, the prime minister, the legislature) and the timing. All of these factors have bedevilled the long process of apologies by the Japanese state to various groups and states and, in this case, Lind has identified an additional problem. Rather than the apology being a 'one off' that resolves strained relations, in Japan qualified apologies were met with domestic opposition and rejection and then another attempt was made to apologize. This resulted in the impact of the apology being dissipated through repetition (Lind, 2008, pp. 93–4).

The second category can be termed the 'substitutional' one. This covers a list of concerns that the apology may only provide a limited or attenuated form of justice, and therefore may be a substitute for a more thorough-going transformation. There are two particular critiques in this area which can be found in the literature. One is that an apology by a state might be a collective national substitute for the judicial pursuit of particular individuals involved in wrongdoing and that an apology lets the transgressor 'off the hook'. This can particularly be a problem in transitional societies or polities and is similar to the critique made of Truth and Reconciliation Commissions (TRCs) in that a focus on apology and reconciliation, often with amnesties involved, is in tension with the pursuit of justice via punishment of the guilty.

The second element here is the critique that the apology may become a 'substitute' for more effective or transformative forms of redress. This is reflected in the populist critique of the apology that governments favour them at times because they are cheap and may rather cynically employ them to placate or mollify groups rather than to address the resource – demanding issue of socioeconomic inequality or marginalization. Theoretically and in practice the apology can be accompanied by a variety of forms of reparation or compensation. The risk is that if nothing concrete or material accompanies the apology it may be interpreted as a cheap gesture. This is a criticism sometimes associated with 'left wing' critics of the apology who wish to emphasize the material over the symbolic as the key to social and political amelioration.

A third area of problems related to the apology in practical politics is that objectives or ends served, or potentially served, by the apology may clash with others that are socially desirable. For example, let us assume that if a well-grounded claim for an apology is granted this represents a manifestation of justice (though justice could well take other forms). Allied to this, the apology may bring about recognition of the cultural identity or history of a previously marginalized group. It may be plausibly argued that justice and recognition are two political goods or virtues. An example of this is the apology by the Rudd administration to Australian aboriginal people which entailed both justice and forms of recognition. A third good present may be that of reconciliation; an example being some of the Japanese interstate apologies which Yamazaki argues were motivated by a desire to mend relations with China and Korea (Yamazaki, 2006, p. 33).

So one can identify justice, recognition and reconciliation as goods that may be realized or promoted by the apology. However, there may be other goods that are undermined by the apology. Therefore, states and governments may have to weigh up these conflicting claims and it may be argued that apologies are not good or bad *per se* but rather states may have to consider them contingently. For example, security of citizens and social cohesion are two other goods that a government may wish to promote or we may argue are necessary in democratic polities.

It is plausible that the promotion of an apology may result in a 'backlash' from others against the group or its supporters wanting the apology, leading to threats or physical harm. Also social cohesion may be undermined in one of two ways. The resentment of the (majority) group against those claiming the apology may widen perceived differences based on group identities and/ or the apology may encourage a form of identity politics that undermines either a sense of national unity or ideas of civic universalism. To offer an empirical example, opponents of an apology by the US government for slavery have invoked the arguments about social cohesion and national unity (Dawson and Popoff, 2004). A possible counter is that this is an argument employed principally by conservatives in an attempt to thwart well-grounded claims for an apology. However, this does not invalidate the general point here that governments may have to make political judgements about whether, and in what way, to pursue an apology. A related point is that it could be argued pragmatically that even if one supports the basic premise that the apology has a legitimate application in the political sphere, in both intra-state and inter-state relations, it should not be pursued or enacted on the basis of an abstract conceptualization of justice but has to be considered contingently in light of other political goods or objectives that states may wish to pursue.

Conclusion

I would conclude with a defence of the political apology. One can accept that some apologies may be insincere or that linguistic ambiguity, evasion or contortion may lessen the impact of others but still argue that apologies are a positive development in that they represent the possibility of reconciliation and that they demonstrate that citizens and their leaders can reflect critically on past actions for which they, or at least some of the citizenry, feel shame or regret. A public declaration of this can attend, at least in part, to the hurt and humiliation of other groups. In this way the apology has the potential to be, in Coicaud's phrase, 'a small yet important part of justice' (Coicaud, 2009, p. 93).

Notes

1 For more detail concerning some of the case-studies mentioned in the chapter see the following texts. For Japanese apologies see Dudden (2008), Lind (2008), Negash (2006) and Yamazaki (2006). For the United States and slavery see Brooks (1999b, part 6), Dawson and Popoff (2004), Nobles (2008) and Torpey (2009). For interned Japanese–Americans see Brooks (1999b, part 4) and Weiner (2005). For the issue of Australian aboriginal peoples see Augoustinos and LeCouteur (2004), Celermajer (2009), Nobles (2008), Smits (2005) and Thompson (2002). For the British apology for the Irish famine see Cunningham (2004).

References

Auerbach, Y. (2005), 'Forgiveness and reconciliation: the religious dimension', *Terrorism and Political Violence,* 17(3), 469–85.
Augoustinos, M. and LeCouteur, A. (2004), 'On whether to apologise to indigenous Australians: the denial of white guilt', in N.R. Branscombe and B. Doosje, eds, *Collective Guilt: International Perspectives.* Cambridge: Cambridge University Press, pp. 236–61.

Brooks, R.L. (1999a), 'The age of apology', in R.L. Brooks, ed. (1999b), *When Sorry Isn't Enough: the Controversy over Apologies and Reparations for Human Rights*. New York: New York University Press, pp. 3–11.

Celermajer, D. (2009), *The Sins of the Nation and the Ritual of Apologies*. Cambridge: Cambridge University Press.

Clarke, S., Hoggett, P. and Thompson, S. (2006), 'The study of emotion: an introduction', in S. Clarke, P. Hoggett and S. Thompson, eds, *Emotions, Politics and Society*. Basingstoke: Palgrave Macmillan, pp. 3–13.

Coicaud, J.-M. (2009), 'Apology: a small yet important part of justice', *Japanese Journal of Political Science,* 10(1), 93–124.

Cunningham, M. (2004), 'Apologies in Irish politics: a commentary and critique', *Contemporary British History*, 18(4), 80–92.

Dawson, M. and Popoff, R. (2004), 'Reparations: justice and greed in black and white', *Du Bois Review,* 1(1), 47–91.

Dudden, A. (2008), *Troubled Apologies among Japan, Korea and the United States*. New York: Columbia University Press.

Fette, J. (2009), 'Apologizing for Vichy in contemporary France', in M. Berg and B. Schaefer, eds, *Historical Justice in International Perspective: How Societies are trying to Right the Wrongs of the Past*. Cambridge: Cambridge University Press, pp. 135–63.

Gibney, M. and Roxstrom, E. (2001), 'The status of state apologies', *Human Rights Quarterly,* 23(4), 911–39.

Govier, T. and Verwoerd, W. (2002), 'The promise and pitfalls of apology', *Journal of Social Philosophy*, 33(1), 67–82.

Honneth, A. (1995), *The Struggle for Recognition: the Moral Grammar of Social Struggles*. Cambridge: Polity.

Lazare, A. (2004), *On Apology*. Oxford: Oxford University Press.

Lind, J. (2008), *Sorry States: Apologies in International Politics*. Ithaca, NY: Cornell University Press.

Negash, G. (2006), *Apologia Politica: States and their Apologies by Proxy*. Lanham, MD: Lexington.

Nobles, M. (2008), *The Politics of Official Apologies*. Cambridge: Cambridge University Press.

Olick, J.K. (2007), *The Politics of Regret: on Collective Memory and Historical Responsibility*. Abingdon: Routledge.

Schaap, A. (2001), 'Guilty subjects and political responsibility: Arendt, Jaspers and the resonance of the "German Question" in politics and reconciliation', *Political Studies*, 49(4), 749–66.

Shriver, D.W. (1995), *An Ethic for Enemies: Forgiveness in Politics*. Oxford: Oxford University Press.

Smits, K. (2005), 'Identity politics redux: apology and deliberation over race in the Australian case', Paper given at Political Theory Workshop, University of Manchester, September.

Thompson, J. (2002), *Taking Responsibility for the Past: Reparation and Historical Injustice*. Cambridge: Polity.

—(2008), 'Apology, justice and respect: a critical defense of political apology', in M. Gibney, R. Howard-Hassmann, J.-M. Coicaud and N. Steiner, eds, *The*

Age of Apology: Facing up to the Past. Philadelphia: University of Pennsylvania Press, pp. 31–44.

Torpey, J. (2009), 'An avalanche of history: the "collapse of the future" and the rise of reparations politics', in M. Berg and B. Shaefer, eds, *Historical Justice in International Perspective: How Societies are Trying to Right the Wrongs of the Past.* Cambridge: Cambridge University Press, pp. 21–38.

Waldron, J. (1992), 'Superseding historical injustice', *Ethics,* 103(1), 4–28.

Weiner, B. (2005), *Sins of the Parents: the Politics of National Apologies in the United States.* Philadelphia: Temple University Press.

Yamazaki, J.W. (2006), *Japanese Apologies for World War II: a Rhetorical Study.* Abingdon: Routledge.

9

Peace-building in Sierra Leone
The emotional dimension

Steven Kaindaneh and Andrew Rigby

Introduction

In recent years the dominant paradigm in post-war peace building can be characterized as the state-building approach (Call and Wyeth, 2008; Paris and Sisk, 2009, p. 3). Theorists and practitioners within this approach have paid little overt attention to the 'subjective' dimension of peace building, focusing instead on the primacy of institution building and infrastructural reconstruction. While acknowledging the importance of creating the necessary institutional and infrastructural foundations for people to recreate 'normal' lives for themselves, one of the arguments of this chapter is that emotions are central to processes of destructive conflict and to 'post-conflict' reconciliation and peace building. The pivotal role of emotions in influencing patterns of political and social life has been recognized more clearly by social scientists in recent years (Goodwin et al. 2001). Unfortunately it is our experience that this awareness and associated theorizing has not spread to the peace-building field. As Neta Crawford observed, 'post-conflict peace building efforts too frequently fail . . . because peace settlements and peace building policies play with emotional fire that practitioners scarcely understand but nevertheless seek to manipulate' (Crawford, 2000, p. 116). It is our contention that an understanding of the emotional dynamics of societies emerging out of violent and destructive conflict will allow theorists and practitioners of conflict transformation to comprehend more clearly the challenges of post-war reconstruction and related efforts to promote coexistence and harmony between those that have been divided through destructive and violent conflict.

In the first part of the chapter an attempt is made to make explicit the emotional dimension of everyday life. This is followed by an emotional history of the civil war and post-war reconstruction in Sierra Leone. Using this case study material the chapter concludes that those who seek to engage in constructive conflict transformation work should factor into their analysis and practice not only the emotional dynamics of any conflict, but also the centrality of emotions in any peace-building project aimed at healing the wounds of division caused by destructive and violent conflict.

What are emotions?

Emotions are 'inner' states associated with a range of feelings, thoughts and actions (Crawford, 2000, p. 125). The word has the same root as 'motive', and of course 'motion'. People are *moved* by their emotions. Emotions are felt, they involve feelings – a generalized state of being that influences one's attitudes, perceptions, interpretive schemas and – of course – one's actions.

The degree to which emotions can 'over-determine' our perceptions and actions varies. Emotions can be 'mild' and they can be 'strong', and when they are strong they can overwhelm us, for however short a time period. This alerts us to the fact that emotions can have different time spans. Some can be short lived, like the spasm of fear when confronted by an aggressive looking stranger who then politely asks for directions, as against the long-term sense of dread experienced by those whose life experiences have proven that they would be wise to expect the worst.

Emotions can have 'targets' of varying degrees of specificity – we can be incensed by the aggression and rudeness of a fellow road user or dismayed at the level of crass materialism displayed by our fellow citizens. Sometimes emotions can be diffuse and without a clear object or target. We might use the word 'affect' to refer to such phenomena as a general feeling of pleasure or of anxiety. Emotions can also have different time orientations – we can feel angry about what we suffered in the past, but we can be hopeful about the future.

Emotions might seem to be 'spontaneous' and 'natural', unmediated by reason. Indeed, some writers incorporate this dimension into their definitions (Jarymowicz and Bar-Tal, 2006, p. 36; Turner and Stets, 2005, p. 21). While such theorists seem to operate with a dichotomous distinction between (rational) cognition and emotions, the relationship between what we might consider to be two dimensions of the mind is one of dynamic interaction and mutual influence. Thus, it is the recognition of an injustice or a wrong-doing that might make us angry, that anger can then act as an interpretive lens through which our ongoing encounters are viewed and acted upon. Indeed, decision-making is dependent on emotions, insofar as without them people are not in a position to attach different values to the alternatives facing them (Collins, 1993).

Moreover, however 'spontaneous' emotions might appear, they have a significant social dimension. Thus, Martha Nussbaum has pointed out how there are 'norms of reasonableness' with regard to the kinds of emotions deemed appropriate to have and to display in response to particular circumstances and experiences (Muldoon, 2008, p. 304; Nussbaum, 2001, p. 10). Hence, as social actors we learn the appropriate emotional response to situations. Furthermore, the manner in which an emotion is manifested behaviourally can be quite standardized within particular cultural groups that share the same 'common-sense knowledge'. We learn to express our emotions in manners appropriate to the cultural milieu to which we belong. Consequently the symbols and gestures by which we express our emotions can be read by others who share our world of meaning. In this sense emotions are socially constructed, however 'natural and spontaneous' they might seem to those experiencing them. Indeed, people can 'control' the external manifestation of their emotions in order to conform to what Hochschild (1979) termed 'feeling rules' and in order to manipulate others in a situation.

Emotions not only influence how we interpret (and act in) the everyday world, they also influence our memory and our understanding of the past. Particular memories can be associated with particular emotions just as current emotions can cause us to recall specific memories from the past. Thus, fear in the here and now may bring up memories of frightening experiences from the past, while the recall of such memories can cause a person to feel fearful in the present. In this sense emotions can be kept alive. Indeed, encounters or situations of a particular kind can act as emotional 'joggers' or catalysts, evoking particular emotions in participants. Monuments and memorials can also perform such a function. While it would be wrong to assume that everyone in such a situation experiences the same emotion – there is no doubt that emotional communities can be generated at commemorative sites and memorial events. In this manner monuments and memorials, as symbols, can guide our memories of the past and, of course, it is these images of the past that shape our understanding of the present and our expectations for the future.[1] All this underlines the fact that emotions can be as much social as personal phenomena. Indeed, there is a contagious quality about some emotions, such as can be encountered in scenes of collective panic and fear. In this manner groups and communities (even nations) can share a dominant emotion. As Jarymowicz and Bar-Tal (2006, p. 374) have observed, 'Emotions can be shared and thus evoked more or less simultaneously in group members. We assume that like individuals, who may be characterized by a dominant emotion, societies too may develop a collective emotional orientation.'

A key role in the production and reproduction of particular collective emotional orientations is played by those moral entrepreneurs that possess the capacity to impose upon wider publics their definition of a situation, and hence the appropriate emotional response. When emotions become 'public' in this way they can be very powerful forces, indeed on occasions emotional communities or networks can span the globe, not only through the channels of the mass media but also through diaspora and other networks. For example, in April 2009 there were demonstrations and public fasts by members of the Sri Lankan Tamil diaspora in many parts of the United Kingdom, Canada and elsewhere who vented their feelings of anger and concern in protest against what was claimed to be the 'genocidal war' waged against the LTTE (Tamil Tigers) by the government of Sri Lanka.

The fact that emotions constitute part of the social bond that can hold people together, while also acting as a causal factor in driving people apart, began to be recognized in a systematic manner by sociologists and social theorists in the 1970s (Turner and Strets, 2005, p. 1). Political scientists subsequently began to explore how to integrate emotions into their analyses, particularly in the study of social movements and the politics of protest (Goodwin et al. 2001; Jasper, 1997). The most extreme form of the politics of protest is when violence is pursued as a means of change. Many of those who engage in violence in pursuit of their aims explain their decision in terms of the 'righteous anger' felt at injustice and human rights abuse which is one of the drivers of struggle for change. Anger and indignation can feed into other emotions associated with destructive and violent conflict, such as hatred of those deemed responsible for suffering and injustice, resentment against those who seem to act with impunity, disregarding all the normal canons of civilized behaviour (Collier, 2004, pp. 563–95). And of course, consequent upon such emotions are the corresponding desires for revenge and vengeance which can continue to live on, long past any formal ceasefire. All these emotions can be permeated by another powerful emotion associated with destructive conflict – fear.

In recent years the impact of such emotions on people's attitudes towards peace processes and associated efforts at peace building in 'post-conflict' situations has been very much the preserve of psychologists interested in the impact of trauma experienced by the survivors of political violence. Typically such studies have sought to assess the levels of post-traumatic stress disorder (PTSD) displayed by a sample of respondents, and attempted to correlate this with their attitudes towards such issues as reconciliation, accountability and the most appropriate forms of transitional justice to be pursued during the peace-building process (Sonis et al. 2009, p. 534; Stover and Weinstein, 2004, pp. 206–26; Vinck et al. 2007, pp. 546–8). However valuable such studies might be to policymakers and peace-building practitioners, they tend to focus on individuals and have little to say about the manner in which publics can come to share particular emotional orientations towards a conflict and subsequent post-settlement attempts to deepen the peace. It is this *social* dimension of collective emotions that is the focus of the remainder of this chapter. In the following section we see how shared emotions among significant sectors of the population came into play as causal factors in the unfolding of the civil war in Sierra Leone.

An emotional history of the civil war in Sierra Leone

Fatalism and Sierra Leoneans

In order to grasp the emotional dynamics that have been so significant in shaping collective life in Sierra Leone, it is important to emphasize a particular emotional feature of Sierra Leoneans – the manner in which people across the country tend to be fatalistic in the way they perceive and respond to issues, especially those relating to conflict and trauma. Most Sierra Leoneans tend to attribute all felt and observable phenomenon to God and it is easy for people to close serious disagreements with the phrase *God dae*.[2] This helps to explain the widespread culture of social forgetting of trauma prevalent in the country (Basu, 2007, p. 239). It also helps us understand the vulnerability of Sierra Leoneans to manipulation, particularly by political leaders. As one close observer of the Sierra Leone sociopolitical environment remarked with reference to local politicians, 'they flood the market with rice, ensure weekend soccer matches and then they can forget about you until their term is up and they ask you for your votes'.[3]

1967–1991: From hope to despair – the path to civil war

The late Siaka Stevens of the All People's Congress (APC) came to power in a landslide victory over the Sierra Leone's Peoples Party (SLPP) in 1967.

The ascent of the APC to power was greeted with joy around the country as people saw the new government as a symbol of national unity, a goal the SLPP had failed to achieve. The collective hope for national development and unity held by Sierra Leoneans soon turned to despair as the new government became increasingly corrupt and dictatorial. The APC destroyed every form of democratic governance by constant vote rigging which finally led to the establishment of a one-party state in 1978 (Abraham, 2001, pp. 206–07). Excessive corruption in the government shattered the economy and rendered state institutions ineffective.

Conscious of the possibility of a coup d'état the APC regime took measures to keep the military weak and divided while strengthening the Internal Security Unit (ISU) of the Sierra Leone Police as the security apparatus for APC officials.[4] As a consequence, many in the military became disillusioned and most personnel looked for 'other things' on the side to make ends meet. Anger and resentment among the military led to talks of a possible military coup, but the high level of suspicion and distrust between members of the forces discouraged rebellious actions. Two attempted military coups d'état by Brigadier John Bangura and Mohamed Sorie Fornah in 1971 and 1975 respectively were violently repressed, resulting in the death of those who were associated with the attempts (Bangura, 2009, p. 3). Among the wider civilian population, especially in the southern and eastern regions which were the traditional support base for the SLPP, the dominant emotions generated by the experience of the APC were disappointment, anger and frustration. Most people regretted voting the APC into power and felt deceived and resentful. These feelings were compounded by a growing sense of hopelessness across the country as the APC destroyed all forms of organized political opposition and entrenched its hold on power. Sierra Leoneans began to wonder whether violence was the only means of freeing themselves from the repressive regime.[5]

Youths were hardest hit by the APC regime as education and career prospects became luxuries for a few whose relatives had access to political resources, with the remainder left facing an uncertain future. These youths expressed their anger and resentment through peaceful demonstrations (to which the ISU reacted violently) or by joining clandestine groups involved in circulating revolutionary ideas, especially those propagated by Colonel Muamar Qaddafi in his Green Book (Humper, 2004, p. 85). Others simply resorted to antisocial behaviour, especially the use of illegal narcotics, thereby providing a ready pool from which politicians recruited them to intimidate political opponents. As the social and economic situation deteriorated further, anger turned into fear as human rights abuses became increasingly common throughout the country. With so much anger and lack of trust in the government, the stage was set for armed conflict in Sierra Leone.

Siaka Stevens retired in 1985, handing over the presidency to Joseph Saidu Momoh, commander of the armed forces. Momoh proved himself to be a weak head of state and under his leadership, corruption increased and state institutions deteriorated even further.

1991 –2000: Mixed emotions and mood swings – the civil war

In March 1991, the rural town of Bomaru in Kailahun district (eastern Sierra Leone) was attacked by a small band of armed men from Liberia, followed by similar attacks in Pujehun district. An organization calling itself the Revolutionary United Front (RUF) led by a former army corporal, Foday Sankoh, claimed responsibility for the attacks.[6] According to Sankoh, the aim of the rebellion was to overthrow the APC and to return the country to democratic governance (Lord, 2000). Although the RUF claimed responsibility for the incursion, many observers attributed the attack to Charles Taylor, who was seeking to punish Sierra Leone for several reasons. Taylor had attempted to use Sierra Leone as a launch pad for his armed rebellion in Liberia but President Joseph Saidu Momoh had frustrated his moves by having him arrested and detained. Furthermore, the Sierra Leone government had agreed to provide an operational base for forces of the ECOWAS Monitoring Group (ECOMOG), the West African peacekeeping force, to intervene in the Liberian civil conflict to restore peace (Abraham, 2001, p. 206). ECOMOG forces had frustrated Taylor's rebel movement, the National Patriotic Front of Liberia (NPFL), and Taylor held Sierra Leone responsible for this setback. In addition, Taylor was concerned that a rival Liberian militia group, the United Liberian Movement for Democracy (ULIMO), was operating from bases in Sierra Leone.

The response of Sierra Leoneans to the armed insurgency was mixed. Some saw it as a welcome move to end years of economic stagnation and repression, others were less sanguine, viewing it as a product of external influences, pointing fingers at Liberia, Libya and later Burkina Faso (Humper, 2004, p. 85). As a consequence, and in the context of the lack of legitimacy enjoyed by the central government and the weakening of the armed forces at its command, there was a failure to mount any robust response and the RUF was able to expand its numbers and territorial control, attracting many recruits from the marginalized youths to whom the rebels offered hope for the future. In the early stages of the conflict the RUF targeted rural communities. Residents who cooperated with the RUF were often spared sanctions, provided with food and rewarded with privileged positions. Those who resisted or whose loyalties were questioned were subjected to degrading abuse and violence. Through this strategy the RUF succeeded in creating divisions among people who had lived together and supported each other for years. Individuals and families who felt threatened by RUF rebels fled for safety. As a consequence there was the spread of fear, distrust and suspicion among people who had once lived together in community.

The military contingents sent to repel RUF advances were ill equipped and poorly motivated. To make matters worse, they were abandoned by their commanders who expropriated rations and other supplies meant for the front-line troops. In April 1992, a group of officers from the front travelled to Freetown to negotiate improved logistical support but the talks turned sour, resulting in a coup d'état which brought the junta – the National Provisional Ruling Council (NPRC) – to power (Boas, 2001, p. 714).

The coup and subsequent removal of the APC was greeted warmly by Sierra Leoneans and their anger, fear and uncertainty were replaced by optimism and hope, feelings that unfortunately did not last for long. People were confident that the junta would end the war speedily and institute democratic governance. The NPRC started off well by stamping down on corruption and enforcing discipline in the civil service, but the effects of the long neglect of the army were still strong. While the NPRC excelled in instituting discipline in most sectors of government, it failed to do so within the army as commanders continued with their corrupt practices, contributing further to the disillusionment of the soldiers under their nominal command. To vent their frustration and anger, the soldiers took to preying on the very civilians they were meant to protect. While some soldiers collaborated with the RUF, others operated as soldiers by day and rebels by night, looting to enrich themselves, thereby earning themselves the nickname *sobels* – soldiers turned rebels (Park, 2006, p. 317). Rural communities were also most affected by the activities of these renegade soldiers. Peaceful citizens accused of supporting the RUF and later the civil defence forces (CDF) were humiliated and in some cases killed. Under the NPRC the civil war spread rapidly to engulf the whole country, causing many to conclude that the junta was colluding with the RUF.

As disappointment, anger and fear grew with the deteriorating security situation, Sierra Leoneans responded in a number of ways. A number of communities formed their own local defence forces, which became known as Kamajors. Although the Kamajors and other local security forces helped to protect civilians, they were also accused of committing gross human rights abuses during the conflict. Civil society organizations also exerted pressure on the NPRC to hand over power to a civilian government, and in 1996 the junta grudgingly organized a general election which brought Ahmed Tejan Kabbah of the SLPP to power. The SLPP election victory was due to two main factors. First, the political party had widespread support from southern and eastern regions of the country, an area mainly inhabited by Mende, one of the largest ethnic groups in the country. Second, Sierra Leoneans wanted the NPRC out, and the SLPP was the only political party strong enough to pose any significant challenge.

The new government was faced with serious challenges – a shattered economy, widespread insecurity and a weak military whose loyalty was questionable. To address the loyalty and insecurity issues, the government decided to reform the army and strengthen the local defence forces, actions that raised suspicion and apprehension within the army and subsequently led to a coup d'état in May 1997 that brought the infamous Armed Forces Revolutionary Council (AFRC) of Johnny Paul Koroma to power (Thomson, 2007).

The initial reaction of Sierra Leoneans to the 1997 coup was anger, but this was soon replaced by fear when the AFRC leader invited the RUF to join the new government. The RUF accepted the invitation. The immediate impact of this coalition was a sudden increase in human rights violations country-wide, forcing many Sierra Leoneans to seek refuge in neighbouring countries. The international community condemned the coup and imposed social and economic sanctions, which only increased the sufferings of those Sierra Leoneans who remained in the country, compounded by growing feelings of fear, anger and despair.[7]

Fear and anger in the pursuit of peace

Between 1996 and 2000 five ceasefire agreements were signed by the government and the RUF, all of which were violated. Sankoh never showed genuine commitment to peaceful resolutions of the conflict as he kept changing his position on agreements, earning him the nick-name 'chameleon' (Abraham, 2001, p. 207). But while people were frustrated by the RUF's unreliability, they were equally angry with the government and the international community for not putting sufficient pressure on Sankoh to end the conflict. Indeed, the Lome Peace Accord (LPA) which eventually laid the foundation for ending the conflict, was initially condemned because it gave blanket amnesty to combatants and elevated Foday Sankoh to the status of vice president, in charge of mineral resources! Placing Sankoh in charge of mineral resources was a cruel irony, considering that the RUF took over a large proportion of diamond mines in the eastern region, using the proceeds to fund and prolong the brutal civil war. These concessions shocked and enraged a wide range of Sierra Leoneans, especially victims of serious human rights violations, who accused the government of betrayal, sacrificing justice for peace and attempting to achieve peace by any means and at any cost. To many people it appeared that the terms of the LPA rewarded the RUF for the atrocities they had committed, while failing to acknowledge the plight of victims of the conflict, and a number of civil society organizations organized protest demonstrations throughout the country. However, as the security situation improved, outrage and disgust with the government gradually dissipated, as Sierra Leoneans began to appreciate the pleasures of peace.

Anger, fear and anxiety were dominant emotions which played important roles throughout the duration of the conflict. During the APC regime, anger contributed to tensions, rebellion and the subsequent cross-border incursion by the RUF. But as the violence persisted, followed by increased loss of life and hardship, people feared that continuation of the conflict was senseless and that it would lead to more suffering. While collective fear can create a platform for violent conflict, it can also be a strong motivation for seeking peaceful means for resolution (Bal-Tal et al. 2007, p. 448).[8] And in the case of Sierra Leone it was this fear of the impact of escalating violence and abuse, and consequent uncertainty about what the future might hold, that caused people to pursue the option of a ceasefire in the hope of a negotiated end to the war.

Peace building through state building: the failure to address the emotional legacy of the war

The dominant concern of new regimes and their international patrons in societies emerging out of destructive and divisive violence is to promote the necessary degree of social order to ensure regime security and legitimacy. This is what might be termed the national reconciliation project. The actual composition of such a project is significantly determined by the balance of power and political forces at the time of transition. In Sierra Leone the conflict was declared over in 2002 with symbolic burning of weapons in various parts of the country. The main thrust of the international peace-building effort was to increase the level of security and restore some semblance of a functioning state. This was approached through three main initiatives. First, a programme to disarm and demobilize combatants; secondly, assistance was provided to enable displaced persons and refugees to return home to resume livelihoods and rebuild their communities and relationships. Thirdly, general elections were conducted aimed at creating a legitimate government.

In addition, two transitional justice institutions – the Truth and Reconciliation Commission (TRC) and the Special Court for Sierra Leone (SCSL) – were established. Each of these different elements of the national reconciliation project aroused mixed emotions across the country as discussed in the following sections.

Disarmament, demobilization and reintegration

The disarmament, demobilization and reintegration (DDR) programme targeted more than 45,000 former combatants from all armed factions. The components of the programme included trading in weapons for cash, training combatants to acquire new skills and providing them with start-up capital for self-employment.[9] Despite the political support and international financial backing, the DDR came under constant criticism from victims and human rights organizations. The privileging of combatants infuriated many Sierra Leoneans who felt that perpetrators were being favoured at the cost of their victims who had lost relatives, limbs and livelihoods. The groups most critical of the DDR were the hundreds of war-wounded, including amputees, who at that time were living in deplorable conditions in over-crowded camps with little or no support from the government. It was only after the security situation had improved and people started to move around once again without fear of armed assault that people began to experience the constructive impact of the DDR programme (Kai Kai, 2003, p. 3).

Return of displaced persons

The end of the civil war and progress made in disarmament of combatants made possible the return of displaced persons to their communities. As noted above, the high level of trust that had existed within village communities before the conflict had been eroded and replaced by fear and suspicion. In many cases the return of the displaced exacerbated the tension between people at several levels. Returnees accused their neighbours who had stayed behind of collaborating with armed men to loot, kill and destroy. On the other hand, those who had remained saw the returnees as opportunists who had chased after relief supplies, and as cowards who had shied away from their responsibility to protect the community.[10] Apart from isolated symbolic reconciliation exercises organized by the TRC, the state largely ignored the emotional needs of survivors at community level. As we shall see later, indigenous institutions responded to these emotional needs, using a number of approaches.

Truth commission and special court

The establishment of the truth commission and the special court, coincidently located in the same neighbourhood in Freetown, also added to the confusion among Sierra Leoneans. The TRC was given good publicity and people were determined to appear before it in order to testify and share their war experiences. But there was a problem. Rumours spread that information provided to the TRC could be used as evidence for the prosecution of those indicted for war crimes. Individuals and groups who could have enriched the historical account of the civil war being compiled by the TRC feared that their testimonies would be shared with the court, possibly resulting in them being called to appear as witnesses in future trials. At a time when former combatants were returning to their communities, people feared that testifying against them in court would re-open old wounds, resulting in the resumption of hostilities (Shaw, 2005, p. 12).[11] As a consequence many people steered clear of the TRC, and even when outreach teams visited communities they returned almost empty handed.

General elections

The first post-conflict general election was conducted in 2002 and aimed at giving all political aspirants a level playing field to participate in post-conflict governance. Pressure was exerted upon the RUF to transform itself into a political party ready take part in the proposed elections. Sierra Leoneans again questioned the government's motive for supporting the RUF, and many interpreted it as continuing the policy of rewarding Sankoh for the sake of peace. In fact the 2002 general election was one of those moments in history when Sierra Leonean's took a collective position on a national issue, refusing to give a political mandate to Foday Sankoh.[12]

While the above efforts aimed at improving the security situation and rebuilding the state and its institutions, they generally failed to address the emotional legacies of abuse and trauma left by the civil war. The truth commission was in the best position to address the emotional needs of victims but it failed to do so for two main reasons. First, it focussed its activities in district headquarter towns that were easily accessible by road, thus excluding rural communities where more than 60 per cent of the population and those most affected by the civil war live. Secondly, most people, especially combatants from rural communities, did not understand the aims of the truth commission and special court and therefore had problems associating with them (PRIDE, 2002). In the vacuum left by the national reconciliation project, rural communities turned to indigenous resources and processes to address emotional issues as a prerequisite for rebuilding relationships. In the following section, we shall focus on those actions taken by traditional institutions to promote coexistence in post-civil war rural communities.

Addressing the emotional legacy of the civil war: community-based indigenous approaches

Throughout the civil war and immediate post-war period very little consideration was given to the feelings of survivors. In most nations emerging from brutal and protracted conflicts, addressing national security is often given priority by concerned governments and their development partners. As a consequence post-conflict reconstruction efforts often seem to prioritize the concerns of former fighters over the plight of their victims. Certainly this appeared to be the case in Sierra Leone. While the UN was directing substantial resources towards the disarmament, demobilization and reintegration of former combatants, and providing the funds to support the truth commission and the special court, victims were struggling all over the country to access basic necessities.

In such circumstances traditional institutions in rural communities were perhaps alone in addressing the emotional needs of survivors.[13] Traditional leaders, especially paramount chiefs, have been criticized as corrupt and undemocratic and implicated as contributing to the causes of the civil war (Fanthorpe, 2005, pp. 28–30). Whatever basis there might be to such charges, it is also clear that paramount chiefs also provided substantial emotional support to war-affected communities, especially those who had been displaced from their homes.[14] The provision of such support to their communities has been an integral aspect of the traditional peace-keeping role of chiefs, and it remained a particularly important function performed by those chiefs who shared the pain and suffering of the displaced throughout the conflict. During the war, when rural communities were displaced, most people found themselves in larger towns in either Sierra Leone or Guinea. The majority of displaced persons were illiterate, with little experience of life outside their village, and therefore had difficulty relating to the bureaucracies of aid agencies supporting war-affected communities. Quite literally they became lost in the crowd. In such circumstance it was frequently the traditional community leaders such as the chiefs and elders who intervened to assist and enable the displaced to access whatever relief aid was being provided.[15]

In the immediate post-war period, with a weak central state and burgeoning tensions at the community level involving returnees and ex-combatants, it was the traditional leadership that intervened to ensure coexistence. While victims were angry, bitter and still suspicious of their neighbours, chiefs were also aware that former combatants and wrongdoers were suffering from guilt, rejection and fear of reprisals. Hence, the first task of the local leadership was to minimize the level of insecurity created by anger, fear and suspicion. This was achieved through the means of dialogue and cleansing rituals with the emphasis upon traditional and religious values that prioritized forgiveness and peaceful coexistence.

Dialogue

To promote coexistence and build relationships, traditional authorities took a number of measures to deal with the complex emotional climate in communities. The first major step was aimed at promoting dialogue at all levels, laterally (between people) and vertically (between people and those in authority). These discussions encouraged community members to share their personal war experiences, thereby creating in effect community-based truth commissions. Compared to the nationally organized TRC, most survivors found this a more comfortable and comforting form of truth telling as it was readily accessible and presided over by people with whom they could relate. Such forms of dialogue helped promote empathy as it enabled victims to begin to understand the circumstances that lead to certain abuse. In such forums it became apparent that during the civil war armed youths, especially new recruits, were often drugged and in most cases under pressure from their bush commanders to commit atrocities. Throughout the dialogue process, traditional leaders guided the community not to be judgemental but to focus on the benefits of confession, forgiveness and reconciliation not only for perpetrators and victims but for the entire community. Through public dialogue and focus on collective benefits, leaders were able to reduce rumours, labelling and finger pointing and in the process help lay the basis for increased trust between people.[16]

Cleansing rituals

As dialogue facilitated confession and forgiveness, traditional leaders moved on to the performance of rituals which included symbolic cleansing and annual remembrance rites. In many parts of Africa rituals are integral to traditional justice systems that are often preferred to other forms of retributive justice such as criminal prosecutions (Allen, 2008, p. 47). Individuals who committed offences such as murder, rape and desecrated sacred places during the war were considered defiled and in order to foster harmony between them and the entire community, including ancestors, some form of symbolic cleansing was necessary. Symbolic purification rites in some communities usually commence with public confession by the perpetrator and a plea for forgiveness from victims and the whole community.[17] Confession can help ease the pain of the guilty and in the process foster reunion not just with the self but also with others and with the entire community. Confession, like forgiveness, can transform relationships (Klenck, 2004, p. 142). Typically in the Sierra Leonean context, once confession has been completed and forgiveness offered, the concerned individual is handed over to the diviner or healer for symbolic washing using water mixed with special herbs. After symbolic washing, drinking water is offered to the individual to drink and to rub on his/her chest. It is at this stage that the individual is considered clean enough to be reconciled with the entire community.

The act of cleansing addresses a number of emotional concerns. By symbolic washing, participating communities are convinced that the cursed are sufficiently cleansed for them to interact with others once again. On the side of the wrongdoer, guilt dissipates as the crime becomes a thing of the past and the concerned individual can now move on, assured of acceptance from the community and ancestors. From the perspective of the community, cleansing and re-admission of the offender into society indicates closure, enabling people to move into the future with hope. Ritual cleansing and healing have been used in other parts of Africa, especially in Zimbabwe where it is used extensively to address traumatic memories (Schmidt, 1997, pp. 1–7).

While symbolic cleansing aims at reconciling individuals with the community, annual rituals are concerned with remembering the past, honouring ancestors and improving the relationship between the community and the spiritual realm. Such annual commemorative rituals have also been used in rural communities in Sierra Leone to bring divided groups together and rebuild social ties that were broken by the civil war. Rituals are facilitated by diviners and typically involve the recitation of the names of ancestors, collective confession on the part of the community, offering of sacrifices (an animal in some cases), prayer and the sharing of food and drink. While these annual celebrations aim at commemorating local heroes and significant events in the past, they are also used as a forum by community members to interact and reaffirm their common identity (Winter, 1998, p. 103). In the process of planning and implementing annual rituals community members also helped lay the foundation for renewing trust and the re-establishment of cooperative relationships. In addition, rituals assured individuals that they had appeased ancestors and as a consequence enjoyed their favour, which in turn gave participants a sense of inner peace, a prerequisite for coexistence and sustainable peace.[18]

Concluding observations: security, trust and hope – the emotional requirements for coexistence

The challenge facing those seeking to promote sustainable peace processes in the aftermath of civil war and other forms of divisive collective violence is to erode the basis for the negative emotions generated by the conflict while laying the foundation for the growth of more positive emotions such as compassion, forgiveness, trust and hope. What this means in practice is that however committed peace-builders might be to some model of a harmonious future, it is imperative that they take seriously the emotions of the survivors of conflict (Obeidi et al. 2005, p. 482). People have to deal with their ghosts from the past before they can be expected to embrace a new future. As Chayes and Minow (2003, pp. xx) have remarked, 'reconciliation may remain elusive or even an insulting notion to people still reeling from the murder of their loved ones or their own torture or rape. . . . Clumsy, premature attempts at reconciliation may do more harm than good.'

As we have seen in the case of Sierra Leone there are certain emotional requirements for peaceful coexistence. The relative success of the DDR programme helped reduce the level of fear in society concerning the return of large-scale violence. The initiatives of indigenous leaders and elders were particularly significant in helping people build on their growing sense of security and attempt to come to terms with their loss and accept the need to live alongside those from whom they had been divided, a process which can be seen as constituting the essence of reconciliation. As Bloomfield and his collaborators (2003, p.12) have written,

> At its simplest, [reconciliation] means finding a way to live alongside former enemies – not necessarily to love them, or forgive them, or forget the past in any way, but to coexist with them, to develop the degree of cooperation necessary to share our society with them, so that we all have better lives together than we have had separately.

What this definition sensitizes us to is the fact that there are different levels of coexistence between those that have been divided, each level dependent on particular dominant emotions.

The 'thinnest' surface level of coexistence might be likened to a form of social apartheid, where people live largely separate lives informed by the general ethos of 'You leave us alone and we shall leave you alone'. As Michael Ignatieff concluded on the basis of his observations of the workings of the

South African Truth and Reconciliation Commission, 'You can coexist with people you cheerfully detest. You can coexist with people without forgetting or forgiving their crimes against you. Cold peace of many kinds does not require reconciliation of a personal kind' (Chayes and Minow, 2003, p. 326). At this level anger and resentment towards the 'other' can be widespread and deeply felt, but kept under control for various reasons (Muldoon, 2008, p. 299–305).[19] For example, a Cambodian woman living in the same village as those she believed responsible for the deaths of her family members during the Khmer Rouge period, confessed more than 40 years later that, 'We feel hot inside with hate and we still want to take revenge. But outside we speak with them' (Agence France Presse, 2009).

At the most superficial level of coexistence the dominant emotion remains that of fear – fear about the return of the violence, the generalized fear that the past is not past, such that the violence and abuse of the war continues to cast its long shadow over the present, and feeds the fear of what the future might bring. So long as people's emotional lives are dominated by this fear they cannot develop the trust necessary for social reconstruction and coexistence in the present. It is the growth of this second emotion, trust, that helps undermine and accompanies the erosion of the fear of 'the returning past' – trust in one's fellow citizens and in the institutions that constitute the context for everyday life. This restoration of trust requires some experience of 'normality' in everyday life, a level of predictability that is dependent upon people sharing a similar interpretive scheme for making sense of and acting in the world, making compatible judgements about the appropriateness of particular forms of behaviour. This is the type of *horizontal trust* between people that is a precondition for 'normal everyday life' (de Greiff, 2008, p. 126).[20] But the experience of normality and predictability as a basis for developing trust also requires an institutional infrastructure that facilitates levels of security and thereby helps generate what de Greiff (2008) has characterized as the *vertical trust* between citizens and their institutions.

Mneesha Gellman, exploring the interrelationship in Cambodia between what might be termed the 'national reconciliation project' orchestrated by the political elite and grass-roots initiatives to promote constructive coexistence, has highlighted the interrelationship between the different 'levels', and in the process has emphasized the importance of developing horizontal and vertical trust as a means of loosening the appeal of victimhood and promoting hope for the future. She writes,

Improved democratic capacity at the national level might assist in rebuilding trust and enthusiasm at the local levels . . . conversely, building trust at the community level will give government the much needed social capital to implement peace building agendas . . . competent leadership and democratic organizations that encourage public input and participation can *motivate people to develop a positive vision of the future rather than cling to past grievances.* (Gellman, 2008, pp. 37–57).

A key indicator of a deep form of coexistence is when people start sharing their hopes for the future, when they start imagining a shared future together and when they start to believe that they have grounds for such hope. Of course, to hope for something indicates recognition that what is desired is beyond our present capacity to bring about. But to 'hope well' is to experience ourselves as agents of potential, confronting our limitations and seeking to move beyond them. As such, there is a strong relationship between hope and social change.

One factor that can contribute to keeping hope alive is being among others who share and support our hopes – being a member of a community of hope. But the creation and maintenance of such a community depends in turn upon there being recognizable grounds for hope. As such there is a very powerful positive relationship between social change and hope – evidence of constructive change on the ground reinforces one's sense of agency and hence one's capacity to hope.[21] From this perspective a major challenge for peace builders is to help create the grounds for hope in societies emerging out of the trauma of collective violence. While in certain circumstances such initiatives can come from external actors and agencies, people can create their own grounds for hope within their own communities. For example, in the case of our research in Sierra Leone a number of cases came to light where levels of trust between community members had developed to such a degree that they had moved to implement community-level economic and infrastructural improvement initiatives – a sign of a shared commitment to and hope for the future. In Bomaru (where the civil war started), victims and perpetrators jointly initiated two community-wide projects in agriculture and road construction, aimed at improving food production and increasing access to social services respectively.[22] Youth in another community (Ngolahun) funded and built a health clinic to address the increasing proportion of maternal deaths experienced after the war.[23] While these projects help to kick-start local socioeconomic activities, they also contributed to bringing divided communities together to work for a better future.

Earlier in this chapter reference was made to the manner in which monuments and other forms of commemoration can act as joggers of particular memories and associated emotions, representing in some condensed form a particular interpretive memory of the past and thereby possessing the capacity to bring particular feelings and emotions to the surface. In similar fashion, the successful implementation of community development projects can act as symbols of what the future might hold, serving as symbols of the efficacy of local people as agents of social change, and thereby functioning as emotional joggers, enhancing individual and collective capacities for hope.

It is on the basis of this analysis that we suggest that peace builders seeking to harness the emotional dynamics of a population in the process of post-conflict reconstruction should be sensitive to the following questions:

i   Do the initiatives anticipated help strengthen the sense of personal and collective security and reduce the fear of a return of the violence?

ii Will the initiatives help foster trust – the horizontal trust in others and the vertical trust in the 'system' – necessary for sustainable coexistence?

iii Will the initiatives help establish the grounds for people to have a shared hope for the future?

Notes

1 Whichever emotions are reproduced on such commemorative occasions, whether it be sadness for loss, resentment, anger, thirst for vengeance, can have a significant influence on future developments and relationships.

2 This is a Krio phrase and translates as 'God exists, knows all and sees all'. The phrase is an indication of both defeat and closure of a fractured relationship, as the victim trusts in God for divine intervention in due course. This attitude is common across the country and has no geographical or religious limitations.

3 Interview, Freetown, May 2009.

4 Due to its extreme brutality, the acronym ISU for most Sierra Leoneans came to stand for 'I shoot you'.

5 Kaindaneh was a high-school student during the APC regime and took part in a number of demonstrations against government decisions and actions.

6 Foday Sankoh had been previously imprisoned by the APC for his involvement in a coup, although he insisted on his innocence.

7 Kaindaneh remained in the Sierra Leone throughout the AFRC regime, working with a humanitarian aid agency in the northern region of the country. 'My team and I were constantly harassed by both government and rebel forces. Personally, I made sure that I always carried my passport and some money in foreign currency (US Dollars) in readiness to cross the border into Guinea whenever situations turned sour. I encouraged staff and friends to do the same and indeed we crossed the border several times for our safety.'

8 Bar-Tal and others have repeatedly emphasized the manner in which collective fear militates against progress to peace in protracted conflicts. In Sierra Leone our research suggests that one of the drivers of civil society pressure on the parties to agree to a ceasefire was the collective fear of the escalating cycle of violence and abuse that would accompany the continuation of the war. This prompts the research question: under what circumstances does collective fear obstruct progress towards the peaceful settlement of armed conflict and under what conditions does the same emotion act as a force for peace?

9 Start-up capital included money, equipment-based skills learnt and business advisory and management support.

10 Discussion with traditional leaders and national NGOs in South eastern Sierra Leone, May/June 2009.

11 Rosalind Shaw (2005, p. 12) concluded that the TRC failed to build upon established practices of healing and reconciliation. 'In Sierra Leone, the TRC set itself in opposition to widespread local practices of social reconstruction as forgetting by valorizing verbally discursive remembering as the only road to reconciliation and peace.'

12 Even though Sankoh had persistently claimed that the RUF was a people's movement, the general elections proved the contrary as it got only 1.7 per cent and 2.1 per cent for presidential and parliamentary votes respectively and failed to get any seat in parliament (See Kandeh, 2003, pp. 202–06).

13 Discussion with communities, including traditional leaders on their experiences as displaced persons and as returnees, Kailahun and Bo districts, May/June 2009.
      The traditional institution in Sierra Leone's rural communities is not just made up of chiefs and elders. Other individuals especially those with rural-based skills like healers, diviners, blacksmith, heads of secret societies all team up with local leaders to address issues affecting the community.

14 During the civil war Kaindaneh witnessed a number of visits by paramount chiefs from northern Sierra Leone to refugee camps in the Forecariah prefecture in Guinea. The aim of these visits was to follow up on the welfare of refugees and to support sub-chiefs in the settlement of disputes that arose among Sierra Leoneans due to the conflicting political positions they held. These visits were useful in resolving conflicts and were appreciated by refugees who generally felt abandoned by elected government officials. (Personal experience).

15 Discussion with returnees in south eastern Sierra Leone, May/June 2009.

16 Discussion with community members and agencies involved in peace-building activities in rural Sierra Leone, Kailahun and Bo districts, May/June 2009.

17 Although confession had already happened during the dialogue phase, a public one is also required as part of the cleansing process.

18 It should be emphasized that despite undertaking these traditional justice coexistence activities, a few communities remained divided. Many ex-combatants fled to the towns, aware that there was no 'home' for them anymore in their villages. An unknown number of orphans and women have attempted suicide as a way of escaping their shame and isolation. See A. Behrendt, *Violent memories still haunt Sierra Leone's war orphans*, http://yubanet.com/world/Violent-memories-still-haunt-Sierra-Leone-s-war-orphans.php (accessed 6 August 2009).

19 Anger and resentment do not lead automatically to acts of vengeance, as Paul Muldoon (2008, p. 304) has observed: 'It is possible to be angry without succumbing to a violent rage that wreaks havoc in an entirely disproportionate and indiscriminate fashion.'

20 de Greiff defines reconciliation as 'the condition under which citizens can trust one another as citizens again (or anew). That means that they are sufficiently committed to the norms and values that motivate their ruling institutions, sufficiently confident that those who operate those institutions do so also on the basis of those norms and values, and sufficiently secure about their fellow citizens' commitment to abide by these basic norms and values.'

21 On the concept of hoping well, see. McGeer, V. 2004.

22 Interviews with community members, Bomaru, 5 May 2009.

23 Interviews with community members, Ngolahun, 7 May 2009.

References

Abraham, A. (2001), 'Dancing with the chameleon: Sierra Leone and the elusive quest for peace', *Journal of Contemporary African Studies*, 19(2), 205–28.

Agence France-Presse (2009), Available at: http://www.abs- cbnnews.com/world/02/12/09/krouge-trial-unlikely-heal-cambodias-wounds (accessed 2 July 2009).

Allen, T. (2008), 'Ritual (ab)use? Problems with traditional justice in Northern Uganda', in N. Waddell and P. Clark, eds, *Courting Conflict? Justice, Peace and the ICC in Africa*. London: Royal African Society, pp. 47–54.

Bangura, S. (2009), '34 years after the execution of Mohamed Sorie Fornah and 14 others', *The Patriotic Vanguard Newspaper*, 21 July, pp. 1–8.

Barker, C., Martin, B. and Zournazi, M. (2008), 'Emotional self-management for activists', *Reflective Practice*, 9(4), 423–35.

Bar-Tal, D., Halperin, E. and Revera, J. (2007), 'Collective emotions in conflict situations: societal implications', *Journal of Social Issues*, 63(2). pp. 441–60.

Basu, P. (2007), 'Palimpsest memoryscape: materializing war and peace in Sierra Leone', in F. de Jong and M. Rowlands, eds, *Reclaiming Heritage: Alternative Imaginaries of Memory in West Africa*, Walnut Creek, CA: Left Coast Press, pp. 231–59.

Behrendt, A. (2008), 'Sierra Leone: Violent memories still haunt war orphans', IRIN, Available at: http://www.irinnews.org/report.aspx?reportid=79519 (accessed 6 August 2009).

Bloomfield, D., Barnes, T. and Huyse, L. (2003), *Reconciliation after Violent Conflict. A Handbook*. Stockholm: IDEA.

Boas, M. (2001), 'Liberia and Sierra Leone – dead ringers? The logic of neo-patrimonial rule', *Third World Quarterly*, 22(5), 697–723.

Call, C. and Wyeth, V. (2008), *Building States to Build Peace*. Boulder, CO: Lynne Rienner.

Chayes, A. and Minow, M. eds (2003), *Imagine Coexistence: Restoring Humanity after Violent Ethnic Conflict*. San Francisco: Jossey-Bass.

Collier, P. (2004), 'Greed and grievance in civil war', *Oxford Economic Papers*, 54, 563–95.

Collins, R. (1993), 'Emotional energy as the common denominator of rational action', *Rationality and Society*, 5, 203–30.

Crawford, N. (2000), 'The passion of world politics: propositions of emotion and emotional relationships', *International Security*, 24(4), 116–56.

De Greiff, P. (2008), 'The role of apologies in national reconciliation processes: on making trustworthy institutions trusted', in M. Gibney and R. Howard-Hassman, eds, *The Age of Apology,* Philadelphia, PA: University of Pennsylvania Press, pp. 120–36.

Fanthorpe, R. (2005), 'On the limits of liberal peace: chiefs and democratic decentralization in post-war Sierra Leone', *African Affairs*, 105(418), 27–49.

Gellman, M. (2008), 'No justice, no peace? National reconciliation and local conflict resolution in Cambodia', *Asian Perspective,* 32(2), 37–57, 47.

Goodwin, J., Jasper, J. and Polletta, F., eds (2001), *Passionate Politics: Emotions and Social Movements*. Chicago: University of Chicago Press.

Hochschild, A. (1979), 'Emotion work, feeling rules and social structure', *American Journal of Sociology*, 85, 551–75.

Humper, J. (2004), *Witness to the Truth: Report of the Truth and Reconciliation Commission*, Vol. 2, Ghana: Graphic Packaging, pp. 3–503.

Jarymowicz, M. and Bar-Tal, D. (2006), 'The dominance of fear over hope in the life of individuals and collectives', *European Journal of Social Psychology*, 36, 367–92.

Jasper, J. (1997), *The Art of Moral Protest*. Chicago: University of Chicago Press.

Kai Kai, F. (2003), 'NCDDR Executive Secretariat Report.' (Archive material).

Kandeh, J. (2003), 'Sierra Leone's post-conflict elections of 2002', *Journal of Modern African Studies,* 41(2), 189–216.

Klenck, M. (2004), 'The psychological and spiritual efficacy of confession', *Journal of Religion and Health*, 43(2), 139–50.

Lord, D. (2000), 'Introduction: the struggle for power and peace in Sierra Leone', in D. Lord, ed., *Paying the Price: The Sierra Leone Peace Process*. Available at: www.c-r.org/our-work/accord/sierra-leone (accessed 15 April 2009).

McGeer, V. (2004), 'The art of good hope', *The ANNALS of the American Academy of Political and Social Science*, 592, March 2004, 100–27.

Muldoon, P. (2008), 'The moral legitimacy of anger', *European Journal of Social Theory*, 11(3), 299–314.

Nussbaum, N. (2001), *Upheavals of Thought: The Intelligence of Emotions*. Cambridge: Cambridge University Press.

Obeidi, A., Keith, W., Hipel, K. and Kilgour, D. (2005), 'The role of emotions in envisioning outcomes in conflict analysis', *Group Decision and Negotiation*, 14, 481–500.

Paris, R. and Sisk, T., eds (2009), *The Dilemmas of State Building: Confronting the Contradictions of Post-War Peace Operations*. Abingdon: Routledge.

Park, A. (2006), 'Other inhumane acts: forced marriage, girl soldiers and the Special Court for Sierra Leone', *Social and Legal Studies*, 15(315), 317–37.

PRIDE (2002), 'Ex-combatant views of the Truth and Reconciliation Commission and the Special Court in Sierra Leone', Available at: http://ictj.org/images/content/0/9/090.pdf (accessed 12 June 2009).

Schmidt, H. (1997), 'Healing the wounds of war: memories of violence and the making of history in Zimbabwe's most recent past', *Journal of Southern African Studies*, 23(2), 1–7.

Shaw, R. (2005), 'Rethinking truth and reconciliation commissions: lessons from Sierra Leone', *United States Institute of Peace, Special Report 130*, Washington, D.C.: United States Institute of Peace, Available at: www.usip.org/files/resources/sr130.pdf (accessed 30 September 2009).

Sonis, J., Gibson, J., de Jong, J., Field, N., Hean, S. and Komproe, I. (2009), 'Probable post-traumatic stress disorder and disability in Cambodia: associations with perceived justice, desire for revenge, and attitudes towards Khmer Rouge trials', *Journal of American Medical Association*, 302(5), 527–36.

Stover, E. and Weinstein, H. eds (2004), *My Neighbour, My Enemy: Justice and Community in the Aftermath of Mass Atrocity*. Cambridge: Cambridge University Press.

Thomson, B. (2007), *Sierra Leone: Reform or Relapse? Conflict and Governance Reform*. Available at: www.chathamhouse.org.uk (accessed on 12 April 2009).

Turner, J. and Stets, J. (2005), *The Sociology of Emotions*. Cambridge: Cambridge University Press.

Vinck, P. et al. (2007), 'Exposure to war crimes and implications for peace building in Northern Uganda', *Journal of American Medical Association*, 298(5), 543–54.

Winter, J. (1998), *Sites of Memory, Sites of Mourning: The Great War of European Cultural History*. Cambridge: Cambridge University Press.

PART FIVE

Politics and the triumph of the therapeutic

10

The therapeutic fantasy
Self-love and quick wins

Tim Dartington

Why does social policy often take such an ill-informed stance in relation to what we know about human nature? In parallel with neo-liberal
tendencies in economic theory, there has been an increasing denigration of
dependency in social welfare systems. The importance of relationships is
being devalued, apparently under threat from an opportunist, individualistic
and self-interested approach to human relations. In British social policy, this
is now called 'personalisation', where those eligible for state-funded support
are to receive personal budgets to commission their own individual care. And
more specifically, helping relationships in nursing, social work, education and
other contexts, are also becoming diminished, short term and instrumental,
like any other customer relations. As a result, much of what passes for health
and social care is not in fact fit for purpose.

As Wouters argues in his chapter in this volume, we supposedly live in a
culture of emotional tolerance where we are 'allowed' to have 'feelings'; but I
believe that this has given rise to a new and distorted view of the therapeutic.
This view derives from an ambivalence about the importance of psychological
understanding in everyday life, an understanding which is either celebrated as
emotional intelligence or derided as 'touchy feely', something deeply suspect
in the 'real world' of socioeconomic relations.

Through this modern therapeutic discourse, grief and mourning have
become acknowledged and respectable processes among today's generation, in contrast to parents and grandparents brought up with stiff-upper-lip
attitudes of not showing feelings. More generally, counselling is widespread
as an acceptable response to loss, trauma and suffering of many different

kinds. However, I would argue that this therapeutic sensitivity, with a respect for the emotional impact of change and loss, has to hold its space alongside a contrary model of human relations, one which is instrumental and ratio-nalist. This other model, in its postmodern and neo-liberal manifestations, reacts strongly against the idea that dependency outside of the family has any positive characteristics. While we may pay lip service to our essential interdependency with others, we are continually invited to act according to an independent agenda of personal and economic growth.

For at least 40 years we have been living through the so-called triumph of the therapeutic (Reiff, 1966) where a new view of the self – 'I feel therefore I am' – has arguably become the touchstone of modern culture (Bell, 1973) and also the justification for a new form of (therapeutic) state (Nolan, 1998). As one headline put it: 'We're All Sick and Government Must Heal Us'. But far from encouraging dependency, this is a post-dependent society (Khaleelee and Miller, 1985) in which the state is preoccupied with the rapid repair of emotional damage through a therapeutic fantasy of quick fixes to the modern human predicament, a kind of attempted makeover to the scars left by per-sonal experiences of stress, suffering and loss (often in early life).

So there is a paradox here. The state draws on this therapeutic culture to justify its actions but simultaneously takes an increasingly behavioural view of its powers of intervention. In the United Kingdom the New Labour govern-ment attempted both the micro-management of human behaviour and the macro-liberalization of systems, so that in one week alone, it put forward new guidelines on under-age drinking, involving Anti-Social Behaviour Orders (ASBOs) for children and the possibility of custodial sentences for parents, while putting forward proposals to turn over the management of failing hos-pitals to private sector firms. The new Coalition Government in the United Kingdom, promising to be less interventionist, has continued to make radi-cal changes to the NHS, while adopting ideas from behavioural economics (Thaler and Sunstein, 2008) to promote the concept of a 'Big Society'.

This behavioural and engineering approach derives in part from the assumption that our actions are mostly instrumental and economically driven. We may even track this to Adam Smith or more recently to games theory, but what is important is the wider economic theory that developed in the second half of the last century linked to cold war paranoia – that chaos is averted and equilibrium achieved by the human capacity to strategize against each other in our own self-interest. The nature of man may then be described according to a resourceful, evaluative and maximizing model, which is more subtle than a simple economic model, but remains firmly centred in individual self-interest (Jensen & Meckling, 1998). This is the intellectual tradition that has led to senior executives being offered stock options so that they are fully committed to shareholder value, and also for example to the internal market in the British National Health Service – looking to achieve results by competition rather than cooperation.

This instrumental model has mathematically subtle theories for analysing systems behaviour but they are psychologically naïve. Lacking any recognition of unconscious process, they are wrong footed all the time by the influence of envy, guilt, shame, love and other emotions on social interaction. These are, in contrast, flashpoints for psychoanalytic interpretations of human behaviour. However the instrumental model does allow for something called 'confidence'. Confidence in the market seems to imply a kind of collective wisdom depending on how people feel about things. Games theory depends on us having to guess what the other thinks and what the other thinks we think, etc. We are said to be suffering from a lack of trust in the volatile markets that we are experiencing at the moment. People in the United Kingdom are thought to be keeping £6 billion in cash in their own homes, while bankers remain, according to a phrase used by Peter Mandelson, the then New Labour MP, 'intensely relaxed' about getting filthy rich. Therapeutic discourse acts as a bridge between the narrow instrumental model of human behaviour, with its assumption of the rational actor behaving according to self-interest, and the reality that people do many kinds of things that we do not want to think about.

If we think of humankind as a paranoid agent of his own self-interest, then the intrinsic importance of human relationships is discounted and discredited. It should not be necessary to have to argue for the importance of relationships, as our ordinary experience as social beings is supported by philosophers from Aristotle to Buber. Theologians consistently argue against personal religion in favour of an essential belonging to a community of faith. Psychologists, poets, dramatists and novelists observe and record the minutiae of human interaction as crucial to ontological meaning. The evidence base for the importance of relationships is therefore strong. How then can there be such a successful undermining of that evidence in current social policy?

One example of such undermining in recent years has been what is happening to the doctor–patient relationship. Michael Balint, a psychoanalyst, in his essay 'The Doctor, His Patient and the Illness' (Balint, 1957), argued that the doctor was himself the treatment, that it was the personal relationship with the patient as much as the prescription pad that made the intervention effective (paradoxically, Balint's book was published in the same year as the first antidepressants became available on prescription in the United Kingdom). I doubt if Balint is much read by those enthusiastic about the latest health service reforms, with the development of polyclinics for the efficient delivery of primary care services to patients who are now recast as the customers of medical services delivered by doctors whose interventions may now be timed by the minute. The latest reforms look to General Practitioner-led consortia to take over responsibility for commissioning services and controlling budgets, and we may see then how attitudes of patients may be further changed towards their own doctors.

There is a difference between highlighting the intrinsic value of relationship, as Balint argued, and what I suggest is now our everyday experience where *the appearance* of relationship is used to achieve a business objective – 'have a nice day'. This is services marketing, where the relationship is used to sell a product. Such commodified relationships have become incorporated into what we may think of as a therapeutic culture of person-centred added value. The consumer-focussed therapeutic discourse is not about a psychodynamic understanding of people interdependently relating to the world they are in. Rather, it acts as a defence against that understanding. The therapeutic, as it is now understood, belongs to the tradition of the Kleenex and paracetamol, an immediate response to a recognizable problem. Blow your nose and you will feel better. Treat the symptoms and the causes can look after themselves. In contrast, the psychoanalytic has as its objective, as Freud famously claimed, the achievement of ordinary unhappiness (Freud, 1895) – and much the same could be said of traditional general medical practice, so it was not to be sniffed at. Object relations theory gives a primacy to relationship in furthering understanding. As Klein said of child analysis, 'the first thing that happens in analysis is that the emotional relation with the parents improves; conscious understanding only comes when this has taken place' (Klein, 1926).

In this post-dependent world, authority is mainly internal and ahistorical, located in the individual self – it is not externally represented by old parental figures and intergenerational dynamics of tradition and innovation. When psychoanalysts and open systems theorists came together in the group relations work of the Tavistock Institute in the 1950s, the conferences they developed had, and continue to have, authority in the title (Miller, 1990). In contrast, the therapeutic fantasy of individual salvation does not take sufficient account of authority – authority in relation to role in carrying out the task of the group, organization or community – or the working through of social relations that are functional to the task.

The weakness of the modern therapeutic approach can be seen in relation to what is now called the parenting deficit. As was shown in the debate on underage drinking, the current approach to issues of parenting is constrained by the language of (children's) rights and (parental) responsibilities. This is silo thinking; look at the child over here, the parent over there. The focus is not on the relationship. But the psychoanalyst Donald Winnicott (1960) said in contrast that there was no such thing as a baby on its own, but always in relation to its mother, and a psychoanalytic approach might ask: what is the authority of the parent in relation to the child? Instead there is a seemingly attractive focus on mutuality, but understood narrowly in terms of an exchange of rights and responsibilities, as if love can be bought and sold in a family market.

A therapeutic fantasy approach to mental health – one which offers a short course in individual salvation – is demonstrated also by the language of 'recovery', which has become popular in UK social policy.

The recovery model has an emphasis on self-management and while this has strengths it also contributes to the diminution of the importance of relationships to others, including a reduced respect for the authority of others derived from their competence and experience. Why should I think that anyone knows better than me about anything? Is not the customer always right?

One example of the constraints on relationship within a therapeutic culture is the management of care workers in relation to service users. In the United Kingdom a home care team, working in the community, is commissioned by the local authority. The care staff are contracted to work a specified amount of time with each service user. The technology now allows for a home visit to be timed to the minute, and management say that this way they can introduce some flexibility. For example, perhaps the service user needs more time on one occasion. The carer can give her the time, and that can be monitored, and taken back from the next visit. In this way management say they are being more responsive to client need. In this way the system is seen to offer more flexibility as a way of asserting more control. This is the seeming promise of the rationalist model. The likelihood is that, left to themselves, some carers would do a lot more than they are contracted to do, because they get into a relationship with the service user. Other carers might exploit any lack of surveillance in the system to do less than they could. That, you might say, is human nature, the good egg/bad egg syndrome. The managerial response is to make both workers the same, to contain the good and coerce the bad to a single standard of a National Vocational Qualification within a National Service Framework. This is benign in its intent but it is also Orwellian in its process. The only way it works with any humanity and respect for relationship is that it is applied in an inefficient and incomplete way. Some very good care is provided despite, not because of these safeguards. Some bad care may also go undetected by the monitoring system.

In the United Kingdom a NHS mental health trust, taking a global view of its recruitment needs, recruited a significant number of staff from an African country. A senior manager had visited the country and had been impressed by the caring that he had seen there. But now he was disappointed: that caring culture had not transferred as he had hoped into the NHS Trust. Of course not, someone informed by anthropology or cultural studies might say – it would be naïve to expect otherwise. My question is different – why is it so difficult to think how an NHS Trust might create a community of care at least as good as – not the same as – a village community in a developing country?

Clearly regulation does not sit easily with relationship. What is spontaneous, idiosyncratic, uncertain in its outcome, does not fit with an agenda of national standards. I am reminded of a story that my children liked, when they were young, where the farmer's wife, being a clean and tidy person, cleaned up the farmyard, and the pig, whom she loved, ran away, deprived of the mud and squelch of his familiar environment. I think of this now as a parable also for organizational life, in a culture of audit.

If you allow carers to have relationships of any significance with service users, things will get messy. Managers act like the farmer's wife and then wonder why the pig runs away. We need the remarkable competence of ordinary people to care for others, and in a risk-averse culture of performance management, we become frightened of that competence and impose mechanisms of control. In contrast what is needed, in the supportive psychological sense, is what psychoanalysis calls 'containment' where the concerns of the other are held and made less toxic, enhancing the other's capacity to live with anxiety and doubt.

In modern organizational life it looks *as if* relationships are all important but this is expressed more through networks than sentient one-to-one communication. Networks have the dynamics of speed dating – they offer a quick and ready way of seeing who might suit our needs just at the moment. In public services this has been expressed through the long-established use of 'bank' staff who work shifts as required. In such ways there has been, as I have said, a collapse of respect for relationship. The modern therapeutic fantasy pictures vulnerable people as self-managing and self-sufficient units rather than people engaged in meaningful relations. While I was researching this chapter I overheard two women talking. One had been visiting her mother in an independent living scheme. She was complaining vigorously that her mother was being forced to do things to demonstrate her progress in being independent, for example, by doing the washing up with two care workers standing over her, and she saw this as patronizing and insulting, more a punishment than support. When she complained to the manager, she was told that they had to demonstrate that they were achieving outcomes such as client independence to justify their funding.

On the ground, this means standing over an old lady doing the washing up. In a care system of this kind, if a supportive relationship that has meaning does develop, this is likely to be deviant from the protocols. I heard an encouraging story of an elderly man returned home from hospital following a stroke that had left him partially paralysed. Formally, he was offered intensive physiotherapy for eight weeks. The therapists contrived to 'lose' his notes so that they could continue to treat him.

The Northfield hospital experiments (Harrison, 2000) during the Second World War led to the development in peacetime of the therapeutic community movement in mental health services. Such collective therapeutic endeavours have always struggled against more orthodox individualistic treatments and now more than ever, with the pressures of local commissioning of mental health services. Patients and clients have been re-allocated the role of 'service users', again to play down the dependency in the role and to maintain the appearance of an autonomous being. This is attractive as an attempt to ensure some parity in what is otherwise an unequal power relationship. The service user is the customer of therapeutic services. In the market customers are assumed to know their own needs and to take responsibility for their own decisions. Except that needs are better defined in this context as wants, subject to cost benefit analysis and open to substitution. Increasingly illnesses are being linked to lifestyle choices, obesity leading to diabetes, cardiovascular diseases associated with diet and stress, alcohol-related diseases, etc. Assessment processes therefore fit uneasily in this process. Assessment of need is in fact increasingly to be understood as practically indistinguishable from the management of resources.

For resource managers the question always is, does the service user fit the criteria for the provision of the service according to a rights and responsibility framework, so that for such and such a reason the user has the right to a service, and the provider agency is commissioned to provide it? If the answer is affirmative then interventions are delivered and monitored as short-term interactions. Cases are opened, shut, reopened according to externally determined criteria. (It reminds me of my father's economy-minded habit of turning off the sitting room light even when we were still sitting in the room.)

Agencies act like call centres, where each operator – 'My name is Susan, how can I help you?' – is interchangeable with the next, 'My name is Kate . . .' The apparent offer, the promise of a relationship is a shallow pretence. My experience of a computer helpline was that the adviser had 30 minutes in which to sort out the problem with me. After that time he hung up, expressing the wish that the problem was sorted, which it was not, and I went through the same process with a second adviser and a third. In each case we had to start again with the same check list of possibilities allowing little time for new learning. This, I suggest, is the essential dynamic of the brief intervention, potentially both inefficient as a quick win and ineffective as a long-term outcome.

Psychoanalysis in contrast can seem extreme in its reliance on relationship. A colleague once said to me, 'After three years the patient told me that she had lost a baby when she was sixteen . . .'. Put like that, it does not seem a very efficient technique and is hard to defend as best value. A neutral observer might even think that the technique has become ritualistic and the purpose has been lost. But at the core of this work there is a respect for the patient's own capacity for learning and the difficulties of learning that contrasts with the urgency of time-limited interventions.

I see the psychoanalytic stance as educational but not didactic in its process. There are a lot of technical and ideological meanings to this, but I am concerned here to emphasize the development of understanding through relationship. A psychoanalytic interpretation may be asymmetric (hierarchical and authoritative) or relational and interactive (negotiating meaning) but in all cases this is a communication through the medium of relationship. It allows for subjective judgement, free of external authority. The intimacy of a relationship requires an open-ended commitment, when you don't know exactly what you are getting into and what you will get out but you have the capacity to stick with it.

The modern therapeutic agenda, as it is now being realized in social policy and practice, is very different in effect from the psychoanalytic project with which it is confused. It is much more concrete and positive in its promises about outcomes, and this serves also to distract from the importance of inequalities. If through a quick psychological fix we can be anything we want, it does not matter that we or anyone else starts at a disadvantage. The argument made persuasively by Wilkinson and Pickett (2009) about the correlation of economic inequalities with a wide range of social ills disturbs the established view and challenges the opportunity agenda and the myth that we are all masters of our fates.

The finding that social mobility has actually decreased with the unleashing of market forces as the driver for change also needs some explaining. It would seem that this kind of freedom – this entrepreneurial space – only suits a small minority of people – or a small part in each of most of us. The majority remains risk averse, having neither the stomach nor the skill to make the best of every opportunity according to a resourceful maximizing model. So the poor actually get poorer – the middle range, where most professionals hang out, more or less stay the same, and the 'top' 1 per cent enjoy exponential increases in their wealth.

Psychoanalytic commentators have noted somewhat uneasily that leaders have narcissistic, even sociopathic qualities. In the *Harvard Business Review*, Michael Maccoby wrote about narcissistic leaders:

Despite the warm feelings their charisma can evoke, narcissists are typically not comfortable with their own emotions. They listen only for the kind of information they seek. They don't learn easily from others, they don't like to teach but prefer to indoctrinate and make speeches. . . . . Perhaps the main problem is that the narcissist's faults tend to become even more pronounced as he becomes more successful. (Maccoby, 2000)

Hedge fund managers, as well as rogue traders that they employed, were the extreme heroes (and now villains) of our times because it seems that they did not understand about risk – their lack of awareness, the ultimate in positive thinking, made them both successful in their own terms and dangerous for the stability of markets (Stein, 2007).

The employer–employee relationship, which is worked out also in manager–subordinate relationships at different levels in the organization, is increasingly understood in instrumental terms. On the face of it, there is a more transparent openness, as described in the 360 degrees appraisal process. There is also the possibility of evaluation of every kind of interaction. When I had a cup of coffee at Paddington Station, I was given a four page questionnaire to complete. The faculty at some business schools and universities are scored by the students after every session and the results published. Feedback becomes a kind of surveillance. As some employees have been slow to learn, emails can easily be monitored. There are scare stories of Microsoft products that will monitor stress levels in the staff during the working day.

It is often remarked how the language of management has taken on quasi-religious formulations: mission, vision. . . . But enthusiasm, religious or secular, is not really welcome, because it is difficult to manage. The voluntary sector, with its not-for-profit organizations created and developed to give expression to deeply held values and commitment, is also continuously suborned by an insistent demand that the organizations become efficient, competitive social businesses. Chief executives move from one cause to another without noticing any conflict of interest, and having successfully competed for government funding, they become government advisers.

Enthusiasms are difficult to manage because for the enthusiast authority comes from the task. From the perspective of the enthusiast it is therefore self-evidently right to carry out an action that serves the task. This can be problematic of course. A partner from one of the major consultancies described to me how the voluntary sector did not understand the employer–employee relationship. Volunteers, local committees, ideologically driven workers, have a tendency to do what they think right – managing them requires an empathy with the other's desires that that can only be carried through by relationship – and if that breaks down, there will be trouble and conflict. Some political groups offer an extreme illustration of this dynamic. Voluntary organizations may be seen to implode, as they experience and react to injustice and persecution within their own membership rather than in the external environment.

In contrast we may think of traditional examples of relationships at work – the master–servant relationship and the craftsman–apprentice relationship (Sennett, 2008). In each case there is a contract that acknowledges dependence in a way that runs counter to the employer–employee relationship. Modern employer–employee relationships are an attempt to realize a relationship without dependence – an organization of 'as if' relationships among independent operators. Their interdependence is not sufficient to ensure real cooperation and their activities are managed by surveillance – typically audit and a performance-related reward system. You are not rewarded for who you are (self in role, which I suggest is our innate preference) but what you do (the robotic payoff). Qualities of loyalty and trust are no longer needed if their advantages can be achieved by technicalities of performance management.

The quality movement introduced the concept that nothing has meaning unless it can be measured. But now the concept has developed – so that anything that can be measured will be, whether it has meaning or not. Hence the paranoia we feel about the collection of data by commercial enterprises on their customers, by government agencies, and of course by employers on their employees: only what is measured is 'real'.

This robotic tendency in human relations – to see the individual as a productive unit that can be made to run at near optimum efficiency – contributes to the stressful experience of people at work, because they are not in fact robotic at all. Experientially, we have good days and bad days, our energy levels fluctuate throughout the day, we get on better with some people than others. This may be stating the obvious, but it is the obvious that is being ignored.

To cover for this discrepancy, we have developed a thriving therapeutic culture at work, which addresses the needs of the human in the robot – for example, counselling services funded by employers, and for more important people in the organization, executive coaching. Employees who are downsized are offered out-placement services. Remuneration is increasingly linked to performance bonuses, as if the individual is a sole trader in a competitive enterprise.

George Bush argued persuasively in his election campaign to be American President, 'It's Your Money'. Except that it isn't, of course: it is a powerful myth that wealth is individually generated and attracts personal moral worth (Singer, 2004). This statement is attractive; in fact, it is essential to the instrumental core of the therapeutic project, because it is a denial of the human interdependence of each of us. The globalization of our economic systems has promoted a fantasy of individual enterprise, while integrating us into an interconnected matrix, of which the sub-prime mortgage collapse has given us some uncomfortable insight – and we enjoy what we think of as the fruits of our labours, although these are now probably made by a suicidal workforce in the sweatshops in China.

Think also of the happiness debate. Increased prosperity has left us unhappy, experiencing the status anxiety and the affluenza that Alain de Botton (2004) and Oliver James (2007) describe in their interpretations of the therapeutic culture.

The attack on relationship is in part an attack on dependency. The problem with acknowledging dependency is that it adds weight to our responsibility for others without any corresponding gain of rights. A dependent workforce, one that has to be looked after, provided with security of employment and compensatory benefits in the event of sickness or injury, makes the organization less competitive. And knowledge work, which can be done anywhere through the Internet, requires less dependency in the workforce than, say, manufacturing processes that are factory based. On the larger stage, a dependent population looking for handouts because they are sick or disabled makes a state economy less competitive in the global market.

We recognize dependency in the nursery and the hospice, but not in between, though it remains a fact that there is not a time when we are not dependent on others for our survival and comfort. The human need for relationship is not of course lost or destroyed in the meantime. We retain a capacity for compassion and a sense of community, linked strongly with an identification with 'people like us', to use Margaret Thatcher's phrase. What might group relations thinking contribute to this debate? It emphasizes groupishness and, following Bion, our hatred of our groupishness (Bion, 1961). Or as Sartre put it, 'Hell is other people'. This contrasts with the Maslovian ideal of self-actualization, a sophisticated development of the notion of the self-made man which emphasizes individual achievement, including a capacity for relationships, but fails to recognize that the individual is also a product of his group identity (Maslow, 1943).

We act all the time as if we are on our own in our achievements, and do everything we can to defend ourselves against the sure and certain knowledge that this is just not true. But hatred of dependency is different from denial. The hatred we can do little about, but the denial is something for us to work with in the development and management of human systems.

The politics of involvement (Miller, 1985) is all about relations with others. We define ourselves by who we are not, the not-us, and then value others by their capacity to be 'one of us'. Cultural difference of all kinds is also about otherness. An organizational culture is 'the way we do things round here.' The institutionalization of health and social care systems, with their increasingly elaborated protocols, has as its primary task the imposition of what looks like a corporate culture at the expense of individual empathy.

Bion's observations on our ambivalence about our groupishness are illustrated in the phenomenon of trade. It could be argued that trade is the originating drive for relationships between groups, and these reciprocal relationships have been described as the beneficent side of human groupishness (Ridley, 1996). It is not only about profit and loss: gift exchange is a reaffirmation of relationship (Mauss, 1924). However altruism, the capacity for generosity in a relationship without thought of an immediate return, is often thought of as still involving a trade-off – it is described as reciprocal altruism, where a current action may be returning a past favour or open up the expectation of favours in the future (Badcock, 1986). But more typically trade becomes a way of seeking selfish advantage under the cover of mutuality – in the way that diplomacy is the continuation of war by other means.

The management of dependency through public welfare is itself expressive of a deep ambivalence about relationship. In Western-type welfare systems the integration of health and social care systems has always been an issue – but we need to understand why they are separated in the first place. And because the split is so deeply entrenched in the organizational culture of our welfare services, we may need to look for a psychological underpinning rather than the rational arguments about efficiency and effectiveness and the political jargon about collaboration and partnership.

What is the real difference that is so difficult to integrate? In the care of older people, social care is primarily about living with loss, compensating for ordinary activities that you can't do any more – because you're ill or disabled – like, you can't eat, go to the toilet, dress yourself, sit, walk, whatever. Health care is more about fighting back against disease and disability, and includes activities that are new and special because you are ill or disabled – often invasive like investigations and surgery, requiring temporary or permanent relocation, and a continuing programme of boundary violation of the self, with injections, as well as changing dressings, monitoring medication and so on. One is called social care and the other is health: there is an arrogance about foregrounding one at the expense of the other but that is what we do.

And so we find that social care, as it is currently organized, is increasingly also about fight – short-term interventions to get you back on your feet – and if you really have dependency needs, these will only be recognized at a late stage when a 'panel', a star chamber that meets in secret and does not publish its deliberations or decisions, determines that the individual is eligible for continuing care. Currently in the United Kingdom, this happens at such a late stage that by then the individual in need may only be able to access palliative care. In the meantime, health and social care agencies both pursue targets for short-term interventions, opening and closing cases which banish any sense of continuity or overview of the person's long-term needs.

The split in the resourcing and management of health and social care is itself reflective of a deeper division between heroic and stoical responses to vulnerability in ourselves and others. This observation may be linked to Kleinian theory about the paranoid-schizoid (heroic) and depressive (stoical) positions in understanding how our internal worlds influence our interpretation of external reality. So, perhaps services around vulnerable people are seen to be influenced by these two states of mind, which are in tension and difficult to synthesize. There are then two kinds of responses to our vulnerability – to accident, illness, trauma, debility. A split is enacted between the heroic and stoical; hopeful and the hopeless; the active and the passive; between fight/flight and dependence; between resistance and acceptance; between an assumed omnipotence and a supposed impotence.

The first position may be characterized as having paranoid-schizoid characteristics. The citizen is aggressive, angry about what has gone wrong in his or her life. We take it personally. The appropriate stance is one of not accepting: the ills that one is suffering are not acceptable. The response is one of fighting back. After all, if you want something enough, you can have it. Failure, if it happens at all, is – or has to be – heroic. Vulnerability is for wimps.

The depressive position, which is also very much our experience in relation to health and social care, accepts more readily that there is good and bad in the world. We have to learn to live with that. Hannah Segal, in her analysis of an elderly man, 73 years old, described how he had come to see old age and death as a persecution and a punishment. In her work with him, he came to think of his approaching death 'as a repetition of weaning, but now, not so much as a retaliation and persecution, but as a reason for sorrow and mourning about the loss of something that he deeply appreciated and could not now enjoy: life. . . . But the mourning and sadness were not a clinical depression and seemed not to interfere with his enjoyment of life. . . . He might as well enjoy it and do his best with it while he could' (Segal, 1986, p. 179). She reports that he lived another fulfilling 11 years.

How do health and social care services work with these two positions, the heroic and the stoical? The policymaking agenda is predominantly heroic, being driven by political urgencies. The stoical agenda is carried more by Janus-headed managers, front-line workers, informal carers, and most importantly those who are at any time in our society its vulnerable population.

There has been an important paradigm shift in the delivery of services. The shift is from meeting human emotional needs to a concern with barriers to opportunity. This is an argument developed by Cooper and Lousada in what they have called *Borderline Welfare*. They make a distinction between deep and shallow welfare:

> The fear is that once we allow real contact with a deprived, dependent, helpless population, any services offered to them will become rapidly enslaved to their needs for all time, draining resources from other important projects, and depleting our autonomy and flexibility as a society and an economy.

They go on: 'It is not dependency that is the problem, but fear and hatred of dependency' (Cooper and Lousada, 2005, pp. 194–5).

There has always been a downwards force of delegation to do with physical care. The opportunities for nurses to do nursing are limited – delegated to relatively much less-trained or qualified care assistants. It is a process that in history and different cultures has been pervasive – it is the culture of the wetnurse and the dalit, where acts of care and compassion, from breast-feeding to the cleaning up of excrement, are delegated to the menial members of society – and, one may observe, from outside of society, with the employment of 'illegals', for example, in the United States and the United Kingdom (Ehrenreich and Hochschild, 2003).

At the same time the professionalization of care leads inevitably to specialisms – a four-year degree course leaves you overqualified to wipe bottoms. The general practitioner, once known as the family doctor, now sees more patients in a morning surgery, with time-limited appointments and extended hours, meeting Quality and Outcomes Framework (QOF) targets, according to Department of Health priorities, but does not have time or motivation to make home visits to the terminally ill. The continued separating out of health and social care systems, despite a rhetoric of integration, is reinforced according to unexamined assumptions of difference, and serves a purpose to establish a hierarchy of need and response, so that – as with processes of institutionalization – everyone knows their place. Cultural differences associated with gender and race, social class and other factors to do with migrant status, also serve to confirm this implied hierarchy in the management of care in intransigent circumstances of non-recovery.

My conclusion, in summary, is this: that a therapeutic culture that indulges the fantasy of personal growth and salvation without the necessity for a committed relationship provides a very necessary defensive environment, psychologically speaking. In helping us to live with the freedoms of a market economy that leave us feeling entrapped, it makes the resultant world of targets and audit sort of tolerable. The freedoms of the market are arguably good for us as customers but get us anxious, overworked or excluded as suppliers of goods and services. In this dilemma, the therapeutic fantasy offers the prospect that we are still free men and women.

References

Badcock, C. (1986), *The Problem of Altruism*. Oxford: Blackwell.

Balint, M. (1957), *The Doctor, His Patient and the Illness*. London. Pitman Medical.

Bell, D. (1973), *Coming of Post-Industrial Society*. New York: Basic Books.

Bion, W. (1961), *Experiences in Groups*. London: Tavistock.

Cooper, A. and Lousada, J. (2005), *Borderline Welfare: Feeling and Fear of Feeling in Modern Welfare*. London: Karnac.

de Botton, A. (2004), *Status Anxiety*. London: Hamish Hamilton.

Ehrenreich, B. and Hochschild, A. (2003), *Global Women: Nannies, Maids and Sex Workers in the New Economy*. New York: Metropolitan Press.

Freud, S. (1895), 'The psychotherapy of hysteria', in his *Collected Works, Standard Edition*, Vol. 2. London: Hogarth Press and Institute of Psychoanalysis.

Harrison, T. (2000), *Bion, Rickman, Foulkes and the Northfield Experiments: Advancing on a Different Front*. London and Philadelphia: Jessica Kingsley.

James, O. (2007), *Affluenza*. London: Ebury Press.

Jensen, M. and Meckling, W. (1998), 'The nature of man', in M. Jensen, ed., *Foundations of Organisational Strategy*. Harvard, MA: Harvard University Press.

Khaleelee, O. and Miller, E. (1985), 'Beyond the small group: society as an intelligible field of study', in M. Pines, ed., *Bion and Group Psychotherapy*. London: Routledge & Kegan Paul.

Klein, M. (1926), 'The psychological principles of early analysis', *International Journal of Psycho-Analysis*, 8, 25–37.

Maccoby, M. (2000), 'Narcissistic leaders, the incredible pros, the inevitable cons', *Harvard Business Review*, 78(1), 69–77.

Maslow, A. (1943), 'A theory of human motivation', *Psychological Review*, 50, 370–96.

Mauss, M. (1924 [1992]), *The Gift: Forms and Functions of Exchange in Archaic Societies*. London: Routledge.

Miller, E. (1985), 'The politics of involvement', in A. Collman and M. Geller, eds, *Group Relations Reader 2*. Washington: A. K. Rice Institute.

—(1990), 'Experiential learning in groups', in E. Trist and H. Murray, eds, *The Social Engagement of Social Science: A Tavistock Anthology, Vol.1, The Socio-Psychological Perspective*. University of Pennsylvania Press/Free Association Books, pp. 165–98.

Nolan, J. (1998), *The Therapeutic State: Justifying Government at Century's End*. New York, NY: New York University Press.

Reiff, P. (1966), *The Triumph of the Therapeutic*. New York: Harper & Row.

Ridley, M. (1996), *The Origins of Virtue*. New York: Viking.

Segal, H. (1986), 'Fear of death: note on the analysis of an old man', in *The Work of Hannah Segal, a Kleinian Approach to Clinical Practice*. London: Free Association Books, pp. 173–82.

Sennett, R. (2008), *The Craftsman*. London: Allen Lane and Penguin.

Singer, P. (2004), *The President of Good and Evil: Taking George W. Bush Seriously*. London: Granta.

Stein, M. (2007), 'Oedipus Rex at Enron: leadership, oedipal struggles and organizational collapse', *Human Relations*, 60(9), 1387–410.

Thaler, R., and Sunstein, C. (2008), *Nudge, Improving Decisions about Health, Wealth, and Happiness*. New Haven, CT: Yale University Press.

Wilkinson, R. and Pickett, K. (2009), *The Spirit Level: Why Equality is Better for Everyone*. London: Allen Lane and Penguin.

Winnicott, D.W. (1960), 'The theory of the parent–infant relationship', in *The Maturational Processes and the Facilitating Environment*. London: The Hogarth Press.

11

The slippery slope and the emancipation of emotions[1]

Cas Wouters

Introduction

This chapter aims at showing how overall trends in Western regimes of manners within the twentieth century, and in earlier centuries, have been connected to general trends in self-regulation. After a preliminary section on my theoretical framework, focusing on three central functions of a 'good society' and its code of manners, I will first concentrate on a long-term trend that was dominant until the last quarter of the nineteenth century: the trend of formalizing manners and disciplining people. Driven by the disciplinary forces of state formation and market expansion, 'dangerous' emotions such as those related to physical violence came to be avoided in increasingly automatic ways, that is, increasingly regulated by the inner fears of a rather rigid and authoritarian conscience. A 'second-nature', that is, a conscience-dominated type of personality was in the making. This process accelerated in the period in which entrepreneurial and professional bourgeois classes entered and came to dominate the centres of power and their 'good society'.

Then, I will focus on the last decades of the nineteenth century, when the long-term phase of formalizing manners and disciplining people turned into a long-term phase of informalization of manners and 'emancipation of emotions': emotions that had been denied and repressed (re)gained access to consciousness and wider acceptance in social codes. This phase has continued throughout the twentieth century to the present. The following fairly recent examples will provide an initial visualization of the long-term processes of informalization of manners and 'emancipation of emotions'.

During the Gulf War fighter pilots, interviewed for TV in their planes before taking off, admitted to being afraid. They did this in a matter of fact way. This would have been almost unthinkable in the Second World War, when such behaviour would have been equated almost automatically with being fear ridden, a condition in which it was thought to be impossible to perform well. Admitting to be afraid was experienced as stepping on a slippery slope: one automatically had to act upon the emotion. The dominant response at that time, in answer to the problem of how to prevent soldiers from giving in to fear may be summarized in a quotation from a 1943 manual for American officers: it is the soldier's 'desire to retain the good opinion of his friends and associates . . . his pride smothers his fear' (Stearns and Haggerty, 1991). Precisely the same pride kept soldiers from admitting they were afraid, especially before an operation. At the time of the Gulf War, all this had obviously changed. Today, it has become quite common to admit feeling this or that, hate or lust, anger or envy, and yet to act quite different, playful and subtle. This implies a rise in the level of demands on self-regulation, a change that can perhaps be most clearly seen in changes in the relationship between the dying and those who live on. Here, the traditional rule that dying patients were to be kept under the delusion that there was a fair chance of recovery – doctors conducting a regime of silence and sacred lies, effecting to hardly ever informing the dying of their terminal situation – has changed to the expectation and, for doctors even the judicial obligation, to be open and inform them (Wouters, 2002). A last example concerns divorce. The traditional expectation that divorced couples would stop seeing each other has changed about 180 degrees into the present expectation to have a 'good after-marriage', that is, to maintain a friendly relationship or work towards developing one (Veeninga, 2008).

At the end of this chapter, in order to capture the observed changes in demands on self-regulation and in personality structure, the sensitizing concept of a 'third nature' is introduced: there was a change from a 'second nature' to a 'third nature' personality. The 'slippery slope' serves as a running example.

On good societies and regimes of manners and emotions

As Norbert Elias (2000) has shown, changes in manners open a window onto changes in the relations *between* people, as well as onto changes *in* people, that is, in their demands for emotion regulation. Therefore, the study of any regime of manners can reveal a corresponding regime of emotions. As a rule, within each society, the dominant code of manners and emotion regulation is derived from sociability within the centres of power and their 'good society', that is, the circles of social acquaintance among people of families who belong to the centres of power, and who take part in their sociable gatherings. As the maintenance and improvement of occupational and political positions of power depends on building trust, that is, on making friends and acquaintances in the field, those involved customarily invite each other to dinner and to other sociable occasions, such as parties. Thus, by participating in the circles and gatherings of good society, they continue to seek the protection and reinforcement of their occupational and political interests.

The codes of a good society have three functions: (1) a modelling function, (2) a representational function and (3) a function to regulate social mobility and status competition. These three functions are also operative in layers of good society further down the social ladder, or in the country or provinces.

(1) As the codes of good society are decisive in making acquaintances and friends, for winning a desirable spouse, and for gaining influence and recognition, they serve as an example or model for all socially aspiring people – they have a *modelling function*. Until the nineteenth century, courts and court society had this function. In comparison with court circles, later circles of good society were larger, and sociability in them was more *private*, which made the modelling function of good society less visible. However, the dominant social definition of proper ways to establish and maintain relations was constructed in these circles.

(2) At any time, the manners prevalent in good society will reflect the balance of power and dependence between established groups and outsider groups in society as a whole. As increasing layers of society became emancipated and more socially integrated, the social codes of good societies came to represent these layers – they have a *representational function*. In order to avoid social conflict and maintain their elevated position, the people in the centres of power and good society had increasingly to take the presence of rising groups into account. As part of this, the former had to show more respect for the ideals, sentiments, morals and manners of the latter. Therefore, the code of a good society tends to spare the sensibilities of all groups represented in them; it reflects *and* represents the power balance between all those groups and strata that are integrated in society at large.

(3) In nineteenth-century good societies, an elaborate and increasingly formalized regime of manners emerged. It consisted of a complicated system of introductions, invitations, calls, leaving calling cards, 'at homes', receptions, dinners and so on. Entrance into good society (or its functional equivalent

among other social strata) was impossible without an introduction, and, particularly in England, any introduction required the previous permission of both parties. This regime of manners not only regulated sociability, but also functioned as a relatively refined system of inclusion and exclusion, as an instrument to screen newcomers seeking entry into social circles, thus helping to identify and exclude undesirables and ensuring that the newly introduced would assimilate to the prevailing regime of manners and self-regulation. Thus the codes of good society also *function to regulate social mobility and status competition.*

The modelling function of good society operates only partly through the medium of social codes or rational individual choice, because differences in manners and sensibilities become ingrained into the personality of individuals – their *habitus* – as they grow up. The same goes for many external social constraints as they are transformed into habitual self-restraint. In this context, Norbert Elias described important connections between the formation of good societies, status motives and the transformation of constraints by others into self-restraints: 'fear of loss or reduction of social prestige is one of the most powerful motive forces in the transformation of constraints by others into self-restraints' (Elias, 2000, pp. 395–6). Once these external social constraints have been transformed into habitual, second-nature self-restraints, the social constraints from which they originated and which continue to back them up, are no longer experienced or perceived as such, nor are the powerful status motivations involved in their transformation.

In contrast to individual social ascent, the ascent of an entire social group involves some form of mixing of the codes and ideals of the groups which have risen with those of the previously superior groups. In the twentieth century, the successive social ascent of larger and larger groups has been reflected in the dominant codes and habitus – being a shorthand expression for the mentality, the whole distinctive emotional make-up of the people who are thus bonded together. The sediments of this mixing process can be found in manners books: the patterns of self-regulation of increasingly wider social groups come to be reflected in the codes of manners. They can be perceived in such changes as in the ways in which authors of manners books address their readers, how they draw social dividing lines such as between public and private, formal and informal and what they have written about social introductions and forms of address. As a rule, any regime of manners and emotions symbolizes and reinforces ranking hierarchy and other social dividing lines, while the same rule has it that changes in these regimes reflect changes in social dividing lines and in balances of power. This helps one to understand why the nineteenth century witnessed an *aristocratization* of the bourgeoisie alongside an *embourgeoisement* of nobility, to be partly succeeded and partly supplemented in the twentieth century by an *embourgeoisement* of the work-ing classes and a *proletarianization* of the bourgeoisie: *informalization.*

The disciplinary forces of state formation and market expansion

The life and career of the bourgeois classes both in business and in the pro-fessions depended heavily on keeping promises, and on the rather punctual and minute regulation of social traffic and behaviour. Accordingly, nineteenth-century manners books placed great emphasis on acquiring the self-discipline necessary for living a 'rational life'; they emphasized time keeping and ordering activities routinely in a fixed sequence, and at a set pace. Thomas Haskell has pointed to the significance of the 'disciplinary force of the market' in connec-tion to the rising norm of promise keeping and the ascendancy of conscience. This 'force of the market provided the intricate blend of ceaseless change, on the one hand, and predictability, on the other, in which a preoccupation with remote consequences paid off most handsomely' (Haskell, 1985, p. 561). An overall change in sensibility occurred via the expansion of the market, the intensification of market discipline, and the penetration of that discipline into spheres of life previously untouched by it. The expectation that everyone would live up to promises – as comprised in contracts made on 'the market' – became a mutually expected self-restraint, which eventually became taken for granted to the extent that it came to function as part of people's conscience.

This type of conscience formation presupposes state formation in the sense that the monopolization of the use of violence by the state, and ensuing pacifi-cation of larger territories, provided a necessary condition for the expectation of promise keeping and living up to contracts to become taken for granted, and engrained in the personality as conscience (Elias, 2000). Taking the devel-opment of these conditions into consideration helps us to understand why it was not until the eighteenth century, in Western Europe, England and North America, that societies first appeared whose economic systems,

> depended on the expectation that most people, most of the time, were sufficiently conscience-ridden (and certain of retribution) that they could be trusted to keep their promises. In other words, only then did promise keeping become so widespread that it could be elevated into a general social norm. (Haskell, 1985, p. 353)

This argument adds to the one put forward by Durkheim in his writing about the order behind the contract: 'For everything in the contract is not contractual'. The order behind the contract, 'in current parlance, is designated by the name, state' (1964 [1893], pp. 211–19). It was in the process of state formation that the commitment to live up to a contract came to be increasingly taken for granted and internalized. This internalization ran in tandem with, and depended upon rising levels of mutually expected protection of people and their property.

The entrepreneurial bourgeoisie largely took this protection by the state, the order behind the contract, for granted. It was their point of departure. Their whole social existence heavily depended upon contracts, contracts regulating the conditions of such activities as buying, producing, transporting and selling. In turn, the making of these contracts, as well as the conditions stipulated in them, depended upon an individual's reputation for being financially solvent and morally solid. To a large extent this reputation was formed in the gossip channels of good society.

The moral solidity of nineteenth-century bourgeois men

A reputation for moral solidity referred to the self-discipline of orderliness, thrift and responsibility, as the qualities needed for a firm grip on the proceedings of business transactions. Moral solidity also pertained to the private and sexual sphere: without demonstrable control over their wives and families, working bourgeois men would fail to create a solid impression of reliability, and ability to live up to the terms of their contracts. Therefore, bourgeois means of controlling potentially dangerous social and sexual competition depended to a substantial degree on the support of a wife for her husband. Her support and social charm could make a crucial difference, as is implied in the opinion that 'nothing makes a man look more ridiculous in the eyes of the world than a socially helpless wife' (Klickmann, 1902, p. 25).

At the same time, these pressures offered specific opportunities for women. Whereas men dominated the eighteenth-century courtesy genre of manners books, in the nineteenth-century etiquette genre, women gained a prominent position, both as authors and as readers (Curtin, 1987). As the social weight of the bourgeoisie increased, middle-class women enjoyed a widening sphere of opportunities. Although confined to the domain of their home and good society, upper- and middle-class women came, more or less, to run and organize the social sphere of good society. The workings of this social formation took place, in large part, in women's private drawing rooms. To some extent, women came to function as the gatekeepers of good society.

In developing the level of trust and respect within a relationship necessary for signing a contract, an invitation into the world of sociability was (and remains) an appreciated strategy. In their relations with friends and acquaintances, with women in general, and with their own wife in particular, men could demonstrate and prove their respectability and trustworthiness. They could show this to a potential client by inviting him and his wife into their home and into the rest of their secluded good society world. Hence, to be introduced, accepted and entertained in the drawing rooms and parlours of the respectable or, in other words, to be successful in the good society, was an important and sometimes even a necessary condition for success in business and politics.

A basic rule of manners among those acknowledged as belonging to the circle was to treat each other on the basis of equality. Quite often this was expressed in what became known as the Golden Rule of manners: do unto others as you would have them do unto you. Some were treated with relative intimacy. Others were treated with reserve, and were thus kept at a social distance.[2] Therefore, the questions who was properly introduced or introducible, and who was not, were equally important. To spot undesirables and to keep one's distance from strangers was a matter of great concern. The prototypical stranger was someone who might have the manners of the respectable, but not the morals. Strangers personified the bad company that would endanger the self-control of the respectable, prompting loss of composure in response to repulsive behaviour or, worse, the succumbing to temptation.

The fear of the slippery slope: the rise of a second-nature type of personality

In the nineteenth century, authors of advisory books came to describe the fall of innocent young men as being instructive of lessons in moral virtue and vigilance. Their repeated warnings against strangers expressed a strong moral appeal, revealing a fear of the slippery slope towards giving in to immoral pleasures. As women were guarded by chaperones, these warnings were directed at young men. A study of a number of such American stories reports that,

> these anecdotal dramas encompass many pitfalls – from seemingly harmless pleasures like dancing to the mortal dangers posed by alcohol – for conduct writers see young men's mistakes not just as individual dangers, but as part of a web of dangerous activity: one slip inevitably leads to the next. (Newton, 1994, p. 58)

Playing a single game of cards with strangers, for example, would 'always end in trouble, often in despair, and sometimes in suicide', an early nineteenth-century advice book warned. In her study of Dutch books of this genre, the author concluded that, by its nature, any careless indulgence in pleasure would lead to 'a lethal fall' (Tilburg, 1998, p. 67). Stuart Blumin also reports on a whole genre of

> purportedly true stories of individual drunkards, nearly all of whom were identified as wealthy, educated, or respectable, or by specific non-manual occupations before they took to drink. Moderate drinking invariably led to heavy drinking and drunkenness, and drunkenness to financial ruin and the destruction of family life. Often it led to the death of the drinker, his impoverished wife (the drunkard in these tales was almost always male), or his children. The loss of respectability, of the ability to pursue a respectable occupation, of wealth, and of family life in a well-appointed home (the forced sale of furniture is a common motif) was crucial to these tales, and spoke clearly and powerfully to the major preoccupations of the upper and middle classes. (1989, p. 200)

Newton concludes:

> Self-control, self-government, self-denial, self-restraint, and discipline of the will are all terms used repeatedly in the conduct book lexicon to reinforce the social construction of masculinity. The true man, then, is he who can discipline himself into qualities of character that lead to material and personal success. This discipline also extends to controlling and subjugating the passions as well. Control of anger, of sexual appetite, of impatience, even of emotion are instilled in the American male psyche as essential to the manly character. (1994, pp. 58–9)

This strong moral advice was intended to teach young men the responsibilities needed not only for a successful career but also, because marriages were no longer arranged by parents, for choosing a marriage partner. Advice betrayed the fear that such choices would be determined mainly by sexual attraction.

Social censorship verged on psychic censorship: warnings expanded to the 'treacherous effects' of fantasy, itself a demonstration of the prevailing conviction that dangerous thoughts would almost automatically lead to dangerous action. The rigorous and violent censorship in stricter and more authoritarian regimes demonstrates the extent to which authorities and others believed in the danger of thoughts, imagination or fantasy. Because of this direct connection between thoughts and actions, warnings against having dangerous thoughts were formulated as powerfully as possible. This kind of high-pitched moral pressure signalled the development of rather rigid ways of avoiding anything defined as dangerous or unacceptable via the formation of a rigorous conscience. It stimulated the rise of conflict-avoiding persons, obsessed with self-discipline, punctuality, orderliness and the importance of living a rational life. For them, the view of emotions came to be associated predominantly with dangers and weaknesses. Giving into emotions and impulses would lead either to the dangers of physical and/or sexual violence, or to the weaknesses of devastating addictions and afflictions. Thus the successive ascent of large middle-class groups and their increasing status and power relative to other groups was reflected in the regimes of manners and emotions. From the pressures of these growing interdependencies and intensified status competition, a particular type of self-regulation originated.

This type of personality was characterized by an 'inner compass' of reflexes and rather fixed habits (Riesman et al. 1950). Impulses and emotions came to be controlled increasingly via the more or less automatically functioning counter-impulses of a rigorous conscience with a strong penchant for order and regularity, cleanliness and neatness. Negligence in these matters indicated an inclination towards dissoluteness. Such inclinations were to be nipped in the bud, particularly in children. Without rigorous control, 'first nature' might run wild. This old conviction expresses a fear of the slippery slope that is typical of rather authoritarian relations and social controls, as well as a relatively authoritarian conscience.

The long-term trend of formalization reached its peak in the Victorian era, from the mid-nineteenth century to its last decade; the metaphor of the stiff upper lip indicated ritualistic manners and a kind of ritualistic self-control, heavily based on a scrupulous conscience, and functioning more or less automatically as a 'second nature', that second-nature type of personality which Riesman called inner directed.

The longing for total belonging and total control

It was particularly in the last decades of the nineteenth century, in the wake of expanding industrialization, that many new groups with new money demanded representation in the centres of power and their good societies. Facing mounting pressures arising from the necessities of social mixing, from increased interdependencies and its intensified competition and cooperation, the advantages of the stiff upper lip diminished. In that *fin de siècle* period, the 'domestication of nature', including one's own (first) nature, increasingly came to trigger both the experience of an 'alienation from nature' (one's own nature included) and a new romanticized longing for nature. The more nature was exploited and controlled, the more the image of an unexploited nature was valued. There was a new interest in mountains and seaside scenery, satisfying many of the new emotional longings: 'The absolute stillness, the dying of the day, the open landscape, all gave a feeling of total belonging, of a quiet ecstasy.' The connection with the rise of a second-nature type of personality seems obvious, for 'the man who endures hardship and deprivations to conquer a mountain single-handed . . . masters both an inner and an outer nature' (Frykman and Löfgren, 1987, pp. 55, 52). These decades saw the genesis of sports as an important part of public life (Elias and Dunning, 1986). It seems likely that most of them became fashionable and popular, at least partly, because practicing them could bring this feeling of total belonging and control. The same feeling was also projected through the romanticizing of a past, with an old harmonious peasant society, where each person knew his or her station in life.

Sociologists Frykman and Löfgren describe a comparable development regarding 'our animal friends': when middle-class people 'had mastered the animal within' and had developed a moral superiority to 'the more bestial lower classes', they felt a growing intimacy with animals and at the same time distanced themselves from them. They developed 'an abhorrence for "natural ways" together with a longing and fascination for "the natural way of life"' (1987, pp. 85–6). There was a quest for spontaneous, authentic, relaxed and informal conduct, which carried the spread of informalizing processes.

Throughout the twentieth century, however, that typical second-nature domestication of 'first nature' survived, despite increasingly losing adherents and vitality, particularly since the 1960s. An early twentieth century example may show how the fear of the slippery slope mirrors the dream of total control:

Each lie breeds new lies; there is no end to it. . . . Do not take that first step. And if you have already turned into the wrong path, possibly have walked it a long way already – then turn around at once, avert yourself. . . . It is better to die than to be false! (Oort, 1904, pp. 10, 14)

A similar rigidity in dividing the world into black and white, right and wrong, is captured in a popular (USA) song of the 1940s: 'you've got to accentuate the positive, eliminate the negative, . . . don't mess with Mister In-Between'. Mister In-Between is the personification of the slippery slope, of course. The first step on his path of vice is the point of no return: the slippery slope is an omnipresent bogey of the second-nature type of personality.

Rising social and psychic control over superiority feelings and displays

At the end of the nineteenth century and in the first decades of the twentieth, old ways of keeping a distance had to be abandoned as many groups of nouveau riche were allowed into the centres of power and their good societies. Further industrialization, including new forms of public transport, demanded more social mixing, at work as well as in trams and trains. Growing interdependency implied that social and psychic dividing lines were opening up, and the new levels of social mixing made it more necessary to achieve greater mastery over the fear of being provoked, pulled down by losing one's self-control and degraded. Social mixing obliged increasing numbers of people to accelerate, steadily, 'down the slippery slope'. Thus, the fear of degrading contact with lower classes and/or with lower impulses had to be brought under more flexible social and psychic control. This was a major incentive to control expressions of superiority.

In the 1930s, some etiquette books, mainly Dutch and German, still contained separate sections on 'good behaviour' towards social superiors and inferiors. Later, these sections disappeared.

Ideals of good manners became dissociated from superior and inferior social position or rank. The trend tended towards drawing social dividing lines, less on the basis of people's belonging to certain groups – class, race, age, sex or ethnicity – but rather, more on the basis of individual behaviour. An example of this process is the waning of references to 'the best people', 'best Society' or 'best sets'. An English manners book of the 1950s declared 'the old criterion of all etiquette writers . . . the best people' to be one of the casualties of a new and gentler code of manners (Edwards and Beyfus, 1956, p. x). In American manners books, these references had not been exceptional until the late 1930s. In the new edition of 1937, however, Emily Post had changed the title of her first chapter from 'What is Best Society?' to 'The True Meaning of Etiquette'. By formulating the latter mostly in terms of individual qualification – that is, in terms of personal qualities such as charm, tranquillity, taste, beauty and so on – Mrs Post had turned the perspective away from the social level to the psychic, or even the biological level. Formulations such as 'the code of a thoroughbred . . . is the code of instinctive decency, ethical integrity, self-respect and loyalty' (1937, p. 2) are examples of social avoidance internalized: from avoiding lower class people, to avoiding layers of superiority feelings.

Display of such feelings would not only humiliate and provoke social inferiors, but also grate on the senses of anyone in good society. Superiority feelings had come to be considered as a lower class of feelings, and to display them as betraying a flaw of the personality. As subordinate social groups were emancipated, references to hierarchical group differences, and to 'better' and 'inferior' kinds of people, were increasingly tabooed. Whereas at one time people of inferior status were avoided, later in the twentieth century behaviour that betrayed feelings of superiority and inferiority came to be avoided: avoidance behaviour was internalized, turning tensions *between* people into tensions *within* people. In the process, the once automatic equation that superiority in power equals superiority as a human being declined to the point of inviting embarrassment. As many types of 'lofty grandeur' came to be viewed as insulting stiffness, a different pattern of self-control came to be demanded: a stronger and yet more flexible self-regulation in which these feelings of superiority were expected to be kept under control. This was a motor in the process of informalization.

The slippery slope rejuvenated

This process of informalization was observed by many authors of manners books. In 1899, for example, a German author wrote that 'social relations have gradually become much more informal, that is, more natural' and added that 'to strive after nature' was 'a general trend in art, science, and living' (quoted in Krumrey, 1984, p. 413). The trend was generally welcomed, until early in the twentieth century, when an English author also expressed a concern:

> The boy of early Victorian days was a ceremonious little creature. He called his parents 'Sir' and 'Madam', and would never have dreamed of starting a conversation at table, and scarcely in joining in it. . . . One would not wish to see the ceremoniousness of those times revived, but it is possible that we . . . err in the opposite direction. (Armstrong, 1908, pp. 187–8)

In this question 'Do we err in the wrong direction?' the old fear of the slippery slope was rejuvenated and has accompanied the whole twentieth-century process of informalization. No longer was it that first step which needed to be avoided, but where *did* solid ground and confidence stop, and the slippery slope become unstoppable? These questions became particularly pressing each time young people had escaped further from under the wings of their parents, revived in particular by each flow of emancipation of young women and their sexuality.

'To strive after nature': the constraint to be unconstrained

As interdependency networks expanded, status competition intensified and the art of obliging and being obliged became more important as a power resource, demonstrations of being intimately trustworthy while perfectly at ease also gained importance. In this sense, processes of democratization, social integration, and informalization have run parallel with an increasing constraint towards developing 'smooth manners'. The expression 'a constraint to be unconstrained' seems to capture this paradoxical development.

This expression resembles that used by Norbert Elias: the social constraint towards self-constraint. Indeed, in the process of informalization the two constraints have become hardly distinguishable: the constraint towards becoming accustomed to self-constraint is at the same time a constraint to be unconstrained, to be confident and at ease. Almost every etiquette book contains passages that emphasize the importance of tactful behaviour, rather than demonstrative deference, and of 'natural' rather than mannered behaviour. However, in processes of emancipation and informalization, some ways of behaving, experienced previously as tactful deference, came to be seen as too hierarchical and demonstrative, in the same way that what had once been defined and recommended as natural came to be experienced as more or less stiff and phony, and branded as mannered. It then became so obvious a 'role' in which so many traces of constraint could be 'discovered' that 'playing' this role would provoke embarrassment. People who stuck to these old ways of relating were running the risk of being seen as bores, as lacking any talent for 'the jazz of human exchange' (Hochschild, 1983). Hence, new forms of relaxed, 'loose' and 'natural' behaviour were developed.

All of this also helps one to understand changes in the practices and ideals in raising children. In the old and new middle classes, parents who themselves had learned to behave in a rather reserved, inhibited and indirect manner, and to conceal their 'innermost feelings behind a restrained observance of conventional forms' (Goudsblom, 1968, p. 30), became charmed and fascinated by the more outright, spontaneous, straightforward and direct behaviour of children. This attractiveness of the (more) 'natural' functioned as a catalyst to the emancipation of emotions.

As 'ease' and 'naturalness' gained importance, and demands for individual authenticity and a socially more meaningful personal identity rose, to behave according to a set of fixed rules of manners increasingly came to be experienced as rigid and stiff, and their performance as too obvious and predictable, as 'insincere', even as 'fraudulent' or as 'deceit'. In its wake, for example, the mourning ritual was minimized (Wouters, 2002, p. 7). This means that traditional ways of behaving and regulating emotions have been losing part of their 'defence' or 'protective' function. The former formal codes had functioned as a defence against dangers and fears which were now diminished, or could be avoided or controlled in more varied and subtle ways – ways in which both social superiority and inferiority were less explicitly and less extremely expressed. Increasing numbers of people pressured each other to develop more differentiated and flexible patterns of self-regulation, triggering a further impetus towards higher levels of social knowledge, self-knowledge and reflexivity.

Emancipation of emotions – rise of a 'third-nature' personality

The period after the Second World War was characterized by decolonization, global emancipation and democratization. These national, continental and global integration processes have exerted pressure towards increasingly differentiated regimes of manners, expanding behavioural and emotional alternatives, and also towards increasingly reflexive and flexible regimes of self-regulation. This was a period of rapidly expanding interdependencies and rising levels of mutual identification, in which ideals of equality and mutual consent spread and gained strength. On this basis, avoidance behaviour came to be less and less rigidly directed at 'lower-class' people and 'lower' emotions, and the emancipation of emotions was accompanied by a shift from conscience to consciousness (to use this shorthand expression).

In the course of the integration of 'lower' social groups within Western societies and the subsequent emancipation and integration of 'lower' impulses and emotions in personality, both psychic and social censorship declined. The fear and awe of fantasy or dissident imagination diminished together with the fear and awe of the authorities of state and conscience. There was a significant spread of more and more unconcealed expressions of insubordination, sex and violence, particularly in the realms of imagination and amusement. But also the politics and policies concerning the beginning and the end of life (sexuality, abortion, euthanasia) and concerning soft and hard drugs have been demanding rising degrees of mastering the fear of the slippery slope from both citizens and politicians. At the same time, provoking the established and protesting against the establishment has not only become emotionally gratifying but has also become politically and economically rewarding. In many countries, political parties have come to thrive on this sentiment and populist politicians pluck the heart strings of the common people by present-ing themselves as very different from these worthy gentlemen of the old political establishment, as counter-politicians so to speak. And the economic viability of provocative clothing brands like 'porn star' (US), 'FCUK' (UK) and 'CCCP' (Dutch) indicate that many people have come to take provocative pleasure in wearing T-shirts and caps with PORN STAR on them, and shirts and sweaters with a great FCUK or, in addition to a small emblem with the hammer and sickle symbol, a huge CCCP on them. A daring competition in provocation has indeed been a motor of the informalization process.

The emancipation of emotions could become dominant only at a moment when social/national differentiation and integration had expanded to a level on which its inherent motor – status competition – increasingly came to demand the 'personality capital' needed for a *controlled decontrolling of emotional controls* and rising mastery of the fear of the slippery slope. Indeed, as most social codes were becoming more flexible and differentiated, manners and emotion regulation were also becoming more decisive criteria for status or reputation. Under this pressure of social competition, people have urged each other to become less stiff but more cautious, that is, more conscious of social and individual options and restrictions, and this has been putting social and self-knowledge in greater demand. The same goes for the ability to empa-thize and to take on others' roles. Respect and respectable behaviour have become more dependent upon self-regulation.

Between the 1950s and 1980s, these processes of social and psychic emancipation and integration accelerated dramatically. Together with the old conviction that being open to such 'dangerous' emotions would almost irrevo-cably be followed by acting upon them, many varieties of the fear of the slip-pery slope disappeared. The dominant mode of self-regulation had reached a strength and scope that increasingly enabled people to admit to themselves and to others to having 'dangerous' emotions, without provoking shame, par-ticularly the shame–fear of losing control, and having to give in. This kind of self-regulation implies that emotions, even those which could provoke physi-cal and sexual violence, have become more easily accessible, while their con-trol is less strongly based upon a commanding conscience, functioning more or less automatically as a 'second nature'. Ego functions came to dominate conscience or Superego functions, and a more ego-dominated pattern of self-regulation spread.

To the extent that it has become 'natural' to perceive the pulls and pushes of both 'first nature' and 'second nature' as well as the dangers and chances, short term and long term, of any particular situation or relation, a 'third nature' has been developing. Increasing numbers of people have become aware of emotions and temptations in circumstances where shame–fears and dangers had been dominant before. Obviously, this emancipation of emotions involves an attempt at reaching back to 'first nature' without losing any of the control that was provided by 'second nature'. Thus, the rise of a 'third-nature personality' demands and depends on an emancipation of 'first nature' as well as 'second nature' and increasing control over the fear of the slippery slope.

The term 'third nature' refers to a level of consciousness and calculation in which all types of constraints and possibilities are taken into account. In this way, social processes in which relations and manners between social groups have become less rigid and hierarchical, are connected with psychic processes in which relations between the psychic functions of people's emotions and impulses have become more open and fluent. A self-regulation via the rather automatically functioning counter-emotions and counter-impulses of conscience has lost out to a regulation via consciousness. As social and psychic dividing lines opened up, social groups as well as psychic functions became more integrated – that is, the communications and connections between both social groups and psychic functions have become more flowing and flexible. Lo and behold: the sociogenesis and psychogenesis of a 'third-nature personality'!

Feelings of superiority and inferiority: a counter-trend?

Several emotions that counted as 'dangerous' have come to be recognized as normal aspects of emotional life. There was, however, one important exception to the expansion of behavioural and emotional alternatives: the social codes increasingly came to dictate that overt expression of inferiority and superiority feelings be avoided. From the 1960s onward, the fear of being tempted increasingly concerns feeling superior or inferior. The avoidance of these feelings and of behaviour that expressed them was a confirmation of social equalization and a necessary condition for informalization to occur. Thus, there was a further curbing of emotions in relation to the display of arrogance or self-aggrandizement, and 'self-humiliation'. These displays were either banished to the realm of imagination, games and sports, or compartmentalized behind the social and psychic scenes. The latter leads to hiding superiority and inferiority feelings and this process can be interpreted as a counter-trend or, at least partly, as a reversal of the direction of the main process.

The fear of displaying these feelings surfaces in all media training, whether for managers or politicians. The need to be informal and down-home friendly, to avoid any impression of superiority, intellectual or otherwise, to avoid jargon and convey inclusiveness to all groups concerned – this all enters into the

basic symbolism of contemporary political and managerial processes. It signi-
fies that feelings of superiority and inferiority are excluded from the emancipation of emotions and that the taboo on displaying these emotions is rather
increasing than decreasing.

Through psychoanalysis and other forms of psychotherapy, a rich tradition of recalling and interpreting sexual impulses and emotions has come into
existence and spilled over into all walks of life. By contrast, there is hardly any
tradition of analysing and interpreting emotions and impulses connected with
the struggle for power and status, particularly feelings of inferiority and superiority. And yet, again and again, from the suicide bomber to the 'president
of war', these feelings appear to be directly and highly significant for understanding why social and psychic conflicts erupt in violence.

From this perspective, a question of major importance concerns whether
processes of emancipation of emotions and *controlled decontrolling of emotional controls* will continue and eventually come to include more feelings of
superiority and inferiority. Will feelings of inferiority and superiority be further
admitted into consciousness, while, at the same time, they come under a
stronger, a more comprehensive, more stable and subtle internal (ego) control,
one that is sharply scrutinized and thus backed up by external social controls?
The answer to these questions strongly depends, of course, on the future of
integration processes and their inherent integration conflicts. Will these integration conflicts remain sufficiently controlled and contained? The opposite,
however, is true also: the control and containment of social integration conflicts depends to a large extent on the degree of control over superiority feelings in the societies of the established; on their degree of informalization.

Notes

1 This chapter is based upon a study of changes in manners books from the end
   of the nineteenth to the beginning of the twenty-first century. It is one of the
   results from a research project of many years, the purpose of which was to
   find, compare and interpret changes in American, Dutch, English and German
   manners books. The project has resulted in two books, *Sex and Manners* (2004)
   and *Informalization* (2007). A different version of this chapter will appear in
   the Sociological Review Monograph: *Norbert Elias and Figurational Research:
   Processual Thinking in Sociology* (Oxford: Wiley-Blackwell, 2011).

2 Domestic servants are an exception, yet preferably treated as if they were
   equals by asking as a favour something that cannot be refused. In his novel
   Snobs, Julian Fellowes explains 'It is all part of the aristocracy's consciously
   created image. They like to pride themselves on being "marvellous with
   servants"' (2005, p. 309).

References

Armstrong, L. (1908), *Etiquette Up-to-Date*. London: Werner Laurie.

Blumin, S. (1989), *The Emergence of the Middle Class. Social Experience in the American City, 1760–1900*. New York, NY: Cambridge University Press.

Curtin, M. (1987), *Propriety and Position*. New York: Garland.

Durkheim, É. (1964 [1893]), *The Division of Labour in Society*. London: Glencoe.

Edwards, A. and Beyfus, D. (1956, 1969), *Lady Behave*. London: Boswell & Co.

Elias, N. and Dunning, E. (1986), *Quest for Excitement. Sport and Leisure in the Civilizing Process*. Oxford: Blackwell.

Elias, N. (2000), *The Civilizing Process*. Cambridge, MA: Blackwell.

Fellowes, J. (2005), *Snobs*. London: Phoenix.

Frykman, J. and Löfgren, O. (1987), *Culture Builders. A Historical Anthropology of Middle-Class Life*. New Brunswick: Rutgers University Press.

Goudsblom, J. (1968), *Dutch Society*. New York: Random House.

Haskell, T. (1985), 'Capitalism and the humanitarian sensibility', *American Historical Review*, 90, 339–61 and 547–66.

Hochschild, A. (1983), *The Managed Heart. Commercialization of Human Feeling*. Berkeley: UCP.

Klickmann, F. (1902), *The Etiquette of To-day* (3rd edn 1916). London: The Girl's Own Paper & Woman's Magazine.

Krumrey, H.-V. (1984), *Entwicklungsstrukturen von Verhaltensstandarden*. Frankfurt/M: Suhrkamp.

Newton, S. (1994), *Learning to Behave*. Westport, CT: Greenwood Press.

Oort, Dr. H.L. (1904), *Goede Raad aan de jonge mannen en jonge meisjes der XXste eeuw*. Utrecht: Broese.

Post, E. (1937), *Etiquette in Society, in Business, in Politics and at Home*. New York: Funk and Wagnalls.

Riesman, D. with Glazer, N. and Denney, R. (1950), *The Lonely Crowd*. New Haven, CT: Yale University Press.

Stearns, P. and Haggerty, T. (1991), 'The role of fear: transitions in American emotional standards for children, 1850–1950', *The American Historical Review*, 96(1), 63–94.

Tilburg, M. van (1998), *Hoe hoorde het?* Amsterdam: Spinhuis.

Veeninga, D. (2008), *Het nahuwelijk*. Amsterdam: Augustus.

Wouters, C. (2002), 'The quest for new rituals in dying and mourning: changes in the we–I balance', *Body & Society* 8(1), 1–27.

—(2004), *Sex and Manners. Female Emancipation in the West Since 1890*. London: Sage.

—(2007), *Informalization. Manners and Emotions Since 1890*. London: Sage.

Index